Strategic Budgeting

Strategic Budgeting

Roy T. Meyers

Ann Arbor

The University of Michigan Press

First paperback edition 1996

Published in the United States of America by
The University of Michigan Press
Manufactured in the United States of America
♾ Printed on acid-free paper
2004 2003 2002 2001 4 3

A CIP catalogue record for this book is available from the British Library.

Library of Congress Cataloging-in-Publication Data

Meyers, Roy T.
Strategic budgeting / Roy T. Meyers.
p. cm.
Includes bibliographical references and index.
ISBN 0-472-10362-8 (alk. paper)
1. Budget—United States. I. Title.
HJ2051.M496 1994
353.0072'22—dc20 94-3056
CIP

ISBN 0-472-08414-3 (pbk. : alk. paper)

Acknowledgments

Three people were especially helpful as I did the research for this book. My two immediate bosses at the Congressional Budget Office, Dick Emery and Marvin Phaup, taught me much about budgeting, and through their personal conduct, much more about virtuous public service. My dissertation chair and graduate advisor at the University of Michigan, John Kingdon, unfailingly gave valuable criticism and support. As many in the discipline know, John is the exemplar of graduate school mentors.

Others who provided especially useful comments or assistance include Joel Aberbach, Tom Anton, Paul Courant, Robert Hartman, Phil Joyce, Harriet Meyers, Tim Muris, Irene Rubin, Allen Schick, Joseph White, and last but not least, Samuel Wilson. Many budget analysts, committee staff, lobbyists, and journalists also shared valuable information.

Thanks especially to my parents. Among many gifts they gave me was the relatively minor one that, as a young kid, I could devour the *New York Times* each morning before school. Those were years when one couldn't help being absorbed with the news of civil rights, of escalation and antiwar protests, and of discredited presidents. With this introduction, my appetite for knowledge about the mysteries of government and politics grew, to the point of fascination with the esoterica of government budgeting. Little did they know what they were encouraging!

Like even the *New York Times,* at some point I will have to make some corrections to what follows. Please blame me for the errors, and not those persons listed above.

Grateful acknowledgment is made to the following publishers for permission to reprint previously published material.

HarperCollins Publishers for excerpt from *The Politics of the Budgetary Process,* 4th edition, by Aaron Wildavsky. Copyright © 1984 by Aaron Wildavsky. Reprinted by permission of HarperCollins Publishers.

The *Washington Post* for excerpt from "As Federal Funding Tightens, Lobbyists Find a Surer Way," June 18, 1989, pp. A1, A14, by Dan Morgan. Copyright © 1989, The Washington Post. Reprinted with permission.

Contents

Chapter 1

Introduction

Persistent fiscal stress now guarantees that funding for many programs will be threatened each year. Consequently, most advocates of existing programs feel they must develop strategies of protection. Advocates of proposed programs must also find strategies to counter the inevitable bias against new spending when times are tight. Strategic knowledge about budgeting is also useful for those who are disturbed by deficits. They want to design controls that will reduce spending, and they need to react effectively to innovations by spending advocates.

The term *strategy* is used in many arenas of competition—business, war, sports, and politics—and there are many definitions of the term. Here, a strategy is a plan or approach that integrates resources, tactics, and goals. For the short run, political actors take resources and goals as relatively fixed; they apply their resources through political actions such as lobbying to increase the probability of reaching their goals. These actions are called *tactics.*[1] Over the long run, political actors modify goals and mobilize resources as well as utilize tactics.

Incremental Budgetary Strategy

Following the 1964 publication of Aaron Wildavsky's *The Politics of the Budgetary Process,* there was a consensus understanding of budgetary strategy—the *incrementalist* approach. Wildavsky drew this term from the work of Charles Lindblom, who had suggested incrementalism as an alternative to the view that government decision making should feature comprehensive planning by experts. In contrast, incrementalist decision making featured a limited search for information ("bounded rationality") and extensive reliance on the political process to set policy goals ("partisan mutual adjustment").

To many, the area of budgeting begged for application of the incrementalist perspective. Most works on budgeting had been written by economists and featured prescriptions of appropriate economic concepts and comprehensive

---

1. In much of the political science literature described below, *strategies* is used for both tactics and strategies. When discussing this work, I follow that usage.

processes for efficiently allocating the government's resources. Despite their virtues, these works were unrealistic descriptions of the process. Into the void flowed Wildavsky's *Politics*. It described "incremental budgeting" as a process of bargaining between institutions under conditions of uncertainty.[2] Uncertainty was caused by general limitations to knowledge, by the complexity of the budget, and by the counterpositioning of the roles of participants. Budgeting participants responded to uncertainty by relying on certain "aids to calculation." They limited the scope of their activities to a small number of items. They learned to seek small increases from the "base," which was the amount provided by the previous year's budget. They developed routine behaviors and expected other participants to behave as routinely.

Wildavsky also argued that budgetary roles were strongly connected to institutional positions. He identified participants within the executive and legislative branches and suggested that these institutional representatives typically, though not universally, acted in specific ways. The agencies were "advocates," the Bureau of the Budget acted as the "Presidential representative," the role of "guardian of the Treasury" was played by the House Appropriations Committee, and the "appeals court" role was taken by the Senate Appropriations Committee.[3]

The book was also filled with lively descriptions of a rich variety of budgetary roles and strategies. Agency budget officials sought to build a clientele of supporters, and to maintain the confidence of those who possessed the authority to make budgetary decisions for their agencies. They also used a wide range of bargaining strategies, such as threatening to cut a popular program in response to an across-the-board budget cut. Wildavsky conceived of two types of strategies: ubiquitous strategies, which were designed to build and maintain clienteles and to gain the confidence of decision makers, and contingent strategies, the proper selection of which depended upon whether the agency aspired to maintenance of the base or growth above it. Many of the contingent strategies took the form of offers and counteroffers ("Cut the popular program," "The ceiling," "You choose," etc.) in a process of bargaining over total outcome levels and individual objects of expense.

Members of Congress and officials of the Bureau of the Budget developed complementary strategies. Through this interplay of strategies over the years, participants gained an understanding about each agency's "fair share," the

---

2. I use the term *incremental* throughout the text to refer to incremental budgeting, and not to the more general model of decision making.

3. The match of role with institution was used by another masterpiece: Richard Fenno's *The Power of the Purse* (1966). This study of the House and Senate Appropriations committees focused theoretically on the congressional committee as a form of political organization rather than on the appropriations process per se, but Fenno did describe in great detail the incremental decision processes that committees routinely used.

"proportion of funds, if any, which are to be increased over or decreased below the base of the various governmental agencies" (Wildavsky 1964, 17). Stable expectations and behaviors resulted in stable, incremental patterns of budgetary outcomes from year to year. (See also Anton 1966.)

One paradox of this understanding was that the *politics* of the budgetary process was not very *political* in the popular (and disparaging) meaning of that term. The actors were strategic, but they were not devious, and although the game was competitive, it was played following strict rules of sportsmanship. Perhaps this was a comforting approach for political scientists who wanted to say something interesting about the budgetary process, yet also fit within the dominant pluralist paradigm. Forget the economists' prescriptions! The real experts on budgeting were the more realistic—and supportive—political scientists!

A final reason for the acceptance of incrementalism was its apparent validation. A small part of the theory of incremental budgeting was soon operationalized in a series of articles by Wildavsky and associates Davis and Dempster. These articles sought to confirm the incremental theory by predicting agency budget requests and congressional appropriations with linear regression equations. The authors found that simple equations—for example, those that regressed appropriations only on the president's requests for these agencies—produced coefficients of determination (r^2) that exceeded .9. They also examined what they called "deviant cases"—the cases with large residuals from the fitted equation—and attempted to identify the causes of these deviations. They concluded that these cases represented "shift points" in traditional patterns of budgeting. Changes in patterns were the result of "cumulative pressures" on the specific agencies (Padgett's term 1980, 361), but the times when these pressures reached a critical mass were generally unpredictable. Listed among the causes of shift points were partisan controversies, new laws, and changes in macroeconomic conditions.

Paradigm Lost

For nearly thirty years, the theory of budgetary incrementalism was repeatedly elaborated, criticized, and tested.[4] Though battered and bruised by critics, and seemingly overtaken by the rapid transformations in budgeting over the past twenty years, the view of budgetary strategy as incrementalist retained some supporters (for example, Pitsvada and Draper 1984). But there are far fewer supporters than there were in the past. Consider one indicator of what political scientists know confidently about budgetary strategies: what they say to stu-

4. Detailed reviews of incremental theory can be found in LeLoup 1978b; Padgett 1980; Tucker 1982; Schick 1983.

dents in their first exposure to political science. I reviewed numerous textbooks for introductory courses on American government and found that they gave very little coverage to budgeting, despite the indisputable importance of budgeting to recent politics and despite the sizable literature on the subject. The normal treatment was a short discussion of budgeting in the contexts of managing the economy or of congressional resurgence. None of the texts mentioned incremental budgeting.

One function of textbooks is to convey facts, and describing the extraordinarily complex process of budgeting may leave little space for ideas. But another explanation may be doubt about what to say. Might not potential majors be disenchanted with the discipline if they were told: "We used to say that budgeting was incremental, but now we're not quite sure how to describe it"?

The problem is that though incrementalism mischaracterizes current-day budgetary strategies in almost every respect, an alternative understanding of budgetary strategy has not emerged. Describing a plausible alternative to incrementalism is the purpose of this book. To do so, I begin by describing the flaws of incrementalism. I then set out the basic assumptions and features of a *budget structure* approach to budgetary strategy.

The Flaws of Incrementalism

Davis, Dempster, and Wildavsky's tests of incrementalism's validity were soon followed by others, most of which were critical. In a devastating critique, Wanat (1974) generated budgetary outcomes randomly and then obtained coefficients of determination with magnitudes equal to those produced by Davis, Dempster, and Wildavsky. Padgett then showed that the tests employed by Davis, Dempster, and Wildavsky were incapable of discriminating between incremental theory and several other plausible theories (1980). Gist argued that much of these presumed incremental budgetary outcomes were the artifact of mandatory program designs, and not the result of a discretionary appropriations bargaining process (1975, 1977; see also LeLoup 1978a).

Other critiques maintained that the Davis, Dempster, and Wildavsky equations were misspecified. An example was the high degree of aggregation of the dependent variables, as the tests measured only the budgetary outcomes for *agencies.* This practice showed incremental outcomes for agencies when nonincremental outcomes at the smaller bureau and program levels canceled each other out (Natchez and Bupp 1973).[5]

---

5. There is no clear choice about the proper level of the outcome measure (Gist 1982). Institutions formulate budgets for both policy units (accounts and programs) and institutional units (agencies). The former are aggregated into the latter. While policy units are more predomi-

Another issue that arose from validity testing was the maximum size of a year-to-year budget increase that would qualify as an increment (the antonym to *increment* was never identified). Bailey and O'Connor (1975) showed that the studies by Wildavsky and Fenno that found incremental outcomes included many annual changes that exceeded 10 percent, but this only stimulated a long debate over whether 10 percent was the appropriate cutoff.

Wildavsky and his associates responded with a strong defense to these challenges. In the article "On Change: Or, There Is No Magic Size for an Increment" (1979), Dempster and Wildavsky claimed that critics misinterpreted the several meanings of *incrementalism.*

> Confusing a method of problem-solving with a process of interaction, a theory of organizational behavior in budgeting with a theory of policy development, a shift in organizational relationship with the size of monetary change, is not surprising. The concepts are closely related. The definitions do reveal differences in priority about what is most worth explaining. Having worked for 15 years on the limited portion of the subject—the United States federal budgetary process—recorded in our forthcoming book we can only sympathize with those who, whatever the cost and confusion, want to understand it all at once. (373)

They went on to define an incremental process as "one in which the relationships between actors are regular over a period of years," even though this process could produce changes in budgetary outcomes of large magnitude (1979, 375). Dempster and Wildavsky justified their selection of unit of analysis by simply stating that they weren't interested in policy, only in relationships between organizations (1979, 374). They also commented on the difficulty of obtaining budget data by individual program, concluding,

> We have preferred to leave the undoubtedly important question of why some programmes grow and others decline to another generation of scholars. No doubt it is true that if one could explain this, one could explain almost anything, but we do not expect a general theory of policies and programmes to be produced in the near future. (1979, 387)

Wildavsky was certainly correct in describing his theory as a theory of strategy and process as well as of outcomes. Yet because he chose to test the theory by measuring outcomes and not by measuring the relative stability of

---

nant as terms of trade, particularly in the legislative branch, agency budget managers are sometimes accorded flexibility to transfer funds between accounts within an agency. See Natchez and Bupp 1973; Anton, Cawley, and Kramer 1980; Fisher 1975; Pitsvada 1983.

relationships, perhaps he shouldn't have blamed his critics for making the same choice!

Let's turn to incrementalism's descriptions of strategy and process. Incrementalism relied on three basic points.

1. Budget actors make simple decisions when confronted with complexity.
2. Budgetary roles are determined by institutional position.
3. Budgetary bargaining is stable and consensual.

All of these points were challenged by empirical research, the highlights of which I now summarize.

Budget Actors Often Make Complex Calculations

Incrementalism stated that budgeting participants focus on the increment and take the base as a given in order to simplify search in the highly complex process of budgeting. But using a time-series data set of planning figures from executive branch budget formulation, Kamlet and Mowery found that "the budgetary base often receives as much attention from OMB and agencies as does the increment—both with respect to the number of negotiated items and to their monetary significance" (1980, 805).

Wildavsky had also asserted that budgeting "veils policy implications rather than emphasizing them" (1964, 136; see also 60), but critics claimed that this argument was reductionist. For example, Caldeira and Cowart showed that increases in crime rates led to higher spending for criminal justice when increases in crime rates were accompanied by ideological receptivity from political officeholders (1980). Kanter studied appropriations for defense and argued that the pattern of outcomes was consistent with a programmatic style of appropriations decision making (1972). Domke showed that service shares of the Department of Defense's appropriations often changed substantially from year to year, and particularly during the first year of an administration. He interpreted this variability as the outcome of presidential program direction (1984; see also Rickards 1984). And finally, Schulman argued that it was improbable or even impossible to budget incrementally for some programs (1975). He developed an ideal type of nonincremental or large-scale policy-making, using the rapid growth of the National Aeronautics and Space Administration (NASA) as an example. In nonincremental policy making, there is relatively comprehensive decision making, rapid growth in budgets and personnel, but also a substantial likelihood of rapid decline. The equilibrium of incremental growth is not the expected outcome for these programs. A working paper by Bassein and Schulman modeled spending outcomes with a nonlinear technique, and then raised

> the possibility that the budgetary characteristics of agencies may tell us more about their different political and administrative circumstances than the incremental model of budgeting would lead us to believe. Cognitive limitations do not render the budgetary process a simple reactive response to a previous year's expenditure level. Non-linear fluctuations are not simply a "break-point" from overwhelming decision-making routines caused by essentially randomized "exogenous" variables. Budgetary outcomes we contend reflect a rich set of purposive strategies—strategies which are far more complex than simply adding a marginal increment to the previous year's base. (1985, 40)

They suggested that explanations for the existence of nonlinear spending patterns may be found through "a reintegration of budgetary research with public policy and organizational studies," with particular emphasis being placed on changes in policy conditions, the relative mobilization of competing political coalitions, and the lobbying techniques used by these coalitions (1985, 41; see also Kiel and Elliott 1992).

Budgetary Roles Are Unstable and Numerous

Also damaged was the idea that particular institutions typically played specific roles. Much of this criticism came from research on the "new Congress." The new Congress was more fragmented and open than in the past, the result of procedural reforms that encouraged collegial decision making, of greater congressional attention to constituency demands, of massive campaign contributions, and of more sophisticated lobbying techniques. These institutional transformations made budgeting more complex than it was during the era of supposed Appropriations Committee hegemony that was portrayed by Wildavsky and Fenno (Schick 1980; Caiden 1984; Ellwood 1985b).

Allen Schick observed that the creation of the Budget committees as a new set of guardians allowed the Appropriations committees to complete their transition to the role of acting as claimants (aka "subdued guardians") on the Treasury (1980). But the Budget committees could not act as strong guardians, particularly in the House, where rotating membership created strong incentives for Budget Committee members to defend the standing committees from which they came and to which they would return. The institutional problem became "Who, if anyone, will serve as the 'guardian of the Treasury' within the Congress?"

In retrospect, it seems possible that the "guardian of the Treasury" concept was a caricature even in the 1950s and early 1960s. After all, even granting the committee norms for fiscal prudence and the selection process for subcommittee memberships, committee members were still politicians who sought reelection, and their committee membership gave them powerful means to increase their chances. The Democratic committee members also were part of a party that was committed to spending more than President Eisenhower (see Morgan 1990; McCubbins 1991, 83–118, esp. 105–8).

The new process also forced some political scientists to note that responsibility for microbudgetary decision making was not solely in the hands of the Appropriations committees that had received so much attention, for "authorizing" committees also participated through their control of "backdoor" or "direct" spending programs. By definition, budgetary outcomes for these programs are not adequately explained by a theory of bargaining over appropriations. The range of programs in these areas was quite wide, including the many business-type programs that were primarily financed through revolving fund collections, the procedure for establishing the compensation of federal employees, the setting of price supports and other agricultural assistance, changes in eligibility requirements and cost-of-living adjustments for transfer programs, and the adoption of user fees. Nor did incremental budgeting theory offer explanations of microbudgeting decisions for tax expenditures, which in many ways are functionally equivalent to "regular" government spending. But while many political scientists knew of the opportunity to research these other spending institutions, only a few responded (e.g., Weaver 1988).

Though the instability and variability of institutional budgetary roles was usually explained as the result of structural change within the Congress, another cause was electoral change. A Republican Senate majority was much less disposed to act as an appeals court. Witness also the many political appointees in the Reagan administration who *supported* OMB passback cuts instead of opposing them (as agency advocates), or the combative, intransigent opposition of Secretary of Defense Weinberger and President Reagan to any OMB-proposed defense-spending cuts. Malachowski, Bookheimer, and Lowery have argued that these cases of ideological clashes with roles suggest that the concept of guardianship be revised.

> We believe that guardianship should be viewed not only in terms of substantive budget actions, but in terms of how it relates to incremental change of the status quo. In periods of presidential advocacy, preservation of the status quo—or rather, incremental change of the status quo—required substantive cuts in the president's requests. But in periods of presidential guardianship, as in the Carter and Reagan years, guardianship as preservation of incremental change would require the opposite: sub-

> stantive additions to the president's requests. This might be thought of as procedural guardianship as opposed to substantive guardianship, which has now become the province of the executive (1987, 347).

Research on OMB documented similarly large changes in its institutional role. The standard description emphasized how the congressional assertion of budgetary responsibility, the operating style of OMB director Stockman, and other important factors led OMB to replace its traditional executive-branch budget preparation procedures with a year-round, legislative budgeting orientation, and its ethos of neutral competence with one of political responsiveness (Heclo 1984; Schick 1984; Mosher 1984).[6]

Competition Is Rife in Budgeting

An initial challenge to incrementalism's consensual bargaining component was written by Natchez and Bupp. In contrast to the absence of raw competition in Wildavsky's work, they found competition central to the process they observed at the Atomic Energy Commission (AEC). Though they shared with Wildavsky the perception that budgets of larger organizational units—departments, for example—were stable over time, they saw great variance at the program level in awards of budgetary resources. This variance was the result of competition among "aggressive entrepreneurs" from the operating bureaus (who were supported by their clienteles). These participants did not accept the fair share as a norm or as a good predictor of likely outcomes. Natchez and Bupp did not describe in detail the actual strategies used by these entrepreneurs or the nature of competition in the budgetary process. They did develop a "prosperity index"—a measure of how the budgetary allocations to programs change over time relative to changes in other programs—and showed that different AEC programs received quite different scores on this index. Gist used this index to demonstrate that agencies experienced a waxing and waning in budgetary fortunes of the same magnitude as did programs, but Gist also claimed that the index was tautological in character, and therefore could not be used to discredit incremental theory (1982).

This challenge was taken up by a series of studies that asked whether assertiveness by agencies—requesting a relatively large increase—is a productive or counterproductive strategy. In contrast to the position of Wildavsky that assertiveness is counterproductive because it reduces the confidence of the guardians in the agency, Sharkansky found that assertiveness was positively related to agency success (1965). LeLoup and Moreland found that the more

6. For fascinating reviews of the failure of the OMB to control the Defense Department's budget, see Center for Defense Information 1982; and Szanton 1985.

assertive programs were cut by greater percentages from their requests, but still grew faster than less assertive programs (LeLoup 1975; LeLoup and Moreland 1978). Left unanswered by these authors, however, was the problem of whether the assertive agencies were simply taking advantage of the temporary, positive climate for budgetary success (see also Kingdon 1966; Bozeman 1977). This importance of context for strategy had previously been suggested by Fenno. He had ranked thirty-six bureaus by their success in avoiding Appropriations Committee cuts from their requests and in obtaining increases above previous years' appropriations levels and found that the agencies that worked to develop the confidence of the Appropriations Committee and those that were assertive in their requests were likely to be successful. But he also concluded that other factors—factors external to the agency-committee relationship—were probably more important causes of success. These factors included the type of functions carried out by the agencies and the social trends that affected agency responsibilities. Fenno concluded,

> In one sense, growth is a function of appetite. In order to grow, a bureau must ask for sizable increases. But, in a larger sense, both growth and appetite are a function of the same set of expectations. To a small degree, these expectations can be affected by aspiration levels generated from within the agency itself. But most important are the expectations emanating from the larger society to which agency, Appropriations committee, and Congress respond. (1966, 396)

Microbudgeting Is Affected by Macrobudgetary Constraints

After the passage of the Congressional Budget Act of 1974, political scientists markedly reordered their research agenda, giving priority to *macrobudgeting*. Macrobudgeting is the process of determining aggregate budgetary goals and conforming the budgetary outcomes for individual programs to these goals. In contrast, *microbudgeting* is the process of allocating budgetary resources to individual programs and agencies. The two are related, of course, but incrementalism focused exclusively on microbudgeting. This perspective was criticized in quantitative studies by Crecine and Bromiley, who showed that the budgetary bargaining process in the executive branch was strongly constrained by the president's fiscal goals (1980), and by Auten, Bozeman, and Cline, who showed that fiscal pressure affected Congressional microbudgeting (1984).

The brave new world of Congressional budgeting introduced many new and complicated procedures and institutions; what little space was left in publications after description analyzed whether these reforms were working. But this quickly led to a debate about the real purposes of the Congressional

Budget Act. Was the act intended simply to promote timely passage of appropriations and tax bills, or to express congressional priorities, or to promote deficit reduction? And did the purpose of the act change as it was informally amended in each year of its use? Answering questions of intent became much easier as deficits grew to previously unimaginable levels during the mid-1980s, and as Congress responded with the Balanced Budget Act of 1985, popularly known as Gramm-Rudman-Hollings. The new, dominant questions became "what are the causes of large deficits?" and "is the government capable of reducing deficits to acceptable levels?"

Attention to macrobudgeting did lead to investigations of how the economic context affected microbudgetary strategies. Economic productivity and income growth were relatively high during the two decades after World War II—the period described in the incrementaliststudies—but trended downward after this period. Schick suggested that incrementalism was an affordable form of budgeting during the earlier period because the economy's growth dividend was available to fund increments above the base. Spending programs were designed to grow, and the public learned to enjoy more benefits without paying commensurately increased taxes. When economic growth slowed, program designs and public expectations failed to adjust (or did so with very long lags), making budgeting more redistributive, conflict ridden, and unstable (Schick 1983, 1990).

Similar effects from fiscal stress were identified for budgeting in state and local governments. In response to taxpayer revolts like the Proposition 13 movement in California in 1978 and several municipal fiscal crises, scholars began to describe what they called *decremental* or *cutback* budgeting (Levine, Rubin, and Wolohojian 1981). Robert Behn succinctly stated the anti-incrementalist perspective of these studies.

> Indeed, the fundamental concepts of incremental budgeting are completely inverted by retrenchment. For example, although the incremental budgeting process is decentralized, decremental budgeting inherently requires centralization. Similarly, the substantive decisions of incremental budgeting are made in a fragmented manner, but decremental budgeting requires a comprehensive package (1985, 155).

A clear model emerged—as economic performance declined, governments suffered fiscal stress, which overloaded existing budgetary institutions. Advocates of controlling spending (or limiting tax or borrowing increases) responded with attempts at centralization, while prospending forces sought fragmentation. Thus Bozeman and Straussman suggested that fiscal stress increased the importance of top-down, executive-coordinated decision making relative to bottom-up, or incremental decision making (1982; see also Fischer and Kamlet 1984).[7]

Would a Modified Incrementalism Be Useful?

Initially, the strong qualities of *The Politics of the Budgetary Process* led many readers to overlook its weaker ones. It captured much that is important about the process of budgeting, particularly the effects of skillful confidence maintenance and clientele development. Of course, these acts are generally advantageous for success in many political processes, and not just in budgeting. In addition, many of the strategies specific to budgeting were so clearly described with telling quotes that they rang true to readers.

On the other hand, these strategies were poorly categorized. Wildavsky described some strategies as being contingent on the aspirations of agencies for outcomes. Some contingent strategies were described as appropriate for agencies that sought to maintain the base, and others were said to be more appropriate for expanding the base. But why would aspiration levels be the sole (or even an important) basis for planning budgetary strategies? For example, classified in the section on expanding the base were "It pays for itself" and "Spend to save." Both strategies seek to persuade decision makers of the benefits of spending and are equally plausible strategies for either maintaining or expanding the base. Most of the other contingent strategies seem logically unrelated to outcome aspirations.

More generally, the criticisms described above are considered to have substantially invalidated incrementalism. Allen Schick has provided a telling evaluation.

> Incrementalism is an extraordinarily elastic and elusive concept. It can be made to fit just about every budgetary circumstance. When expenditure trends for particular activities and projects were shown to include budgetary decreases, the concept was reformulated into one that deals with total spending by agencies, so that incrementalism could coexist with declines in particular programs. When big dollar shifts were shown to occur in some agency budgets, incrementalism was redefined in terms of "the regularity or irregularity of the change in size, not the absolute amount of the changes themselves."

7. But Stewart has suggested that historical experience in the Congress does not fully support this model. While analysis of structural changes and policy decisions from 1865 to 1921 confirmed the model in most situations, there were occasions of "expansionary centralization" and "retrenching fragmentation" (Stewart 1988, 1989). For other historical analyses, see Wander 1982; Huitt 1963; Fisher 1975. See also Ferejohn and Krehbiel 1987.

> . . . Incrementalism says more about what budgeting is not—and cannot be—than about what budgeting is. It asserts that budget makers cannot reexamine every item in the budget every year. They cannot pit all programs against one another in a competition for scarce funds. They cannot canvass all the options that might merit consideration. They cannot look much beyond the next budget to gauge the effects of current decisions on future programs.
>
> To do these things would overload the budget process, require more data and calculations than can be handled in the time available for preparing the budget, and would open intractable conflicts over money. So rather than being "rational" and comprehensive, budget makers are incremental. But within the broad expanse of the increment, incrementalism offers little explanation as to how decisions are made. It does not deal with how the increment is divided, with "who gets what," which Wildavsky pinpointed as the all-important issue in budgeting. It does not explain why some programs grow more than others, and why shares in the budget change over time. It does not explain why spending increases are big in some years but small in others. It says very little about budget outcomes, other than that they are incremental (1983, 3; see also LeLoup 1978b; Berry and Lowery 1989; Berry 1990).

By 1984, when *The Politics of the Budgetary Process* was published in its fourth edition, Wildavsky acknowledged in a long prologue that the incrementalist model was now less powerful. He blamed the development of an insatiable desire for spending among politicians, a ready justification for spending in excess of revenues from Keynesian economists, and a strategic response by spending advocates—in his model, agencies. His description of this response is worth quoting at length.

> Annualarity signifies predictability; this norm is not only desirable but feasible; the budget *will* last a year. With this common expectation, agencies are impelled to make accommodation with central controllers, like the Office of Management and Budget (OMB). Though not spelled out, this is the mutual understanding: because the Treasury promises to pay the amount passed in the budget, agencies will exercise restraint in requests and try to stay within the allotted amounts. To break that implied contract is to court a number of consequences. When the Treasury cannot guarantee payment of the allotted amount, agency political activity increases—not merely to get all that it asked for but also to keep it. If the budget sends a signal to "get it if you can," early accommodation is unwise, resulting in delayed decisions and enhanced uncertainty. Agencies that find such uncertainty intolerable will try to escape from prior restraints by making

> larger demands, and so there will be more left when cuts come. Thus initial bids become ever less reliable as a true gauge of agency expectations. Rather than remain within the appropriations process and absorb the inescapable uncertainty, program advocates seek to escape by making direct drafts on the Treasury (called "backdoor spending," or entitlements); by loans or loan guarantees; through shifting functions to "off-budget" entities; through special funds and "earmarked taxes"; and by imposing regulations on private parties, which then must bear the cost even though it does not appear in the agency budget. Inevitably, as funds available to the Central Treasury shrink, representing a lesser proportion of the total; and, without direct control over loan guarantees, entitlements, and the rest, grows less able to calculate how much is being spent—the Treasury tries to impose a harsher regimen on what is left, tempting agencies and program advocates to attempt further escape measures (1984, xviii–xix; see also Kettl 1989).[8]

Then, in 1988, Wildavsky published *The New Politics of the Budgetary Process* (a second edition emerged in 1992). This was a remarkable book in many ways. It was as readable as the original work, broader in coverage, and often insightful. It also contained many factual and interpretive errors. For example, he wrote that "the annual *balance sheet*—the outlays—is not the same as *commitments*—the budget authority" (1992, 13). This is a totally confused description of basic financial and budgetary concepts. Outlays measure the net liquidation of obligations (usually with cash), while a balance sheet records the assets, liabilities, and equity (or surplus) of an organization. Or, for example, the discussion of trust funds features the Commodity Credit Corporation, which is not a trust fund. The entire discussion of trust funds has little to do with the actual characteristics of trust funds.

More importantly, Wildavsky largely abandoned the incremental theory of the previous book, labeling as "classical" (and therefore somewhat out-of-date) the strategies, roles, and norms that were at the center of the book. The criticisms of incremental budgeting theory were ignored, perhaps as a battle best forgotten (see Caiden 1990, 229).

"Budget Structure" Strategy

My alternative description of budgetary strategies draws on lessons learned from these criticisms of incrementalism. For example, it does not emphasize role conceptions that are based on institutional position. Rather, it simply

---

8. Given the nonparticipation of the Treasury Department in the microbudgetary process except when its own or highly related accounts are involved, the reader should interpret Wildavsky's use of "Treasury" as metaphorical.

classifies participants based on their goals for spending. *Spending advocates* seek to increase or maintain funding for programs. *Controllers* resist spending advocates, either because they oppose the purposes of the spending advocates' favored programs or because they would like to limit total spending (or the taxes and borrowing that finance spending). Both spending advocates and controllers try to influence *decision makers,* who as leaders of the government or as their delegates are legally authorized to make budget decisions.

My conception does resemble previous research by making a simplifying assumption about behavior.[9] The past work assumed that organizational membership determined an actor's role.[10] Agency bureaucrats were budget maximizers (Blais and Dion 1991). Members of Congress acted as claimants for the interests that supported them, except for those few members who were on the committees that were supposed to "guard the Treasury." The Budget Bureau staff represented the president, who primarily tried to avoid reelection-threatening recessions.

Those who made such assumptions realized that the goals of political actors are often much more complex. Agency bureaucrats, for example, not only want their funding to grow but also desire (at the least) predictability and autonomy, both of which can be threatened by funding growth (Bozeman and Straussman 1990, 56–61). Similarly, I realize that actors who are spending advocates for some programs are controllers for others, and that ignoring goal conflicts may limit what can be learned about these actors. On the other hand, by classifying participants on the basis of their goals for spending, it is easier to focus on the strategies and tactics that they use.

Another lesson from the criticisms of incrementalism is that we must recognize that budgeting is an especially competitive process. The competition may not always be zero-sum because of some flexibility in defining the effective limit on spending. Nevertheless, political and financial constraints on governments eventually produce zero-sum conflict. Winners and losers are relatively easy to identify in budgeting.

To understand this competition, I use a group perspective, viewing the competitors as coalitions of organizations and actors that support or oppose spending for specific programs. There are usually more spending advocates than controllers. Membership in coalitions is not fixed; while there are usually core supporters that lead, coalitions may also contain temporary members who help out every now and again. The core members of a spending advocate coalition are usually the responsible agency and one or more interest groups.

---

9. One of the central methodological issues in modern political science is whether it is useful to assume that political actors have simple or complex goals. The typical choice is between narrow self-interest or a mix of self-interest and altruism. See Mansbridge 1990.

10. On the utility of role conceptions, see Searing 1991.

At times, though, an agency may oppose spending for one of its programs because this spending may not fit with its preferred mission.

The core members of controller coalitions are usually OMB and the Budget committees. They are sometimes joined by organizations that oppose particular spending programs; an example is how railroads typically oppose highway spending. But even OMB directors and others who usually act as controllers sometimes act as spending advocates.

Coalitional strength changes with the mobilization or demobilization of political resources. Important resources include an active membership, money, and expertise. They are used to influence the selection of actors who have the authority to make decisions and to persuade them to support the coalition's goals. (Again, these tactics of resource mobilization, bargaining, and argumentation are usually effective in most political processes—not just in budgeting.)

A third lesson from criticisms of incrementalism is that we need a better understanding of strategies that are budget specific and those that challenge the budgetary status quo. Incremental strategy relies heavily on general political tactics that I just described. Coalitions should mobilize resources to demonstrate clientele support. They should also try to earn the trust and respect of decision makers. Incremental strategists become budget specific when they suggest that the appropriate way to request appropriations is to politely ask for just a little more.

An alternative strategy instead features disrespect of budgetary authorities. This strategy uses tactics that respond to, and seek to change, the structure of the budgetary process—the characteristics of the process of budgeting that shape budgetary behaviors. It is useful to think of this structure as it applies to individual programs. Each program has its own

method of *accounting* for its spending,
decision procedure used to provide it with spending authority,
policy design that guides how it may acquire and spend funds for different purposes, and
commonly-perceived *effects* of its spending.

Spending advocates learn how certain budgetary characteristics provide advantages to programs, and they try to have the most advantageous budgetary characteristics applied to their programs. They try to change accounting practices to reduce the reported costs of programs. They attempt to develop and transmit believable rationales for programs, in hopes of offsetting accounted-for, process-controlled costs with a level of perceived benefits that justify these costs. They avoid macrobudgetary controls when possible. They shop for microbudgetary decision procedures that place few hurdles in the way of spending and contain few competitors for the funds that they covet. Finally, they try to design the budgetary operations of programs so that funds are received from several, stable sources and spending is dedicated and automatic.

Unfortunately for advocates, controllers often respond to these tactics. They control spending by making costs more visible and by showing that spending isn't effective. They develop procedures that require programs to compete against each other for funding. They argue for periodic reviews of all programs. And they propose that programs be redesigned to make them more flexible, in order to respond to fiscal stress should the need arise.

The structure of the existing budget process is the product of this dynamic competition between controllers and spending advocates. Current accounting standards were accepted both because they were perceived to defensibly represent the effects of financial transactions *and* because they permitted the resolution of the budgetary competition in the previous period. The schedule for the current budget reflects a calculation of how much time is needed to complete the mechanical steps of budget decisions *and* an admission that previous competitions have sheltered some programs from the threat of annual budget cuts and focused attention on others. Participants in the process and their methods for making decisions and resolving conflicts are determined in part by constitutional rules, but also by the previous competition over how much power should be delegated to central budget agencies and committees. (See also Jones and Euske 1991.)

A fourth lesson from criticisms of incrementalism is that budgetary actors vary in the complexity of calculations they make. Incrementalism is right in suggesting that actors do not act rationally, if rationality is defined as possessing complete information and strong computational powers. The participants in the dynamic of control and advocacy are often confused, using inappropriate tactics and developing poorly designed strategies. But they do learn, and some learn better than others. Those who can understand how new contexts make certain tactics likely to succeed show skill in the strategy of budget structure.

A final lesson from the criticisms of incrementalism is that the difficulty of testing budgetary theories provides clues about budgetary strategies. This is the subject of the next chapter, which begins by evaluating the methodologies used in quantitative studies of budgeting by political scientists. I show that most studies wrongly assumed that government-reported budgetary data are reliable and valid measures of who got what.

The third chapter expands on the budget structure strategy that I just outlined. It ties the potential effectiveness of budget-structure strategies to some paradoxical social expectations for the budgeting process. The four following chapters catalog budget-structure tactics. Chapter 4 shows how spending advocates and controllers have dueled over budgetary accounting practices. Chapter 5 describes how they battled over budgetary decision processes. Chapter 6 describes typical conflicts over budgetary policy designs. Chapter 7 covers the role of program argumentation in budgeting, detailing arguments used by advocates and controllers about the effects of spending. The final chapter describes an agenda for structural reform of the budget process.

An appendix includes short discussions of the methodology used to produce the book and of the potential validity of the budget structure model. To briefly anticipate those discussions, this book is highly place and time specific. It is based primarily on participant observation of budgetary strategies used in the federal government during the 1980s.

Chapter 2

Strategy behind the "Fog Bank"

> Budget data is like a fog bank. The current system gives one a feel for a tier of numbers, one or more times removed from the actuals. You can trust it as far as you can trust *Pravda*!
>
> (A long-time budget technician, 1985)[1]

Political scientists certainly have not shared this perception. As Wildavsky wrote, in budgeting "the outcomes are specific and quantifiable" (1964, 126). They were free, replicable, interval level, and spanned a long time. With such measurement simplicity, which self-respecting scholar wouldn't boot up the computer?

But I argue in this chapter that there is much truth in the budget technician's claim. Budgeting is a process that features money, yet most budgetary research ignored *how* the government counts its money.[2] This led to mismeasurement of outcomes, which impaired many tests of budgetary theories. In addition, the emphasis on testing existing theory slowed recognition that *bad* data is *good* for some participants in the process. This is surprising, for social scientists have long recognized that government statistical series must be interpreted with care—statistics are generally collected and reported under the direction of the powerful, who sometimes prefer not to share accurate information with others (see, for example, Alonso and Starr 1987; Stone 1988, 127–46; Tufte 1977).

To make these points, this chapter compares federal budgetary concepts with the outcome measures used in research studies. Much of the chapter's material is technical, but this is necessary to explain the actual dynamics of the structural strategies. I describe the case of the Farmers Home Administration (FmHA) to illustrate how previous studies failed to accurately measure budgetary outcomes for this agency. These studies used government-reported budgetary data for FmHA, even though FmHA spending projections were

1. Regarding *Pravda,* note when this statement was made.

2. The main exceptions were Leonard's book (1986) on "quiet spending," which he defined as "any use of public financial resources without appropriation," Ippolito's book (1984) on credit spending, and an important conference paper by Ellwood (1985b), which showed how tests of macrobudgetary and political business cycle theories often used inappropriate data.

routinely misleading. Erroneously reported budget outcomes were the *intended* result of the strategy used by FmHA supporters, who compensated for their poverty of traditional political resources by skillfully manipulating budgetary procedures. The chapter then briefly describes how spending advocates for rural electrification used a similar structural strategy despite their comparative wealth of traditional political resources.

Measurement and Analytical Conventions in Quantitative Studies

The dominant statistical paradigm in the quantitative investigations of budgeting expects data to take the following form: a relatively large set of observations, linearity in parameters and variables, stability of cases over time, and independence of cases. The early quantitative studies used simple linear regression to model yearly or within-year changes; later studies often used simultaneous equations. Time series were for periods of ten to thirty years, and researchers often employed a selection rule that required an observation within each period. Sample sizes usually exceeded thirty cases. When researchers introduced numerous independent variables into equations to compare the causal strengths of different factors, they typically pooled cases within years to increase the power of statistical tests.

The most sophisticated studies in this framework have been those by Malachowski, Bookheimer, and Lowery and by Kiewiet and McCubbins. The former documented changes in the advocacy, guardian, and appeals court roles over the 1948 to 1984 period (1987). Kiewiet and McCubbins found an incremental pattern of small increases over the period of 1948–79 for the appropriations for thirty-seven agencies (1985a). They also modeled the effects of a large set of expected determinants, such as partisan differences, transitions between administrations, inflation, and unemployment, and confirmed their expectation that congressional-presidential interactions are largely accommodative. In another study, they concluded that presidents have more influence on spending "when the president desires to spend less than Congress than when he would rather spend more" (1985c). A third study confirmed the hypothesis that Congress is more generous in election years than in off years (1985b; see also Kiewiet and McCubbins 1991).

Aside from some notable improvements in statistical techniques, the studies that I just summarized differed little from the earlier ones by Fenno and by Davis, Dempster, and Wildavsky (Berry and Lowery 1989, 450). Tucker, a critic of the methodological quality of the earlier research, concluded that "progress in model building would be stimulated if critics of incrementalism would devote less effort to disconfirmation by identifying counterexamples and more effort to identifying superior models" (1982, 335).[3] In my opinion, doing so will require relaxing some of the measurement and analytical conventions of these studies. Take, for example, the sample selection rule that excluded cases for which observations could not be made in every period of the time series. This eliminated the problem of missing data that would have complicated analyses, but also ruled out some cases—new agencies, dead agencies, reorganized agencies—which would be nonincremental by definition! For example, Malachowski, Bookheimer, and Lowery describe their data set:

> The data used in the analyses to follow represents an updated version of the set used by Fenno (1966) in *The Power of the Purse,* covering the years FY48 through FY84 for those agencies studied by Fenno that were not later absorbed by reorganization or allowed to lapse through legislation. *Thus 14 of the 36 domestic agencies studied by Fenno are not included in the data set.* (1987, 332; emphasis added)

Another stability assumption was implicit—that spending outcomes were constant in meaning, being devoted to the same programmatic or organizational purposes. This eliminated the inferential problems that would have resulted if substantial program metamorphoses had occurred, ignoring the strong possibility that they had. In housing programs, for example, there seems to be a rapid pace of program modification and replacement through passage of new "sections of the act." Unfortunately, there is no easy way of demonstrating the rate of instability in the budgetary universe. In my interviewing a number of informants in the budget agencies and committees expressed the belief that substantial change is a normal condition. Several recounted stories of the large effort required to keep the computerized program and account structure up-to-date.[4]

Another simplifying assumption is that accounts are independent of each other. In fact, many budget accounts are substantially interdependent. Some receive or pay significant amounts through intragovernmental transfers. An extreme example is the Census Bureau, which was included in many of the quantitative studies. Census conducts surveys for other agencies, and its fortune waxes and wanes with those of the paying agencies. In 1985, 51 percent of

3. See also Gist 1982; Berry 1986, 1990; and Berry and Lowery 1989.

4. There are no historical archives that record changes made in this structure, probably for lack of any utility to the operations of the agencies and committees. An estimate of a maximum level of instability could be made by recording the number and purposes of budget accounts and programs changed in a program area. See Bickers 1991; Kaufman 1976; and Anton, Cawley, and Kramer's description of "core" and "barometer" programs (1980, 106).

its obligations were performed for other agencies.[5] Another type of interdependence is when account outcomes are partially determined by the conditions that affect spending in other accounts *and* by the spending in these accounts. This occurs particularly in budgets for income-security programs, because eligibility for programs is often tied to eligibility for other programs. Budget agencies respond to such interdependence by formally estimating offsets.

Along with doubt about the stability and independence of cases should come greater skepticism about linearity. The statement by Davis et al. that "the budgetary process of the United States is equivalent to a set of temporally stable linear decision rules" is simply implausible for the many programs that are directly related by law to conditions that show cyclical or other nonlinear patterns of change over time (Davis, Dempster, and Wildavsky 1966, 537). Indeed, it would be surprising if unemployment insurance or farm subsidies didn't track cyclical labor and commodity markets.[6]

But the convention that government-reported data is reliable is most open to challenge. When the quantitative research began, data were typically taken from the Brown Books, which are annual publications of the Appropriations committees, and from presidential budget documents.[7] It is unclear whether any of these investigators ever looked into how these figures were generated. Let us do that now by reviewing one agency's budget accounts—those for the Farmers Home Administration. FmHA is admittedly an extreme case, one that was chosen to dramatize the inadequacy of the measurement conventions. But it is not unique.

Budgetary Outcomes for the Farmers Home Administration

The Farmers Home Administration is an agency of the Department of Agriculture (USDA).[8] It has described itself as the "world's biggest governmental loan agency" (Farmers Home Administration 1980, 10).[9] It provides agricultural credit to relatively needy borrowers, subsidizes rural housing construction and rents, and finances construction and operation of rural development projects.

5. In 1985, total receipts by accounts from other accounts exceeded $150 billion.

6. Such cyclicality has been demonstrated by Bassein and Schulman 1985 for a small set of outcomes (measured as reported outlays).

7. The "Brown Books" are an annual Senate document known as *Appropriations, Budget Estimates, Etc.*

8. Useful sources on FmHA include Ippolito 1984; Shillingsburg 1979; Gilbert and Smith 1976; Schussheim 1974; U.S. Department of Agriculture 1985; Chite 1989; and Drews 1982.

9. The World Bank, at the very least, might dispute this claim.

FmHA's budget authority and outlays were $18.3 and $11.1 billion respectively in 1985, and as of the end of this year had a portfolio of outstanding direct loans with a principal of $65 billion.[10] (1985 is used as a reference year in this chapter because it is the last year for many long-standing budgetary accounting practices before the Balanced Budget Act [Gramm-Rudman-Hollings] changed them.)

FmHA received regular attention in the research that tested budget theories. Some studies (mistakenly) bundled FmHA's appropriations with appropriations for other USDA agencies (for example, Davis, Dempster, and Wildavsky 1966). Fenno was the first to look at FmHA separately, when he compared appropriations requests and outcomes for a sample of thirty-six agencies and found relatively few changes of large magnitude over a twenty-year plus time period (1966). However, he measured only the salaries and expenses account (known as its S and E account) for FmHA, which funds its basic administrative expenses. The S and E account included 29 percent of FmHA's outlays in 1966; the proportion declined to only 3 percent in 1985. The balance of FmHA's spending was made up of its loans and payments for agricultural credit, housing, and rural development assistance. Fenno found that FmHA's S and E appropriations grew at comparatively slow rates in the House (2.8 percent) and Senate (4.7 percent). Many later studies used Fenno's sample frame, modifying it a bit for changes in organization. Some of these studies reported specific findings for FmHA, while some others were prevented from doing so by the pooling of cases within years.

During this period, FmHA carried out a variety of programs through more than a dozen budget accounts, and one might reasonably expect the outcomes for these programs and accounts to vary. Therefore, the following analysis will be restricted to one major component of FmHA's budget—the Rural Housing Insurance Fund (RHIF). RHIF was one of the largest budget accounts for FmHA activities, constituting approximately 36 percent of FmHA's outlays in 1985. The programs financed by RHIF were typically not cheap. Many "rural housing direct loans," for example, were extended at 1 to 3 percent interest for 20- to 50-year terms. In 1985, OMB calculated that the present value of the subsidies associated with these loans ranged from 13 to 76 percent of the face values (these are averages for different types of loans).[11] Most of the rest of FmHA's budget—the activities in the Agricultural Credit Insurance Fund (49 percent of FmHA outlays in 1985) and the Rural Development Insurance Fund

10. OMB, Budget of the U.S. Government, Special Analysis F: F56–7. When budget data is cited by year, the data is for the federal fiscal year. The fiscal year started on 1 July until 1976, when 1 October became the starting date. The period from 1 July 1976 to 30 September 1976 is known as the Transition Quarter, or TQ in tabular presentation.

11. OMB, Budget of the U.S. Government, FY87, Special Analysis F: F-33.

(10 percent of FmHA outlays in 1985)—resemble the operations and accounting of RHIF.

Budget Concepts circa 1985

Before examining the RHIF in detail, I will describe basic federal budgetary concepts from 1985. Figure 2.1 shows these concepts and some of their interrelationships.

Obligations are legal commitments to spend money, whether in the present or the future. Obligations are liquidated when checks, cash, or certain in-kind benefits (valued in dollars) are disbursed. Such liquidations are called *outlays.* (Prior to the Congressional Budget Act, outlays were known as *expenditures.*)

Authority to obligate funds comes in a variety of forms. Most authority is defined legally as *budget authority.* As defined in the Congressional Budget Act, budget authority itself comes in several forms–*appropriations, borrowing authority* (authority to spend debt receipts), *contract authority* (authority to enter into contracts in advance of the receipt of funds to cover these obligations), and *entitlement authority* (authority to make payments to individuals who are legally entitled to benefits even if funds have not already been provided in appropriations acts).

Excluded from the definition of budget authority is the legal authority to insure or guarantee debts, even though outlays often result from such authority. In addition, many accounts receive payments directly from the public, and these collections may be used to finance new obligations. In so-called *revolving funds,* offsetting collections are *deducted* from new obligations to arrive at the budget authority figure. Another type of obligational authority that is not recorded as budget authority are funds provided by *transfers* from off-budget governmental agencies or from on-budget accounts. Some programs have no need for budget authority in some years because of their reliance on these sources.

Further complicating the situation is the fact that there are different varieties of appropriations. Appropriations that are *discretionary* require annual action to become available. Other appropriations are *permanent* in the law, meaning that funds will be available for obligation without further legislative action. In most accounts, the *receipt* of permanently appropriated funds (dedicated taxes, for example) is counted as budget authority, but in other accounts, the *use* of permanently appropriated funds (to pay entitlement benefits, for example) is counted as budget authority.

Some provisions in appropriations acts are *not* counted as budget authority, however. In accounts that receive dedicated revenues as a source for financing, appropriations may be used to *limit* the expenditures of these funds for certain purposes. The administrative expenses of the Social Security Administration are constrained in this manner. Other appropriations not scored as

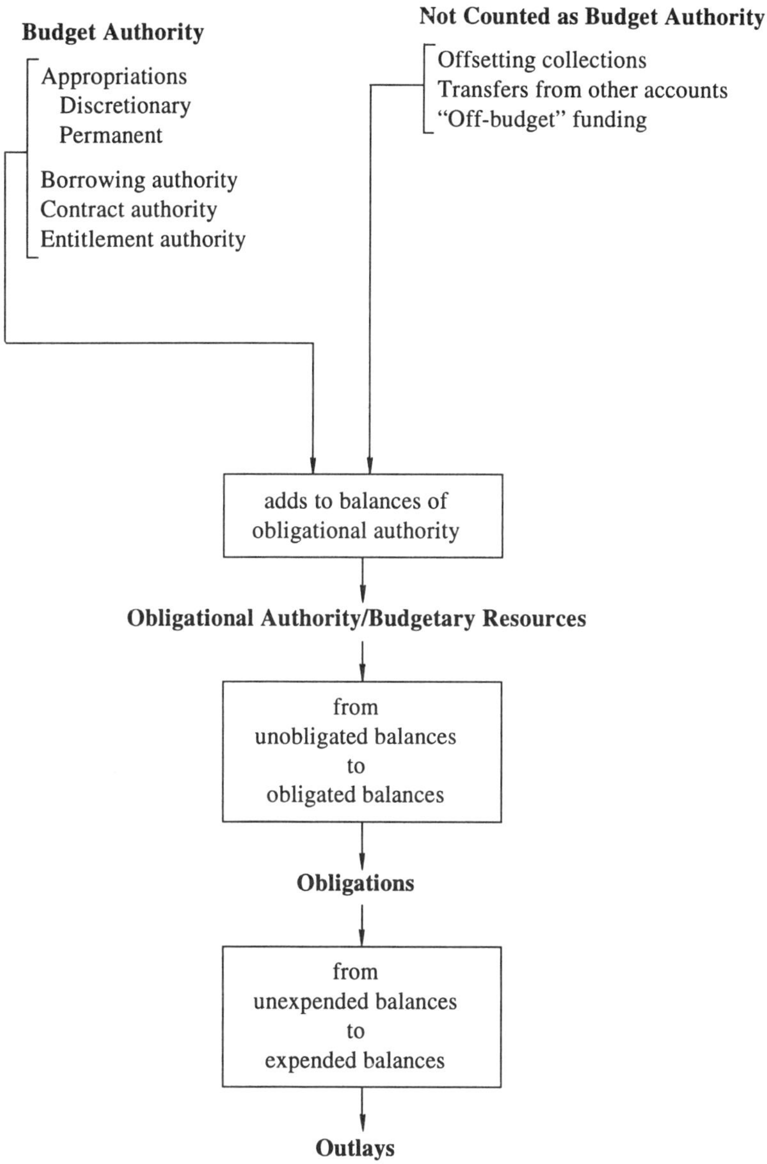

Fig. 2.1. General model of 1985 budget concepts

budget authority are those that are used to "pay off" obligations that have already been counted as budget authority—to liquidate contracts, retire the debt from use of borrowing authority, and to make up deficiencies from unfunded entitlement payments.

Concepts for the *flows* of authorities and funds—crucial to an understanding of budget documents—are shown in figure 2.1. Reading toward the bottom, conversion of balances from unexpended to expended status represents the *spendout* of obligations. In most budget accounts, the spendout rate is not controlled. In certain accounts, however, the rate of outlays is changed by varying the rate of obligations or the receipt of financing. The obligation of funds from a stock of obligational authority draws down unobligated balances and adds to obligated balances. Some authority may never be used, however, or may lapse if granted for only a definite period of time, or may be rescinded by statute. Receipt of new budget authority or other funds by an account increases its stock of balances of obligational authority, a stock that is sometimes described as *budgetary resources.*

The Illusion and Reality of RHIF

Table 2.1 shows RHIF's appropriations, budget authority, outlays, and new loan obligations over the period 1966–89. Five simple observations about these data follow.

1. The trend in appropriations is not an incremental one, using the (either discredited or abandoned) standard of annual increments of less than 10 percent—only a fifth of the year-to-year changes meet this standard. On the other hand, the trend in loan obligations is relatively incremental, with half of the year-to-year changes meeting or approaching 10 percent.
2. RHIF appropriations grew fastest in the 1980s, but loan obligations were *declining* at this time.
3. In some years RHIF received *no* appropriations, yet continued to create loan obligations.
4. In most years budget authority amounts are much larger than appropriations amounts.
5. In most years outlay amounts are smaller than budget authority amounts, and in some years are *negative.*

How can these data be explained? Table 2.2 can help guide us to answers. This table is the Program and Financing Statement for the RHIF reproduced from the fiscal year 1982 budget appendix. A *P and F* is prepared for each budget account and includes most of the important financial information that can be found in the budget documents. Unfortunately, P and Fs are complex

TABLE 2.1. RHIF Budgetary Outcomes (actual dollars in millions)

Year	New Loan Obligations[a]	Outlays	Budget Authority[b]	Appropriations
1966	146	31	100	100
1967	388	31	0	0
1968	514	49	73	0
1969	503	10	105	1
1970	765	125	31	31
1971	1,229	−186	1	1
1972	1,613	169	86	24
1973	1,655	−232	78	53
1974	1,480	1,290	1,576	90
1975	2,360	−898	126	126
1976	2,439	1	122	122
TQ	642	514	1	1
1977	2,590	89	506	176
1978	3,303	449	669	330
1979	3,649	184	790	334
1980	3,587	1,717	2,280	351
1981	3,314	−130	594	562
1982	3,444	1,246	2,004	658
1983	2,951	1,828	2,100	1,214
1984	2,776	2,340	2,604	1,621
1985	2,718	2,385	2,522	1,948
1986	1,825	3,235	3,034	1,978
1987	1,716	798	2,434	2,434
1988	1,845	3,611	6,594	3,114
1989	1,845	3,611	4,837	3,837

Source: Budget of the U.S. Government, Fiscal Years 1968–91.

[a]Data for new loan obligations are drawn only from one line in each year's Program and Financing Statement. This line was labeled "loans obligated," "loans from the fund," "from fund for later sale," "loans made from fund," or "loans obligated, excluding financed sales from inventory." This is the most reliable and least complex measure, but it slightly understates loan obligation totals in each year.

[b]New obligational authority for 1966 and 1967.

and can be confusing, so the text identifies line numbers and columns to guide readers.

Appropriations are on lines 40 and 60. For the RHIF account, appropriations were made to recapitalize the fund for the losses and interest subsidies of two years beforehand. That is, *the appropriations for this account, treated as the object of an incremental bargaining process in all of the cross-budget quantitative studies, were generally treated as relatively mandatory by all budgeting participants.*[12] As a result, one might expect to discover a strong correlation between requested and actual appropriations.

12. Exceptions occurred in fiscal years 1986 and 1987, when the Congress appropriated less than was required to fully recapitalize the fund for prior losses.

TABLE 2.2. Program and Financing (in thousands of dollars)

	Identification code 12-4141-0-3-371	1980 actual	1981 est.	1982 est.
	Program by activities:			
	Capital investment, funded:			
	1. Loans made:			
	(a) Payment of delinquent installments	891	800	700
	(b) Advances on behalf of borrowers	15,501	18,000	21,000
	(c) Loans from the fund	3,587,311	4,022,000	4,251,000
	2. Purchase of loans from investors	114,957	220,000	125,000
	3. Purchase of certificates of beneficial ownership	2,882,297	2,387,000	894,000
	4. Interest on loans purchased from investors	–9	100	100
	5. Collateral acquired by default	12,884	19,300	24,100
	6. Judgments	3	—	—
	7. Disbursement of loan repayments to investors	83,520	98,800	55,000
	Total capital investment funded	6,697,355	6,766,000	5,370,900
	Operating costs, funded:			
	1. Administrative expense	—	3,000	3,000
	2. Interest on certificates of beneficial ownership	1,502,415	2,087,000	2,623,000
	3. Premium interest for investors	6,685	4,300	3,500
	4. Interest on participation certificates	6,247	6,246	5,394
	5. Amortized discount on participation certificates	10	10	10
	6. Interest expense on withheld collections	4,781	5,000	4,750
	7. Interest on borrowings	88,945	136,800	105,100
	8. Interest supplements	3,631	3,400	2,500
	9. Rental assistance payments	31,283	111,000	151,000
	10. Homeownership assistance payments	—	—	1,000
	11. Certificates of beneficial ownership and insured loan sales expense	11	13	12
	12. Compensation for construction defects	588	2,000	2,000
	13. Other expense	2,579	1,300	1,480
	Total operating costs, funded	1,647,175	2,360,069	2,902,746
	Total program costs, funded	8,344,530	9,126,069	8,273,646
	Change in selected resources (undelivered orders)	480,522	369,577	465,578
10.00	Total obligations	8,825,052	9,495,646	8,739,224
	Financing:			
	Offsetting collections from:			
11.00	Federal funds: Investment income from participation sales fund	–6,436	–6,470	–5,628

TABLE 2.2—*Continued*

Identification code 12-4141-0-3-371		1980 actual	1981 est.	1982 est.
	Non-Federal sources:			
14.00	Repayments on loans held by the fund	–746,163	–900,000	–1,050,000
14.00	Loan repayments received on behalf of investors	–83,520	–98,800	–55,000
14.00	Repayments on advances	–9,031	–12,000	–15,000
14.00	Sale of loans	–78,073	–60,000	–50,000
14.00	Proceeds from sale of acquired property	–9,311	–15,000	–22,500
14.00	Payments on judgments	–79	–150	–200
14.00	Insurance premiums	–676	–600	–500
14.00	Guarantee fees	–7	–20	–25
14.00	Interest revenue	–935,438	–1,057,009	–1,164,162
14.00	Principal attributed to subsidy recoveries	–2	–400	–2,000
14.00	Subsidy recoveries	–5	–800	–3,000
14.00	Fees and other revenue	–2,373	–1,883	–1,983
15.00	Off-budget Federal entities; Sale of certificates of beneficial ownership	–4,681,000	–7,341,130	–4,161,380
22.98	Unobligated balance transferred from participation sales fund: Fund balance	—	—	–23,843
23.98	Unobligated balance transferred to participation sales fund: Fund balance	7,259	4,567	3,729
31.00	Redemption of debt	—	—	23,843
32.47	Balance of authority to borrow withdrawn	—	609,367	—
39.00	Budget authority	2,280,199	615,318	2,211,575
	Budget authority:			
	Current:			
40.00	Appropriation (definite)	320,209	504,318	653,967
40.00	Appropriation (indefinite)	31,283	111,000	152,000
60.00	Appropriation (indefinite)	—	—	—
67.10	Authority to borrow (42 U.S.C. 1487 (h)) (indefinite)	1,928,706	—	1,405,608
	Relation of obligations to outlays:			
71.00	Obligations incurred, net	2,272,939	1,384	2,207,846
	Obligated balance, start of year:			
72.47	Authority to borrow	2,422,378	3,151,085	2,511,718
72.98	Fund balance	312,656	139,855	1,521,413
	Obligated balance, end of year:			
74.47	Authority to borrow	–3,151,085	–2,511,718	–3,917,326
74.98	Fund balance	–139,855	–1,521,413	–755,499
90.00	Outlays	1,717,035	–740,807	1,568,152

RHIF also had permanent authority to borrow indefinite amounts from the Treasury on an unsecured basis. This *borrowing authority* is shown on line 67.10. Borrowing authority allowed RHIF to receive funds from the Treasury without first going through the appropriations process. Borrowing and appropriations add to the total for *budget authority* on line 39. For 1981, the Carter administration estimated that RHIF would receive $615 million in budget authority.

RHIF's major form of program *obligations*—loans—are shown on line 1c, under "capital investment." The estimate of loans for 1981 was roughly $4 billion. But compare this obligation level to the estimate for *outlays*—on line 90—of a *negative* $741 million. That is, in the same year when RHIF would be committing itself to obligate $4 billion of loan funds, with only $615 million in budget authority, the budget estimated that RHIF would actually be taking in cash! How could this happen?

First, it's important to understand that RHIF was a *revolving fund*—legally authorized to collect payments on old loans and use these funds to make new loans and grants. Only the net financing needs were recorded as requiring budget authority. This practice was justified by the principle that budget authority should only show the net draw by an account on the general revenue of the Treasury. Repayments of principal and interest on old loans are shown on the entries for line 14. When repayments of old loans were large, revolving fund status could lead to big differences between obligations and budget authority.

Second, the Administration also estimated the RHIF would receive an additional *$7.3 billion* of funds *transferred* from the Treasury that would not be counted in the budget authority figure! This was shown on line 15, "Off-budget Federal entities: Sale of certificates of beneficial ownership." By packaging loans into securities called Certificates of Beneficial Ownership (CBOs) and by selling the CBOs to an *off-budget* bureau of the Treasury called the Federal Financing Bank (FFB), RHIF effectively could redeem the principal of loans and relend this principal. The flow chart of figure 2.2 should make these transactions clearer. RHIF received funds that were roughly equivalent to borrowing from the Treasury (there were minor differences in interest rates and other loan conditions), but that were *not* counted as borrowing from the Treasury. Complicating this transaction is a repurchase of old CBOs (line 3 under capital investment) and interest payments on outstanding CBOs (line 2 under operating costs)—the reasons for these payments by RHIF to the FFB are not important here—that reduced the net take by the RHIF from the FFB to about $4 billion.

In the annals of the manipulation of budget accounts, the 1981 estimate for RHIF is a classic case, if only for its magnitude. The RHIF's financing and accounting arrangement allowed the Carter administration to estimate in-

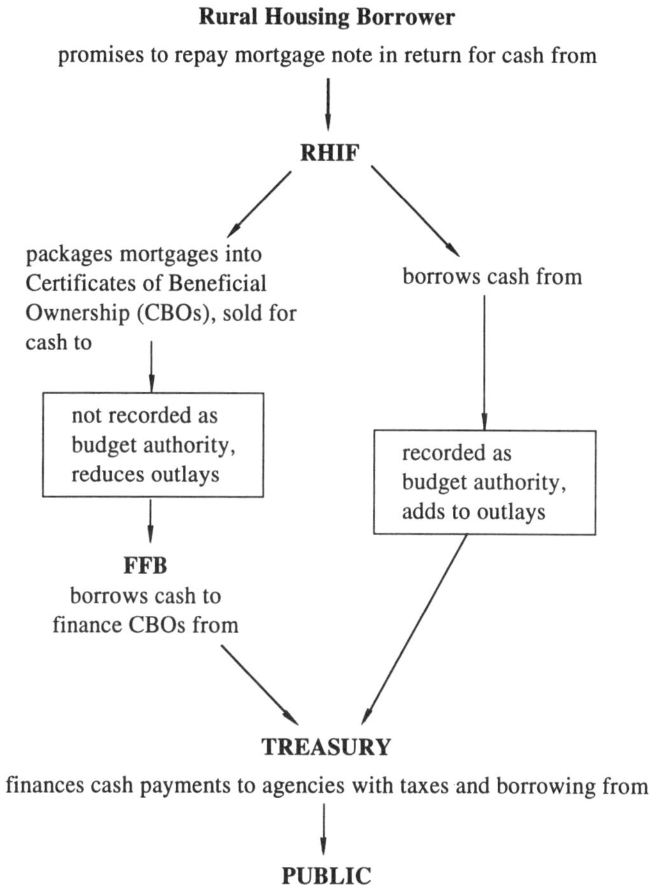

Fig. 2.2. RHIF-FFB-Treasury financial flows

creased obligations, but with a decline in budget authority and a massive decline in outlays. It may not be coincidental that this extreme plan was proposed in the previous year, ten months before the Presidential election. *But table 2.1 suggests that 1981 was not a novel year for RHIF's budget.* From the Johnson to the Carter administration, RHIF obligated increasing amounts on program activities without corresponding increases in outlays, budget authority, or appropriations. Most of the spending was financed by borrowing from the Treasury and from the public directly, and most of this borrowing was not recorded in the budget in a visible way. It was not until the Reagan administration that RHIF's borrowing was made more visible, and as a result RHIF's program obligations and other budgetary outcome measures began to track more closely.

Here is a more detailed story of RHIF's budgetary development. RHIF was created as a revolving fund in 1949. It was financed by appropriations and borrowing from the Treasury through 1957. In 1958, to raise additional funds, FmHA started selling its high-quality loan assets to investors. In effect, the promise of a reputable FmHA borrower to repay principal and interest was sold. These sales continued at a fairly low volume for the next seven years. Then, during the preparation of the fiscal year 1966 budget, as President Johnson realized the Vietnam War was beginning to cost some money and was feeling pressure to keep the outlay total under $100 billion, he told the Bureau of the Budget to find a way. Manipulating the RHIF accounts was one solution. By this time, RHIF had nearly run out of good paper to sell, and few investors would buy the promises of repayment from farmers on the brink of insolvency. To solve this problem, a new mechanism was invented. The lower-quality loans were pooled, provided with the federal government's assurance of their value, and sold in the securities market. These sales were known as *participation sales.* They were encouraged by the 1966 Participation Sales Act, which made it easier to package the loans, and which appointed Federal National Mortgage Association (FNMA), then part of HUD, as sales agent.[13]

These sales were in fact not sales, because FmHA actually kept ownership of the loans, the risk of defaults, and the responsibility for servicing the loans. The participation sales were actually a costly means of borrowing from the public. They did produce a political benefit, however, because this borrowing was not counted as part of Treasury borrowing—instead, it *reduced* the reported deficit. They also increased the budgetary resources of RHIF, which the administration supported anyway and which doubtless overjoyed housing advocates.

Unfortunately for FmHA and LBJ, the participation sales were criticized heavily in the press and on Wall Street. To deflect the criticism, LBJ appointed a Commission on Budget Concepts. In 1967, the President's Commission on Budget Concepts, over the objections of Budget Director Schultze, complained that

> net expenditures in Federal loan programs shown in the current budget have been correspondingly reduced by several billion dollars in each year and anyone looking at recent budget presentations could have been left

13. The Bureau of the Budget developed this approach by modifying a recommendation of 1962 Committee on Federal Credit Programs, whose intent was to graduate FmHA borrowers to private credit.

> with an erroneous impression as to the extent of increase in direct loans outstanding. (1967, 54)

The commission therefore recommended that FmHA and other agencies show the sales as borrowing from the public, which was done for the fiscal years 1967 and 1968 actuals. In addition, in 1968 FNMA was privatized, and no authority was granted to its successor, the Government National Mortgage Association (GNMA), to make participation sales for FmHA. Therefore, if FmHA wanted to retain its financing, it had to go back to borrowing directly from the market, and that is what FmHA wanted to do. Its advocates then amended the Housing Act of 1969 to require that the direct sale of RHIF loans be treated as the sale of loan assets, and not as borrowing from the public. This reversed the Commission on Budget Concepts' recommendation. Table 2.1 shows the subsequent drop in budget authority as a percentage of obligations. When the Housing Act expired, this language was incorporated into appropriation bills.

In 1973, President Nixon declared a moratorium on housing programs and impounded funds from rural development and from emergency disaster programs, including those in the RHIF. One of the responses was the Congressional Budget and Impoundment Control Act. The act established much tighter controls on borrowing, including the requirement to treat borrowing from the Treasury as budget authority, which in most previous years was hidden in the books. Table 2.1 shows how budget authority consequently peaked in 1974. Fortunately for RHIF, in the previous year, an even better source for covert financing had been created in the Treasury Department.

The Federal Financing Bank's initial role was to pool all agency debt—that of the Small Business Administration, the Export-Import Bank and sixteen other agencies—so that it could be sold to the public by the Treasury Department. The Treasury was quite upset about the borrowing premiums paid by agencies and about the lack of coordination by agencies with the Treasury when they went to market. The FFB was to serve as the Treasury's coordinator for all agency debt. It was to be an off-budget agency, in order not to count loans twice—once in the originating agency's account and a second time in the FFB's account.

In 1974, the FFB made several offerings to the public, but then it discontinued this practice and started borrowing directly from the Treasury (Ippolito 1984, 54). The effect on RHIF, when combined with the loan asset sales language, was to provide off-budget Treasury financing for RHIF—financing that was functionally equivalent to appropriations but was not counted as appropriations. This opened the floodgates for a very rapid growth in RHIF obligations. RHIF reduced its on-budget borrowing from the Treasury and borrowed off-budget instead, with plenty of support from the rural-oriented Carter administration.

The Reagan administration took a strong ideological stand against FmHA (except in election year of 1984). This is reflected in one of OMB director Stockman's most famous statements: "For the life of me, I cannot figure out why the taxpayers of this country have the responsibility to go in and refinance bad debt that was willingly incurred by consenting adults." (He thought that FmHA's "fair share" was 0.) Starting with the 1984 budget, OMB began to treat RHIF's FFB transactions as borrowing and redemption of borrowing, which meant that RHIF's budget authority was completely recognized in the budget. The administration also threatened to veto appropriation bills that contained excessive obligation limits. Then, in 1985, Gramm-Rudman brought the FFB on-budget.

Was this the end of the line for RHIF? Not at all. Its advocates had quickly understood the impact of on-budget treatment and began to search for another financing method. In an eerie repeat of the asset sales experience of the later 1960s, this search joined with the desire of budget controllers to "reduce the deficit."

Senator Moynihan started the debate in May of 1985 when he proposed an amendment to the budget resolution that he characterized as a "deficit reduction proposal of the clearest and most straightforward kind"—$8 billion worth of loan asset sales in each of three years.[14] Waving endorsements from First Boston, Lazard Freres, and Shearson Lehman, he also claimed that the loans would be sold "without recourse," that is, without a government guarantee of payment in case of borrower default. (A recourse provision gives the purchaser of a loan asset the legal right to claim payment on the underlying loan from the government if the borrower does not meet the loan's repayment obligations.)[15] But effective recourse would be created by the sale's "overcollateralization," as a group of loans would be reserved to substitute for defaulted ones. This would ensure that purchasers would be paid and would allow the government to maximize its short-term revenues from the sale. The sale would also provide an acceleration of financing for the loan funds (including RHIF) that would be selling their assets.

Moynihan's proposal was voted down by 71–26, but it reminded decision makers of the possibility of an easy way around the Gramm-Rudman constraints. A loan sale mandate was included in the 1985 reconciliation bill, which cut off RHIF's access to the (now on-budget) FFB and provided that loan assets should be sold to the public with recourse, that is, with guarantees

---

14. *Congressional Record* 7 May 1985, S 5473–85.

15. See Haas 1988a for a good description of the self-interested support of investment bankers for loan asset sales.

of payment. But a delay in enacting this bill and the administrative complexities of returning to public sales slowed implementation.[16]

OMB responded with a proposal in the next budget for a "pilot program" of loan asset sales, which were to be made without recourse. The motivation for the pilot program was complex. The pilot program was favored by OMB director Miller as a method of privatization, and by budget examiners as a prod to encourage better administration of loan programs and as a tool to develop market estimates of the cost of credit subsidies. But the apparent deficit-reduction effects were not ignored. Even the Deputy Director of OMB in a memorandum to the Cabinet confessed that one objective was to "increase unified budget offsetting collections in the year of sale" (Wright 1986). Loan asset sales produced this effect by accelerating effective recognition of loan repayments—the stream of expected payments from future years would be reflected in the price paid by purchasers. This was an offer that decision makers found too good to refuse, even though it promised to make future deficits larger. The 1986 reconciliation act required asset sales for a variety of programs; the conference report recommended that "various sales arrangements should be considered so as to ensure that the government realizes the best possible net return from the sale of these assets made in a fiscally responsible manner."[17] The effect of the RHIF loan asset sales can be seen in table 2.1 in the reduced outlays for 1987 (Rauch 1986b).

In the midst of this, OMB and Congressional Budget Office (CBO) technicians sought ways to control loan asset sales. They agreed to score all loan sales with recourse provisions as being equivalent to borrowing (which would prevent any "deficit reductions" from these sales) and to score nonrecourse sales as offsetting collections (these would be allowed to "reduce the deficit"). But this rule, which became known as the binary rule, was challenged by a broad coalition of agencies, members of Congress, and even the GAO, which maintained that sales without recourse "could artificially depress proceeds" (1986). In addition, the 1986 reconciliation act had required that FmHA protect the rights of borrowers to receive interest credits and delay repayment. These concerns stimulated extremely complex negotiations between FmHA, OMB, the Congress, affected interest groups, and financial advisors. The RHIF sale went forward only after the loans were divided into a "senior/subordinated structure," which was similar in many respects to the Moynihan overcollateralization technique mentioned above; yet OMB did succeed in limiting the extent of recourse in the plan (V. Clark 1987).

---

16. OMB ruled that all of RHIF's existing assets were committed to back previous loans from the FFB.

17. Report 99–1012, the Omnibus Budget Reconciliation Act of 1986, 17 October 1986, 261.

Like the participation sales charade of two decades earlier, criticism of this round of loan asset sales, along with the other doubtful savings enacted in 1986, greatly embarrassed budgetary decision makers. An initial response was the prohibition of most new loan asset sales in a provision of the Balanced Budget Reaffirmation Act of 1987. Only sales that had been "routine" prior to the act were allowed, and OMB followed a strict interpretation of this rule. But not all spending advocates were willing to live by those limits. In 1989, for example, the influential House Veterans' Affairs Committee reported a bill to finance a new Mortgage Indemnity Fund by selling loans with a guarantee that the federal government would repurchase loans that went into default. The chairman of the committee, Mississippi's "Sonny" Montgomery, complained that

> two years ago, the committee learned the Congressional Budget Office and the Office of Management and Budget had agreed to change the treatment of receipts from loan asset sales. CBO and OMB ordered this scorekeeping change without seeking our committee's view or those of other committees with jurisdiction over loan asset sales. . . . The Committee believes that if loan asset sales are to continue, they should be conducted in such a way as to maximize cash proceeds to the program. Therefore, the committee bill would require that regardless of sales methods—with or without recourse—proceeds should be accounted for as offsetting collections. . . . By adopting what is essentially a change in scorekeeping rules, this provision results in savings that are approximately $300 million higher than the reconciliation instruction to the committee required by the fiscal year 1990 budget resolution.[18]

A potentially more permanent control was enacted three years later in the Budget Enforcement Act of 1990. "Credit reform" shifted the basis of accounting for credit programs from cash to accrual, recognizing as a budgetary cost only the present value of the subsidy provided by a loan. Under credit reform, the complicated financing transactions that have played such a major role in FmHA's budgetary history will now not affect the deficit, substantially decreasing the incentive to use them. (Credit reform is described in more detail below.)

FmHA Outcomes Mismeasured/FmHA Strategy Misperceived

In FmHA's case, appropriations, budget authority, and outlays are quite misleading indicators of "who got what." As an OMB staffer complained in an

18. *Congressional Record* 6 June 1989, H 2289–96.

interview, "FmHA is always a complete mess to us. At times in the past, even after our full budget-year review, its numbers haven't tied together—they just didn't add up mathematically."

Of course, FmHA's formal budget outcomes were not completely irrelevant. Regardless of the fact that appropriations, budget authority, and outlays were not good measures of how much money FmHA received or spent, these measures were symbolically important. Because many participants in the process considered these measures to be meaningful, then in a very important sense they were. Advocates could complain that FmHA wasn't being supported and decision makers could claim that it was being carefully restrained, even if these characterizations were far from the truth. In addition, even though the measures were quite imperfect, they did not totally mislead. One year's appropriation might have been only a small portion of FmHA's financing, but at least that portion counted in the spending totals.

This measurement failure also misled many academics about the budgetary politics of FmHA. An example is the findings in the otherwise sophisticated study by Auten, Bozeman, and Cline (1984). They found a strong *increase* in appropriations for FmHA when there was greater Republican strength in the Senate. Although this is a surprising result given the low-income beneficiaries of FmHA programs and the occasional strong Republican opposition to these programs, Auten, Bozeman, and Cline did not discuss this finding specifically. The material above, on the other hand, supports a reasonable hypothesis that could explain this apparent anomaly. Because Republicans didn't like the program, they shut the off-budget spigot, forcing advocates to find on-budget resources. This created the illusion of more support in the appropriations process but actually indicated an attack on FmHA's financing. As a member of the Reagan administration said to me,

> Beyond 1982, Stockman had a conversion "beyond the barn," and became a leading exponent of honest budgeting. The supply-siders were on us for pessimistic assumptions, but actually many of the deficit increases were technical because we were backing out gimmicks.

My account misses a great deal as well, of course, for a complete review of RHIF's budget history would discuss other factors that significantly influenced its spending over the years, including agricultural and general recessions, elections, a good deal of racism, and the distributive design of its programs. But the selective history documents a skillful structural budget strategy that relied on mastery of the technical rules of budgetary accounting—a strategy that was ignored by all of the quantitative studies. Throughout its history, RHIF's supporters sold the fiction that the program carried out activities that were close to costless to the federal government, even while it was using billions of federal dollars. For example, the 1985 edition of its "autobiography" said that FmHA was a "leading force in spreading the outreach of nongovernmental lending institutions into rural sections" and stated that its money came "from private investors through sale of Government securities," not mentioning that these were Treasury securities!(U.S. Department of Agriculture 1985, 1–2). Yet in the scholarly literature on budgeting, only nonquantitative works by Ippolito and Leonard (which were oriented toward showing the limitations of budgetary accounting and procedure rather than describing process) discussed FmHA or similar cases in depth.

Another important observation about FmHA's strategy is that it apparently compensated for a low level of political resources. The organized supporters of RHIF were small builders, rural bankers, and the National Rural Housing Coalition, which had a professional staff of one.

> What makes him different from other high-roller lobbyists is that he has no money to feed into political kitties, and that his cause—housing of the poor—has been under almost constant assault by the Reagan administration since 1981. The surprise, probably, is that while the administration has cut about $2 billion—that is, about half—from subsidized rural housing programs, it has failed to eliminate the programs from the USDA budget as it has proposed to do in each of the last two years. . . . That failure is explained in part by Rapoza's ability to goad a large but often somnolent rural grass-roots network into appealing to their senators and representatives for help. In 1982, 1985, and again this year, in league with the influential home-builders' lobby, the coalition has blunted assaults on loan and rent-subsidy housing programs.[19]

This popular analysis followed the pluralist logic of incrementalism, ignoring the budget-structure tactics that protected the programs for decades. In contrast, when I asked budget participants about FmHA, their responses typically began with raised eyebrows, grimaces, and sly grins. They explained outcomes for FmHA, with emotions ranging from anger to admiration, as the result of its success in dodging the bullet of honest budget accounting and in locking in stable financing sources.

A Similar Strategy for Rural Electrification

In contrast to RHIF, the Rural Electrification Administration (REA) was rich in the political resources that enable incremental strategy. The cooperatives that

---

19. Ward Sinclair, "For Lobbyist, Eyes Have It: Robert Rapoza Pulls Shoestrings for Subsidized Housing," *Washington Post,* 2 May 1986, sec. A.

supported it were geographically dispersed throughout the country, and able to divert enough financial resources into political activity to be represented by the National Rural Electric Cooperative Association (NRECA), which was one of the largest lobbying organizations in Washington. The NRECA's inside lobbying was supplemented with mass membership campaigns: co-ops placed inserts in monthly bills that criticized opponents as "enemies of rural America," which certainly was not an attractive label to members of Congress. Yet the REA's advocates used budget-structure strategies that were quite similar to those used in support of RHIF. After briefly reviewing the REA's budget history, I suggest some explanations for the similarities.[20]

A time series of REA's financing and spending is shown in table 2.3. REA made moderately and deeply subsidized loans to cooperatives in rural or formerly rural areas for electricity and telephone services. Its financing was as complex as RHIF's. Like RHIF, REA made participation sales in the mid-1960s. Growth in appropriations in the early 1970s made it a natural target for Nixon's impoundment campaign. Congress responded by declaring the REA off-budget in 1973. The Congress also created a revolving fund to finance REA's programs, set *minimum* loan levels in appropriation acts, converted some direct loans to guaranteed loans financed by the FFB, and required OMB to count the receipts from REA's sale of loan assets to the off-budget FFB (packaged as Certificates of Beneficial Ownership) as offsetting to outlays. These strategies made REA a prime target of budget controllers. Even worse in the eyes of controllers was the audacity of REA's advocates, who claimed in national advertisements that proposed cuts in REA's budget would not reduce the government's budget deficit! This was literally correct, but *only* because controllers were barred by statute from counting REA's programs in the budget. REA's advocates also crowed that "not a single lender has defaulted," which given the munificence of the loan terms was understandable but really not praiseworthy.[21]

The Reagan administration proposed significant reductions in REA's programs in 1981 (Senate Committee on Agriculture, Nutrition, and Forestry 1981). While not very successful, this attack set the stage for a debate of a proposal by REA's advocates to establish its "self-sufficiency." REA had been borrowing from the FFB at interest rates that were higher than it received on the loans it extended to the co-ops. Over time, lending with a negative spread depleted the balances in the REA's revolving fund. To save the revolving fund,

---

20. Useful sources include unpublished CBO and OMB memos; Ippolito 1984; U.S. Department of Agriculture 1984; Doyle 1979; and Morrison 1983.

21. Some co-ops did default beginning in 1985, due largely to an (industrywide) inability to accurately forecast oil prices and the costs of constructing nuclear generating plants (S. Morrison 1988).

TABLE 2.3. REA Budgetary Outcomes (actual dollars in millions

Year	Direct Loan Obligations	Guaranteed Loan Commitments	Outlays	Budget Authority	Appropriations
1966	413	0	373	466	12
1967	472	0	424	474	12
1968	470	0	508	447	12
1969	470	0	486	452	13
1970	470	0	511	478	15
1971	487	0	565	482	16
1972	571	0	567	686	17
1973	763	0	499	650	17
1974	759	974	17	17	17
1975	900	1,406	19	20	20
1976	1,000	563	21	21	21
TQ	0	17	5	5	5
1977	1,083	2,764	22	22	22
1978	1,167	500	23	24	24
1979	1,250	3,695	24	25	25
1980	1,175	2,523	27	27	27
1981	1,100	444	28	28	28
1982	1,099	400	29	30	30
1983	1,101	0	28	30	30
1984	2,081	0	28	30	30
1985	3,801	0	244	500	247
1986	2,953	0	339	1,914	129
1987	1,033	582	–204	294	49

Source: Budget of the U.S. Government, Fiscal Years 1968–89.

Note: Data show on-budget outcomes for salaries and expenses and loan programs, excluding Rural Telephone Bank and rural communications fund activities.

the co-ops proposed that the Treasury redefine the liabilities of the REA—its borrowings from the FFB—to instead be REA's equity! This debt forgiveness would have been worth about $8 billion over the terms of the outstanding debt. It would have also allowed REA to use the new equity as collateral for new loans, starting the fund on the road to insolvency all over again.

This proposal was almost enacted, despite its truthspeak character (Wehr 1984a, 1984b; Dion 1983). The cause of its defeat was the surprising but determined opposition of Senator Simpson of Wyoming, a state with many REA-assisted co-ops. Simpson conveyed his threat of a filibuster in a "Dear Colleague" letter that was notable for its bluntness.

> When this remarkable agency first embarked upon its mission in this country it was a stunning thing to observe. It literally changed the face of America. But after the extraordinary effort had been largely completed—when over 99 percent of rural America then received electrical energy—

> then some very creative financiers, accountants, lawyers and businessmen entered the fray. The complexity of the financing schemes and revolving fund capers of the REA would make an atomic scientist blanch. For they will have your eyes whirling like slot machine wheels as they patiently describe the remarkable and complex financing procedures of REA. . . . I would hope you might lay back on this one and take a very close look at it. If you mull around in it long enough you might see how an extremely sophisticated special interest lobby has taken a most magnificent program and through use of a remarkable array of scalpels, wrenches and sledge hammers has fashioned a bizarre blend of on-budget/off-budget financing and subsidy packages through use of the Federal Financing Bank and other methods over these many years that would greatly and deeply disappoint, sadden and distress the creators of rural electrification in this country.[22]

Following this loss, the Gramm-Rudman-Hollings Act placed the FFB and REA back on-budget. Yet REA's supporters rebounded, shifting their lobbying efforts in support of a new proposal to allow co-ops to prepay outstanding loans without a prepayment penalty. This tactic will be described in chapter 4.

While REA's advocates relied on accounting and financing tactics, they also skillfully argued that REA's spending was "worth it." In chapter 7, I will quote a macroeconomic analysis prepared on REA's behalf, suggesting that the argument was outlandish. Yet it was not the only misleading argument made by REA's advocates, who had to offset the perception held by many analysts that there was no need for REA's programs using reasonable standards of equity. Its original purpose of wiring the country had long been fulfilled, and rural consumers who were served by REA-assisted co-ops paid *less* on average than did urban consumers. But this was not the image put forward by REA's advocates. The NRECA scoured the country for the few remaining consumers lacking electricity and featured them in national ads like one run in June 1992.

> Christina Rael is 74, still runs a few head of cattle in Catron County, New Mexico, and right now she's thinking of getting rid of that old washboard of hers. Reason is she finally has a washing machine and the electricity to run it.

Along with this old standby came arguments that REA could fulfill a new mission: economic development. Readers of the NRECA ad could call to request a glossy report that "documented" the spinoffs from a variety of co-op economic development projects.

---

22. It's more likely that the creators of REA would have smiled in self-recognition. See Caro 1982, 516–28.

The question is: why did REA's advocates, like RHIF's advocates, use a budget-structure strategy instead of an incremental strategy? I identify three factors, all of which I will discuss extensively in the next chapter. First, *tactical opportunities* were present. Accounting practices for credit were flawed. A Democratic Congress was receptive to proposals to limit the discretion of a Republican administration. And many decision makers were conditioned by historical forces to be receptive to arguments about the positive effects of REA's spending.

Second, the REA coalition's mobilization of political resources and bargaining with decision makers proved insufficient protection from *threats by controllers.* REA's advocates faced budget cuts unless they did something else. What evolved was a dynamic of control and advocacy. The program profited from a flawed accounting practice and generous financing design, controllers proposed reforms, and its advocates resisted, suggesting alternatives that provided similar advantages. The perception that the program was effective was challenged and rebutted. The program escaped from the budgetary decision process, but controllers tried to bring it into an arena where it would face stiff competition. In REA's dynamic, the advocates often kept at least a step ahead of controllers.

Third, REA's advocates did so in part because they possessed the technical *skill* to carry out a budget-structure strategy. When threatened, they had the ability to take advantage of tactical opportunities. Not only did they understand how to present their case to members of Congress and how to pressure them, they also understood how prepayments could provide new financing and how to design biased macroeconomic studies. Some of the REA's leading advocates built this skill over years of supposedly "guarding the Treasury" as Appropriations Committee members and staff.

Summary

At the beginning of this chapter, budgetary data was likened to a fog bank. Previous studies—in which budgetary data was treated as high-quality data—didn't contemplate the possibility of a fog bank. Instead, they beheld a sunlit city of classical proportions.

This chapter showed that the fog bank does indeed exist and suggested several perspectives from which to peer through it. What lies underneath the fog bank is more like a modern metropolis than a classical city. Furthermore, as the RHIF and REA examples showed, some of the buildings in the metropolis resemble buildings designed not by a Renaissance man like Thomas Jefferson, but by the evil genius in Fritz Lang's movie *Metropolis.* The following chapters walk into this metropolis, in search of the actual architects and their methods.

Chapter 3

The Structure of Budgeting and Strategies for Budgeting

Most imposing physical structures are designed by a hierarchically organized yet small group of architects. The imposing institution of government budgeting has had more designers, who certainly haven't been organized or in agreement about a final design.

The terms *institution* and *structure,* used similarly above, are popular in social science (March and Olsen 1989; North 1990). Many scholars have observed, however, that there is no consensus about what these terms mean (for example, see Ostrom 1986). Some use institution and structure to describe attributes of organizations or constitutions, and others use them more broadly to encompass commonly accepted rules or patterns of behavior. Some prefer an ordering of concepts, with higher-order institutions composed of both the structure provided by attributes of systems and the rules that provide incentives for behaviors. Others use the terms institution, structure, and rules interchangeably.

I share the perspective that institutions, structure, and rules are important determinants of political behaviors, but I do not seek to resolve the conceptual uncertainty related to these terms. Rather, I first specify some social expectations for the budgetary process that distinguish it from other political institutions. The critical observation is that though these expectations are strongly held, they are often unrealized. I then discuss how budget-structure strategies take advantage of the gaps between expectations and performance, and how they often create these gaps.

The Distinguishing Characteristics of Government Budgeting

What does society especially expect of government budgeting? I identify three important features—the budget process is expected to *use definitive information, follow a routine schedule,* and *demonstrate central control.*

In reaction to these assertions, many readers are probably sputtering, and with good cause, "What, is he crazy? What about the gimmicks? What about the missed deadlines? Why do I feel that no one is in charge?" Good questions.

Clearly, the budget process often fails to meet the main expectations for it. Then why even bother to identify these expectations? The main reason is: whether or not these expectations are actually met, they establish the structure of budgeting.

Definitive Information

One distinctive feature of the budget process is that it uses a *standard*—a definite measure established by authority. Recalling David Easton's definition of politics as the "authoritative allocation of values" (1951, 129), the expectation in budgeting is that "values should be valued in dollars." In the federal government, the budgetary standard is an *expenditure* standard—cash payments of programs count the most. Expenditures are totaled and subtracted from revenues to arrive at the bottom line of the deficit.

Budgeting uses a standard more than any other government decision-making process. For example, contrast budgeting with regulation. The budgetary accounting system compares programs on the basis of the costs to government. Would it be appropriate to compare regulatory policies solely on the basis of the costs borne by the regulated? To date, the political system has concluded that it would not (see Cooper and West 1988). Rather, there is a free-for-all over which information can be considered. For some regulatory programs, statutory constraints require that benefits be offset against costs, but for other programs costs must be given less weight. There is no standard.[1]

Support for a procedural standard implies agreement over the goals of a process. A sufficient goal for the expenditure standard is that the government needs to manage its cash flow so that it can pay bills when they are due. But many people expect the budget to fulfill other goals: minimizing government spending, managing fiscal policy, fostering appropriate resource allocations, and preventing fiscal burdens from being shifted onto future generations. The paradox is that though there is a strong desire for a budgetary standard, each goal implies a different one. Consider the goal of allocating resources efficiently. To meet this goal, one must weigh not only the expenditure costs of inputs, but also the social benefits and costs of outcomes and the social costs of inputs. Because the correlations between government expenditures and these social values are often low, the expenditure standard is a poor proxy for a resource-allocation standard.

When participants have numerous goals for the budgetary process, the current standard for the process may be perceived as *one* of several *alternative*

1. A case can be made that a standard is often used in comparisons of national military capabilities. In the United States, these analyses are known as *net assessments*, and they quantify munitions and manpower so that different force structures can be compared on a "threat" metric. For a description of the assumptions behind this form of analysis, see deLeon 1987.

standards, rather than as *the* standard. And once the definitive nature of the budgetary standard is lost, the uniqueness of the budgetary process will be diminished. Knowing this, advocates of the budgetary process try to protect the standard. But they must usually acknowledge that any standard fails to perform some functions that are important to the government and can be performed by alternative standards. They are reduced to arguing that the current function is the most important for the budgetary process to fulfill. While there is agreement on the desirability of a *single* standard, much effort is expended attacking and defending the *particular* standard in use.

Another important informational characteristic of the budgetary process is its reliance on experts to produce standard-relevant information. The expectation is that "budget information should come primarily from budget experts." They are relied upon for evenhanded ("neutrally competent") application of the budget standard to different programs. In comparison, to contrast budgeting with regulation again, the opinions of regulatory experts seem to be challenged with greater frequency. Why might this be the case?

Some budgetary transactions are relatively difficult to challenge—it is much easier to count checks and cash, for which there are accounting records in hand, than to measure regulatory costs and benefits. But many of the government's financial transactions are relatively complex, which suggests another reason for the expectation that budgetary experts will be influential. This reason is the recognized importance of the financial stability of the government. Because accountants and economists can help protect the financial stability of the state, they encourage others to pay deference to them (Mosher 1984). Yet deference to experts comes hard to Americans. Widespread public participation is the rule in public policy-making, and this creates pressures to open up budgeting as well. Along with this *interest* in challenging the experts there is often the *ability,* for in the capitalist United States financial expertise is probably more widely distributed than in any other country. Application of a standard may require skill and practice, but many participants meet these conditions.

Routine Schedule

Another distinguishing expectation for the process of budgeting is its routineness. Not only is the *information* used in the process to be highly structured, but so is the *timing* of decisions. The strong expectation is that "budgeting should follow a schedule." The formal schedule is set out in statutes and in documents such as budget circulars. Often practitioners assume slippage from these schedules, but they expect that decisions will be made even if made a bit late. Budgeting is not only part of the "recurring agenda"; it is the most recurrent (Walker 1977).

The scheduled nature of the budget process is *not* unique because the stages for interaction between participants are structured in advance. In this sense, budgeting is not much different from other decision-making processes, such as rulemaking under the Administrative Procedure Act (published proposal, review and response, modification, final publication and application, adjudication) or the constitutionally defined process of lawmaking (passage, veto, override). What is unique is the expectation that once a budgetary decision is made for a program, another budgetary decision will be made for the same program within a relatively short period of time. That is, one can identify an expected, and short, *periodicity* for most budget decisions—a regular length of time between decisions. In the federal government, a year is the modal periodicity. Discretionary appropriation programs are reviewed annually, consistent with the annual schedule for macrobudgeting that requires submission of the President's budget and consideration of the budget resolution. The expected periodicity for mandatory programs is more varied (approaching the procedural equivalent of infinity for an "untouchable" program such as Social Security).

Such periodicity does not exist in most other policy-making processes.[2] Consider regulation again. Regulations take longer to develop than budget decisions, and once they are made, there is usually no expectation that they will be revised in a specified period of time. Revisions will undoubtedly take place, but at unpredictable times—as the result of legal challenges, new legislation, or political and administrative turnover.

Why should the budget process follow a routine schedule? Return to the importance of financial stability for state maintenance. Lengthy periodicity is risky because it permits inattention to unanticipated threats such as revenue shortfalls or the rapid growth of spending. Leaders find that they can deal efficiently with these problems when they schedule regular choice opportunities (Cohen, March, and Olsen 1972). Moreover, prudent lenders come to expect such active management by their debtors.

A routine schedule for budgeting can also reduce conflict and build trust between institutions that have opposing views. Wildavsky argued convincingly that a set periodicity for budgeting was functional for participants—the "norm of annuality" helped participants complete bargains because it provided for a standard length of contract.[3] More generally, Robert Axelrod's study of repeated Prisoner's Dilemma games shows that the more frequent the interaction, the more likely that cooperation will develop (1984). Budgetary bargainers with low levels of trust calculate that they will enter into a deal, but

2. Personnel evaluations are performed annually, but the policy content of this process is relatively low.

3. Wildavsky actually used the term *annualarity* (1984, xviii).

only for a short period of time; then they design contracts that contain the boilerplate of "one-year money."

One might observe in recent years that the only routine quality of the federal budgetary schedule was its regular violation. The norm of annuality has limits, in that the conflict-reducing effect of the norm may not offset the value of making a decision out of phase or declining to decide in phase (Caiden 1982).

Furthermore, the value of a routine schedule is self-limiting. Above I used the language of the garbage-can model of decision making, in which leaders can create choice opportunities through the regular schedule (Cohen, March, and Olsen 1972). But it is the nature of regular choice opportunities to attract more problems and solutions than originally intended, because this routineness can allow problems and solutions to be considered when their "normal" opportunities are less frequent. The common metaphor is that budget bills are the "last train leaving the station." The timing paradox of budgeting is that it demands more energy than expected, and a process that is intended to be routine often turns out not to be.

Central Control

The third distinguishing factor of budgeting is that it is used to demonstrate responsive control of government finances. The expectation is "responsible budget decisions should be made by powerful but accountable leaders." The paradox here resides directly in the norm, in the opposition of power and accountability.

Many observers have commented on the centrality of competent financial management to the maintenance, and even the existence of the state.[4] In the United States, for example, conflict over the adequacy of the federal government's taxing power, and over the institutions that would control the nation's finances, helped define the early history of the nation. Anticipating this conflict, Alexander Hamilton began a series on public finance issues in *The Federalist Papers* with the following analysis from Number 30:

> Money is, with propriety, considered as the vital principle of the body politic; as that which sustains its life and motion and enables it to perform its most essential functions. A complete power, therefore, to procure a regular and adequate supply of revenue, as far as the resources of the community will permit, may be regarded as an indispensable ingredient in every constitution. From a deficiency in this particular, one of two evils

4. For a provocative summary, see Levi 1988. See also Webber and Wildavsky 1986; Burkhead 1956; Schick 1966.

> must ensue: either the people must be subjected to continual plunder, as a substitute for a more eligible mode of supplying the public wants, or the government must sink into a fatal atrophy, and, in a short course of time, perish. (Madison, Hamilton, and Jay 1961, 188)

Historical analyses generally begin with the observation that, for collectivities to become states, they had to collect enough revenue to provide for the common defense. As ambition for state performance increased—citizens and leaders desired expanded governmental institutions, a reallocation of social resources, and better-managed economies—or as fiscal crises threatened, new power centers were established and then strengthened. These were the fiscal institutions delegated responsibility for formulating and carrying out financial policies, subject to the consent provisions required by their principals. Delegation permitted the use of financial expertise and the control of demands for excessive spending. Absent such controls, spending growth led states to tax too heavily, which created revolts that threatened state power.

Fiscal institutions have usually not restricted themselves to this state-maintenance function. Because a state's financial resources can be converted into political resources, an adept fiscal institution can effectively control the state. This poses a threat to the leaders of other institutions in the polity, who worry that central control over the nation's finances will not only help maintain the state but also build the fiscal institution into the dominant power. Their natural reaction is to try to control the fiscal institution.

Conflict over the power of the fiscal authority is central to much political history. Of course, the patterns differ across states. The most cited example of development is from British history, with the progression of constraints on the crown from the Magna Carta through the Civil List to the eras of Peel and Gladstone, when a complete fiscal policy became the center of the party program (Burkhead 1956). In the United States, many historians have focused on the Budget and Accounting Act's centralization of responsibility with the executive budget.[5] The more recent budgetary histories of political institutions in the United States typically highlight the difficulties faced by the Congress in wresting delegated spending authority from the presidency and in delegating power internally to members who will act as the "guardians of the Treasury." These stories are several orders more complicated than the development of the executive budget, but are central to any understanding of the institution of Congress and of congressional-presidential relations.

Although controversy over the control of fiscal powers is an essential characteristic of budgeting, it is not as special as are the acceptance of a

---

5. Fisher has shown that the development of delegated authority was much more complex than the simplistic but popular model of a "dramatic cleavage" in 1921 (1975, 9–35).

decision standard and a routine schedule. Maintenance of the state depends at least as much on military competence as on financial competence. But both leaders and citizens do place great weight on financial competence in evaluating government performance. An example can be cited from a period of great budget stability in the United States—the two decades after World War II. In his review of budgeting in Illinois, Thomas Anton demonstrated that a process of budgeting was desired in part because it gave symbolic assurance that a center existed—that in a constitutional order of separated institutions, there were actors who were *perceived* to be serving as controllers and who were also *thought to be* accountable (1967).

More recently, public confidence in budgetary institutions has turned to despair, with poll responses judging leaders harshly for budgeting failures. Unfortunately, citizens also generally oppose most policy changes that could significantly reduce budget deficits, and leaders then perceive that they are dealing with a nearly unmanageable problem. They worry about posterity's judgment—"this was the group that led the United States into its disastrous fiscal policies." They search—in vain?—for ways to delegate power to institutions that would remain accountable to the public yet also be sufficiently powerful to reduce the deficit against the wishes of mobilized interests.

Budgeting in Brief

In sum, budgeting is an institutionalized process: almost everyone expects that the finances of the government will be managed, that fiscal powers will be delegated, and that regular budgetary procedures will be followed. But look beyond this general accord, and one typically sees recurrent conflict over the specific means by which these expectations will be met. In other words, it is usually safe to assume that the norms of budgeting are less resilient than often supposed. Rather than typically exhibiting equilibrium, budgetary structure develops over time and frequently features paradox. This perspective generally resembles an institutionalism described by Orren and Skowronek.

> Let us begin with a proposition about institutions that is uncontroversial, that institutions are comprised of structures and rules that persist through time, and it is this persistence that distinguishes institutions from mere behavior or uniterated games. A stubborn skepticism about the potential for system integration in an institutionalized polity yields a corollary, however: that institutions, both singly and in their interactions, will characteristically manifest ordering principles that are conflicting and contradictory in their tendencies. As opposed to operating as the "glue" of politics, holding things together and forming a whole, institutions are here

> the catalytic—the "soup"—of change and development. (Orren and Skowronek 1991; see also Riker 1980; Stone 1988)

Budget Structure Strategies

To this point, I have suggested how expectations for the budgetary process produce its basic structure—the type of information that is considered, the expected timing for decisions, and the allocation of authority to decision makers.[6] With this framework, it is now possible to describe how the strategies of spending advocates and controllers both respond to and create budget structures.

Begin by considering the structure of budgeting for an individual program. At any point in time, each program has its own

> method of *accounting* for its spending,
> *decision procedure* used to provide it with spending authority,
> *policy design* that guides how it may acquire and spend
> funds for different purposes, and
> commonly perceived *effects* of its spending.

These characteristics affect the decision makers who are brought together routinely to allocate funds among programs. While decision makers certainly consider the political strength of coalitions that support and oppose programs, the process forces them to focus on formal accounts of costs. They are also expected to further social goals when budgeting; to do so, they rely heavily on popular, informal arguments about the relative effectiveness of programs. Accounting practices and perceived effects thus jointly influence evaluations of the costs and benefits, and thus the desirability, of spending.

Budget decisions are also affected by decision procedures and policy designs. Decision procedures determine which programs will be competitors or collaborators, how program-level decisions to spend are timed, and whether these decisions are constrained by macrobudgetary control procedures. Budgetary policy designs govern the ease by which decisions to spend are made and are carried out.

For many programs, it is often conceivable that they could have different budgetary characteristics than their current ones. Consider a program that transfers income to a set of individuals. It could be funded through the appropriations process, or it could be funded by revenues that are dedicated to the program and offset against obligations in a "revolving fund." The program

6. See Ostrom (1986) for a discussion of how an approach of this type permits the specification of an institution.

could be justified as a "welfare" type of income transfer to deservedly needy individuals, or instead be portrayed as an investment—as a way to prevent larger expenditures on these individuals in the future.

Spending advocates learn that certain budgetary characteristics—the latter ones in the example above—provide advantages to their programs. They use budget structure tactics when they attempt to convince decision makers to accept the most advantageous budgetary characteristics. For example, they try to change accounting practices to reduce the reported costs of programs. They attempt to develop and transmit believable rationales for programs, in hopes of offsetting accounted-for, process-controlled costs with a level of perceived benefits that justify these costs. They avoid macrobudgetary controls when possible. They shop for microbudgetary decision procedures that place few hurdles in the way of spending and contain few competitors for the funds that they covet. Finally, they try to design the budgetary operations of programs so that funds are received from several, stable sources and spending is dedicated and automatic. When spending advocates use these tactics frequently, they rely on a budget-structure strategy.

The set of conceivably adoptable budgetary characteristics that could increase an individual program's budget, or protect it from challenge, are *tactical opportunities* for spending advocates. Identifying tactical opportunities is inherently complicated—they vary by budgetary characteristic and interact in context. Given this complexity, it often takes a special skill to recognize tactical opportunities; this type of skill is discussed in detail below.

Nevertheless, it is possible to speculate about some general features of tactical opportunities. First, the level of acceptance of a current budgetary characteristic is important. For example, if an accounting practice is traditional, accepted in theory, and honored in fact, it will be harder to change than one that has been recently violated or questioned.

Second, the programmatic plausibility of a suggested alternative budgetary characteristic also affects whether a tactical alternative exists. Some policy designs preferred by spending advocates will be thought by decision makers to be plausible mechanisms for solving policy problems; others will not. For example, loans might typically be seen as an appropriate tool with which to subsidize businesses, but not for those who would seem to have little ability to repay. Similarly, off-budget status or exemption from budget preparation requirements might be less likely for clear governmental activities (defense, for example) than for those activities at the margin of publicness (preferential financial intermediation, for example).

In part, who is doing the deciding establishes the relative acceptance of current practices and the perceived plausibility of suggested alternatives. Policy and budget analysts generally possess well-developed ideas about policy designs and the effects of spending and have a good understanding of accounting rules and decision procedures. Consequently, they are most skeptical of spending advocates' suggestions for new budget structures. Most elected officials do not approach this level of knowledge, leading them to accept policy designs and claimed effects that technical specialists would not.

Tactical opportunities are also likely to change over time. Agenda change is one reason. For example, if a program can be portrayed as a solution to a problem that has just been given political priority, it will likely prosper in budgetary competition.

Another developmental limit on the availability of tactical opportunities can be understood by borrowing the concept of a "niche" from biology.[7] Many species survive competition by finding niches with large carrying capacities—ones with plentiful food and few predators. By and large, budgetary competition appears similar—covert, not cutthroat. Coalitions usually do not seek to directly and visibly capture a portion of a competing coalition's budget. Rather, they seek to obtain protected positions that guarantee them access to budgetary resources regardless of the threatening conditions that exist when fiscal stress is high or when controllers attack. Once in a niche, they seek to prevent others from gaining it.

An example is provided by a variant of the tactic of dedicating funds: obtaining a checkoff from income tax returns as a source of financing. At the state level, this tactic has diffused widely, leading to a decline in funding for its original beneficiaries.[8] At the federal level, this danger was recognized by the Democratic sponsors of public financing of presidential elections. Confronted with a proposal by Republicans to allow a checkoff for antidrug programs, the *Washington Post* reported that Senator Long successfully argued against the amendment by saying that the checkoff for drugs "would 'confuse and dilute the effectiveness' of the existing $1 income tax checkoff to help finance presidential election campaigns."[9]

The Dynamics of Control and Advocacy

Continuing with the analogy of budgeting to evolutionary processes, the logic of evolution suggests that over time budgeting should become more com-

---

7. Bassein and Schulman suggested the applicability of the niche concept to budgeting (1985). For other uses of selection models in social science, see Kingdon 1984, 122–51; Nelson and Winter 1982; and Kaufman 1985.

8. Gold 1986, 8, 11; and Cass Peterson, "More Funds Urged for Nongame Conservation," *Washington Post,* 13 November 1986, sec. A.

9. Edward Walsh, "Senate Approves Antidrug Measure," *Washington Post,* 16 October 1986, sec. A.

plex.[10] Even casual observation of the budget process of the past two decades suggests that this is the case. In particular, accounting rules and decision procedures are denser and more comprehensive.[11] This complexity developed through a dynamic of control and advocacy.

In this dynamic, controllers seek to develop accounting rules that accurately measure costs, educate decision makers about the effects of spending, support decision procedures that fairly compare alternative methods of reaching goals, and design programs that work yet still retain budgetary flexibility. They recognize programs for which these goals are not being met, and they try to bring these programs under control. For programs whose costs are underestimated, for example, they reapply accounting rules or develop new ones. They challenge hype about the effects of spending, reestablish periodic review, and alter program designs.

In response, spending advocates seek to avoid these attacks. They argue that new accounting procedures overestimate costs or they develop new program designs that would not be subject to the proposed accounting treatment. Spending advocates may also initiate the dynamic by proposing new budget structures that protect or increase a program's budget. Controllers respond, most strongly when they feel that a structural tactic is likely to diffuse. But contrary to the social expectation that the budgetary process demonstrates central control, controllers do not always succeed. There are a number of reasons.

Consider the quality of accounting rules. Accounting rules should be the most developed budget structure—after all, the main purpose of the process is to control spending, and the expectation is that a decision standard will be used to control spending. However, it is sometimes the case that accounting theory is insufficiently developed to tell controllers how to measure spending—there is no consensus decision standard. In chapter 4, for example, I describe how some structural tactics succeeded because time is a conceptual bugaboo to controllers. Time creates uncertainties about future technologies, about future prices, about the strength of government commitments in the future, and about the future actions of beneficiaries.

Nor does the obvious expertise of controllers always lead members of Congress and other decision makers to accept their recommendations. These decision makers are expected to rely on experts to inform them about the

---

10. Kaufman proposes that a finding of increasing organizational "density" over time will validate an evolutionary perspective to organizational theory (1985, 139–54).

11. In later editions of *The Politics of the Budgetary Process,* Wildavsky claimed that the norm of comprehensiveness had weakened. As I will discuss in chapter 4, the meaning of comprehensiveness had actually expanded. In 1966, when the budget was supposedly based on a desire for comprehensiveness, the "unified budget" didn't even exist.

finances of programs. When spending advocates approach or match controllers' expertise, they can manipulate accounting practices and fool decision makers. In private financial markets, similar attempts at fiscal illusion are usually recognized and stock prices adjust to this new information (Kaplan and Roll 1972). In government, however, there are fewer incentives for spending advocates to expose the fiscal illusions created by their competitors. By and large, tattlers can't profit when they expose others—unlike in the private sector, they can't sell the stock of a program short and capture the gains when fiscal illusion is exposed. In fact, spending advocates who expose fiscal illusions that benefit others may be penalized. By exposing fiscal illusions, they increase perceptions of fiscal stress. Fiscal stress creates pressure to cut spending, including the tattlers' favorite programs. Tattlers may also alienate proponents of the programs that they exposed and be penalized with retaliation.

A third reason spending advocates escape controls is the pressure of the routine schedule. Decision makers want to be perceived as having met the expectation that budgets will be completed on time. They may thus accept some accounting gimmicks late in the budget preparation process; to do otherwise might encourage many spending advocates to stall indefinitely. As an OMB political appointee explained,

> There are three stages in which the gimmicks have differing importance. The first is in the Spring Preview when you take a serious analytic look at the programs. No gimmicks then. The second is during Director's Review, when the focus is towards how to squeeze the President's program into a small bucket. December [the third stage] is pure gimmicks. I'd sit down with [the Director and a top technician], when the White House staff were convinced we'd lost the election with this budget, and we'd fix it. We'd always do net outlay gimmicks, and we'd boost the income tax receipts and slow down the military's miscellaneous procurement accounts.[12]

Controllers may go along with this in the belief that demonstrating the routine nature of budgeting will help them actually control spending in the future. But

---

12. A classic case is the offsetting receipt account into which payments for leasing and drilling on the Outer Continental Shelf are deposited. A former Interior Department official was quoted in 1982:

> There is a long history at the Office of Management and Budget of bumping up the OCS revenues to make budget figures look good. This goes back a lot of years. I know in the 1960s and 1970s when I was there, every time we sent our estimates over to the OMB, they came back a little higher.

Hilts, Philip, "$18 Billion Offshore? Far Out! Oilmen Say," *Washington Post,* 14 February 1982, sec. A.

this practice creates tactical opportunities for programs over the long run. As the same OMB appointee later said,

> Through the years we developed accommodations with the ag people. You're just less inclined to screw them because they came up with one billion in revenues you know didn't exist. (See also Mowery and Kamlet 1984; Stockman 1986.)

A fourth reason controllers fail to dominate spending advocates is the nature of the delegation of fiscal authority. Earlier, I suggested that budgeting was paradoxical in that leaders of the state recognized the need for an effective budget process, but also feared an excessive delegation of power to controllers. Leaders must pay heed to some important logic of political organization: those who benefit directly from spending almost always mobilize more easily than the current taxpayers and future citizens who finance this spending. Even those politicians who are ideologically disposed toward control, and who head institutions that carry out control functions, can't ignore this reality. Consider the role conflict faced by House Budget Committee chairman Leon Panetta when the Loma Prieta earthquake cracked his district—he needed politically essential help from the Appropriations Committee after having fought it for years. Panetta resolved his dilemma when he joined the other California members of Congress in pressing for multi-billion-dollar emergency assistance but also opposed waiving legal provisions that would count this spending against the deficit (Calmes 1989; Hook 1990). Most politicians don't ever want to be in such an uncomfortable position, and they ensure this by refusing to act as controllers.

Cross-pressured politicians can respond to the greater mobilization of spending advocates by reining in the career budget technicians who typically believe most strongly in the control function of the process and perform its most crucial technical functions of accounting and scorekeeping. Numerous examples in the following chapters show how technician-controllers in the politicized OMB were subjected to such pressure. Many were disgusted by orders to bend the rules, but realistic enough to know they had to follow those orders. Other career budget technicians in CBO and GAO were more protected but still were not entirely insulated from political pressure.

Pressured controllers respond by trying to design exceptions that would not serve as precedents for similar exceptions, or in a way that it will be easy to reverse later. A good illustration of this approach is given by an internal memo from one OMB technician to another.

> We find it difficult to respond to the Senator's argument that we are inconsistent, since we obviously are inconsistent. As we understand the

> guidelines, we are not allowed to argue publicly that we undo the damage caused by [a politically inspired OMB exception to an accounting rule], but we are free to seek to avoid any further evasions of the budget discipline. The approach suggested in the attachment seeks to skirt within this guidance by "grandfathering" the current mess but arguing against any new evasions.

Fiscal stress is the final reason spending advocates sometimes escape controls. This is counterintuitive, for fiscal stress should empower controllers in several important ways. In the incrementalist model (as modified by Crecine and others), fiscal stress leads spending advocates to reduce requested increases. In the budget-structure model, fiscal stress provides controllers with a rationale for toughening accounting practices and shortening the periodicity of budget reviews. Perceptions of fiscal stress can be increased by triggering events such as the October 1987 stock market crash, which by demonstrating the possible costs of fiscal irresponsibility stimulated the Congress to close some of the loopholes in Gramm-Rudman-Hollings. Similarly, recurrent debt ceiling votes aided controllers by demonstrating fiscal stress and by establishing procedural opportunities for adopting new controls.

The effects of fiscal stress are not all procontroller, however. While some spending advocates may respond to fiscal stress by reducing requested increases, fiscal stress may also stimulate many other spending advocates to attempt budget structure tactics. In addition, the symbolic effects of perceived fiscal stress apparently do not always benefit controllers. On some occasions when budgetary aggregates have approached "magic thresholds"—$100 billion in outlays, a $2 trillion national debt—controllers have accepted gimmicks proposed by spending advocates in order to delay the crossing of these thresholds.

Skill

The dynamics of budgetary competition are further complicated by variation in the budgetary skill exercised by competitors. Eugene Bardach discussed skill by first noting its importance: "The picture of the political process that moves from resources to influence to success seems to be missing something" (1972, 9).[13] Then he defined the "skill factor" as "a quality of political action. The action is political problem solving, and the qualities of skill are efficiency,

13. Many standard works in political science emphasize the concept of skill. To pick just three of many possible examples: Neustadt told presidents they needed to be persuasive (1960); Matthews described how senators who adapted to folkways were most influential (1960); and Kingdon showed how entrepreneurs coupled problems, solutions, and politics to land places on the agenda (1984).

inventiveness, and creativity, the relevant criteria depending, of course, on the type of problem" (1972, 5).[14]

Although it is difficult to develop strong statements about budgetary skill, it appears that many practitioners and observers, following Justice Potter Stewart's aphorism, "know it when they see it."[15] They recognize stars: Jamie Whitten, for example. Nick Kotz commented on Whitten's tactics for opposing antihunger spending, especially for minorities, in his muckraking 1969 book.

> With his wily ability to juggle figures and cloud ideas, Whitten has convinced officials unfamiliar with his technique (and lacking intimate knowledge of the facts) that he is quite a reasonable man—especially when the conversation turns to hunger and the food programs. (Kotz 1969, 93)

After Whitten's politics became more liberal, his continuing obfuscations increased his fame.

> One of Whitten's shrewdest talents, many colleagues think, is his manner of public speaking. He talks with the dynamic cadence of a Southern planter. But his syntax is often complex and anachronistic, and he can speed up the tempo so that words and phrases become incomprehensible. When he is speaking on the floor, veteran reporters have learned to duck down next to the small speakers that carry sound in the gallery in hope of catching a phrase or two of information.
>
> Some members think he speaks that way for a reason.
>
> "You can always tell how much money is involved by how hard it is to understand him," [House Republican Lynn] Martin said. "Whenever I've had a private conversation with Chairman Whitten, I've been able to understand him."
>
> Whitten merely smiles at the allegation. "People say they can't hear and they can't understand what I say," he said. "I'm not trying to fool anybody. After all, I'm from north Mississippi. I'm a Yankee member of the delegation." (Rapp 1987a, 1054–55; see also Rauch 1986a)

Not only was his speaking style obscure, but so was the accounting for the programs he oversaw as chair of the Agriculture Appropriations Subcommittee

---

14. David L. Weimer suggests that researchers observe deviations from standard practice that lead to better-than-average outcomes. But he also argues that measuring outcomes and dealing with contextual variation greatly complicate this method (1992, 240–45). See also Riker 1986.

15. For other examples of skillful spending advocates, see Matlack 1991; Rauch 1991; and Thomas B. Edsall, "Bringing Good Things to GE," *Washington Post,* 13 April 1985, sec. A. For portraits of less-skillful advocates, see Demkovich 1981.

(which included FmHA and REA). Whitten's skill was less evident when he sought to describe the effects of this spending; he usually recited tired, unpersuasive stories about the effects of depression agricultural programs. (See Benenson 1993.) But if Whitten's star dimmed for these tactics, other notable stars glowed during the 1980s. For example, congressional insiders greatly respected Henry Waxman's skill at designing programs and taking advantage of decision procedures, or the ability of House Ways and Means staffer Wendell Primus to justify spending with the committee's annual publication known as the Green Book (Kosterlitz 1989; Haas 1991a).

These advocates were skilled not only in their ability to adapt to others' expectations in budgetary bargaining. (To some degree, it was the opposite—many controllers couldn't stand them.) They also knew how to *identify* tactical opportunities and *take advantage* of them.

Technical expertise is a crucial component of this type of budgetary skill. The fine details of alternative budgetary characteristics are not, to say the least, often matters of common knowledge or interest. They are instead the special province of the "hidden cluster" (to use Kingdon's phrase) of budget-process participants—technical experts in accounting, government decision procedures, and policy analysis and implementation. Congressman (and later Secretary of Defense) Les Aspin showed the importance of technical expertise to budgetary skill with the following complaint about a spending advocate's argument

> A few weeks ago I wrote a memo for Congressmen explaining some of the difficulties in cutting defense spending this year because so much of what we are being asked to appropriate is not due to be spent until later years. In his budget briefing for the press February 6, Mr. Carlucci stood my argument on its head. He said 31 percent of outlays in fiscal year 1983 would come from prior year appropriations while 62 percent would be for immediate operations, such as personnel and O. & M., and thus, he implied, untouchable. That would leave only 7 percent or $15.1 billion of new money. Trying to have his cake and eat it too, Mr. Carlucci then argued that even if you cut all of that $15.1 billion, you would save less than a quarter of that because three-quarters of that money is not until later years . . . the Deputy Secretary has managed to switch from outlays to budget authority in midparagraph and thus totally bollixed his line of logic.[16]

To paraphrase Carlucci's argument, there was no use in cutting defense spending because "we're going to spend some money, some additional money is

16. *Congressional Record,* 24 February 1982, E 542.

already obligated, and most of the rest won't be spent until much later, so there's no use cutting that, either"! When phrased in technical language, such arguments can successfully confuse unsophisticated participants.

Technical expertise is not uniformly distributed among coalitions. Resource-rich coalitions can hire more technical experts and thereby learn more about tactical opportunities. But abundant resources are not necessary for coalitions to learn. Poor coalitions can observe and copy the tactics of another coalition. Diffusion also occurs through exchanges of tactical information by members of different coalitions. A budget technician noted the extent of diffusion after he commented on the importance of the report of the President's Commission on Budget Concepts.

> It's the only study of its kind. The way the rest of the budget concepts are developed is that we say "These are our rules." We had two people who were our gurus, and I trained at their shoulders. That worked fine until eight to nine years ago, because we had all the smarts. Now, the Budget committees, CBO, and others are as smart, and all of a sudden we found ourselves talking across to them, not down. And with what they're coming up with, I'm beginning to lose sleep!

Although technical expertise is important, it is not sufficient for use of a structural strategy. Knowledge of tactical opportunities must be transformed into actions to have the desired effect. Political scientists have long observed that advocacy coalitions often have trouble shifting tactics. New tactics can require different skills, making some leaders superfluous. Or some coalition members may find proposed new tactics unacceptable. These factors can slow or prevent a coalition from changing course.

But the problem is more general, for the practical relationship between an incremental strategy and a structural strategy is often puzzling. Consider a hypothetical spending-advocate coalition that is considering a proposal to use an accounting tactic. The proponent of the tactic might argue that by creating fiscal illusion the favored program can have a larger budget. But then a skeptic raises the question of how this will affect the mobilization of resources for the coalition. "How can we show our members what we have done? If we tell them in our newsletter that we're getting twice what is recorded in the budget, that bastard at OMB will get a copy and embarrass us!" And the proponent might reply, "Don't worry. With the extra money coming in to our members, we can double our dues and spend it on campaign contributions." Who's right?

Also, the relationship between different structural tactics can be problematic. The skeptic continues, "If we do what you suggest, we also won't be able to spread the news that this program works. If it doesn't cost that much, how can it possibly be successful?" And the proponent retorts, "No paradox there—we'll make the program's *efficiency* our central message." Again, who's right?

The skill that can successfully resolve such strategic dilemmas efficiently, inventively, and creatively, to use Bardach's criteria, is largely *intuitive.* It is built by experience in a variety of situations from which lessons are drawn, lessons that are used to understand the context of a new situation. The intuitively skillful can tailor a fiscal illusion tactic so that it is not *too* gimmicky, reducing the probability that it will provoke a response by controllers. The intuitively skillful can stretch the truth to rationalize a program without being outlandish, taking account of different levels of skepticism in various audiences. And the intuitively skillful know how much discretion to give program administrators so that they can fend off controllers.

Some proposals seem to lack this ability. One example was created by an advisory panel on embassy security that was chaired by a legendary bureaucrat, Robert Inman. This proposal could win an award for the use of the most structural tactics at once. It would have created an independent Property Board to own and operate embassies, take fees from the sale of visas, add borrowing from the Treasury, deposit these funds in an uncontrolled revolving trust fund, and use the funds to build new embassies. The amazing thing about this proposal was that the subterfuge was probably unnecessary. Following the loss of life at the Beirut embassy, even an internal OMB memo said, "There is no question concerning the need for secure embassies. If additional funds are required, State should simply submit its program for improved security and seek appropriations through standard channels." The plan's complexity actually engendered suspicion that the program wasn't needed.[17]

Another example is the embodiment of a fiscal illusion tactic—the Pentagon's black budget. The black budget was so nicknamed because unless one had a high-level security clearance, one couldn't know the costs of specific special-access programs. There is overwhelming evidence that programs were classified black to protect them from budgetary controls, for even advocates for defense spending publicly voiced this belief. As a House Armed Services Committee staffer concluded: "the best example of stealth technology is where the Air Force hid the money" (D. Morrison 1987a, 1986b; Maroni 1987). But by the late 1980s, defense advocates came to believe that they had kept programs in the black for too long. With a reduction in the security threat, the old tactic of "it's too early to tell, it's too late to stop" might not work, because the black status of the programs had prevented advocates from widely broadcasting arguments that this spending would be cost-effective. For example, after

---

17. Joanne Omang, "Protecting Embassies Stressed," *Washington Post,* 5 February 1986, sec. A.

huge cost overruns on the B-2 were finally revealed to the general public, Northrop began to run ads saying

> The B-2 Is Elusive.
> Understanding It Doesn't Have To Be.
>
> The B-2 bomber has been rightly described as a revolutionary airplane. And like all revolutions, it takes time for its significance to be universally recognized.
>
> The fundamental—and unprecedented—capability of the B-2 is to carry a devastating payload over long distances while eluding detection by even the most sophisticated air defenses.
>
> This ability will give pause to any foe. And in time of crisis it will be a stabilizing force. A recallable weapon, flying undetected towards its objective. At a measured pace that buys time for reason to prevail. Time for an adversary to consider.
>
> For over a decade the B-2 has been supported by both parties and by four administrations.

In other words, "We should have told all of you earlier, please don't stop!" (D. Morrison 1989, 2012).[18]

In contrast, is it any wonder that the Legislative Branch Appropriations bill shows great structural skill?

> Congress finances its own operations with a bill built more on tradition than logic. That's putting it kindly: skeptics call the measure a monument to obfuscation.
>
> Trying to follow the legislative branch spending bill's $2 billion through its various line items is like trailing a cat through the labyrinthian passageways of the Capitol itself. A taxpayer or reporter who wants answers to basic questions—how much Congress spends on its committees; how many aides members have; how much Congress spends on travel; even how much the members' salaries and fringe benefits add up to—will have to look elsewhere. And look hard.
>
> Such elemental questions, if they can be answered at all, require the cooperation of congressional officials and deep dives into public records—a level of effort not required with other spending bills. Perusing the bill and the Appropriations Committee reports that accompany it likely will only confuse. (Kuntz 1991a, 111)

---

18. While the B-2 survived at a smaller buy, a similar black program, the Navy's A-12, did not.

Summary

There are strong social expectations for government budgeting that recognize the importance of responsible budgeting for the stability of the state. Budget participants respond to these expectations by establishing a range of methods of characteristically budgeting for individual programs. These methods advantage or disadvantage programs in budgetary competition by affecting perceptions of the costs and benefits of spending, by choosing competitors and collaborators for programs, by exposing programs or protecting them from macrobudgetary constraints, and through other effects.

Some skillful spending advocates seek to change the structure of budgeting for their programs when tactical opportunities are present. They are frequently unsuccessful because controllers usually oppose structural tactics. In addition, some spending advocates can't recognize tactical opportunities—they believe that the incrementalist norm of the fair share is widely held. But their more skillful competitors do not; they search for and sometimes exploit tactical opportunities to change budget structures, stealing the march on the trusting incrementalists. As they succeed, structural budgetary skill diffuses, reducing the expertise advantage of controllers. Victories by spending advocates accelerates spending and increases fiscal stress. Greater fiscal stress empowers controllers but also stimulates spending advocates to escape controls.

The next four chapters provide numerous examples of structural tactics and illustrate the validity of this structural model of strategy.

Chapter 4

The Costs of Spending: Smoke and Mirrors Accounting Tactics

A common, offhand remark in the budgeting world is: "There are only [pick a low number] people in Washington who really understand how this account works." Such statements deserve more reflection than they usually receive. If they are true for more than a few exceptional programs, then there is an important implication: not until one delves into the intricacies of budgetary accounting—and manages to stay awake—will one understand one of the most important aspects of budgeting.

Unfortunately, those who stay awake will probably feel as if they are trapped in a recurring nightmare. Typical nightmares feature creepy, crawly creatures or violent criminals; their equivalent in budgeting nightmares is *fiscal illusion.* In this book, I use the term fiscal illusion to mean "the misperception of actual spending."[1] But unlike the exaggerated fears of most nightmares, fear of fiscal illusion is not phobic. This chapter will show that fiscal illusion is common and usually intentional.

To summarize my argument, recall that each budget process features a desire by leaders of states to exercise control over spending demands. Absent control of these demands, spending tends to accelerate, producing heavy tax burdens that lead to taxpayer rebellions. If taxes are instead limited when spending is not, expanded borrowing must fill the gap, but then credit markets charge premiums to cover the greater risk of delinquency and default and may even close off access to credit. Since either scenario threatens their power, leaders recognize that they need regular opportunities to allocate limited financial resources among competing claims. They therefore establish a routine schedule for budgeting. They also promote acceptance of a budgetary decision standard that is definitive.

This chapter focuses on the federal government's budgetary standard. In the last chapter, I argued that the ideal of a decision standard requires, first, an accord over the fiscal goal that the standard of measurement is to support, and

1. In public finance, the term *fiscal illusion* is more commonly used to describe revenue-raising methods that are perceived to extract less revenue than they actually do, such as income tax withholding and indirect taxes like gasoline excises.

second, institutional expertise. Experts are necessary because of the inherent complexity of public finance; they reduce complexity by developing accounting rules and making the inevitable judgment calls. But their work will be too difficult if participants in the budgetary process are not in accord about their main goal. Such agreement is necessary because of the principle in accounting that "form follows function." This means that accounting practices should be determined by the planned uses for accounting information. For example, businesses present financial information in one format to report on their solvency and in a different format to report on their annual income. Similarly, if governments are to report on both long-run creditworthiness and short-run cash flow, they *must* use different formats to best communicate the truth about both outcomes.

At this point, it is useful to more fully describe the President's Commission on Budget Concepts, which was briefly mentioned in the budgetary history of FmHA in chapter 2. (In general, studies of budgetary politics have ignored the commission's work.) As stated previously, President Johnson appointed the commission to deflect criticism of administration gaming of budget concepts.[2] The commission issued its report in late 1967, and some of its important recommendations were incorporated in the 1969 budget.

The commission's relative success, unrepresentative of most commissions, can be laid in part to its high-powered membership, which included the current and previous secretaries of the Treasury, the director of the Bureau of the Budget, the comptroller general (the head of the General Accounting Office), the chairmen of the Appropriations committees, and noted academics and businessmen. Its staff was expert, and the commission used an extensive study process that relied heavily on outside authorities. But its success was all the more notable because it confronted the most important conceptual issues of budgetary accounting and reached agreement on many of them, despite a lack of previous high-level attention to these issues. Only the first Hoover Commission (of 1949) had devoted much attention to the problem of the budgetary decision standard, and though its proposal to require accrual accounting was put into law in 1950, this statute was never implemented. Until 1967, budget concepts were by and large the province of a small group of technicians in the Bureau of the Budget.

Among the commission's recommendations were that accrual accounting be adopted, that loan subsidies be estimated separately, that offsetting income against spending would be proper only in some situations, that capital budgeting was inappropriate for the federal government, and that debt should be

---

2. Some budget folklore suggests that the commission wanted to use trust fund surpluses to hide administrative budget deficits. Yet this motivation is inconsistent with the fact that almost all of the commission's recommendations would increase budgetary honesty.

reported in a certain format. These recommendations were specific and made with confidence. Yet this chapter shows that the commission's recommendations failed to eliminate conflict over the basic issues of budgetary accounting. The primary effect of the commission's good work was it offered technicians in the Bureau of the Budget and OMB some rhetorical protection, who learned to cite the report as close to Holy Writ in debates over proper accounting practices.

No recommendation was made as strongly nor had more effect than the commission's call for a *unified* budget. This unified budget was meant to be comprehensive, including all financial activities of the government.[3] Prior to adoption of the unified budget, presidents used different aggregate budget measures. One measure was the *administrative* budget, which included only appropriated accounts, and another was the *consolidated cash* budget, which added most nonappropriated accounts (like trust funds) to the administrative budget. A third budget aggregate measure that received attention during the 1960s was one consistent with the accounting assumptions of the National Income and Product Accounts (NIPA), the statistical series used for macroeconomic analysis. In some years, presidents featured the administrative budget format, and in others, the consolidated cash or NIPA budget format, with the choice of which format to feature being largely influenced by the relative sizes of the deficits reported by each format—that is, the format that produced the lowest deficit received the most space in the president's budget. In addition, when the administrative budget was featured, the exclusion of trust funds from this budget gave these funds a free ride for the year. This treatment had encouraged the establishment of some programs as trust funds.

The commission had a sophisticated understanding of the difficulty of developing a budgetary decision standard. An extensive quote from the commission's report introduction and summary lays out its basic analysis and recommendation:

> What is the budget of the United States? Fundamentally, it presents the essential ingredients of the financial plan of the Federal Government for the coming year. This plan has many aspects and must serve many purposes:
>
> It sets forth the President's requests to Congress for new programs, appropriation of funds, and changes in revenue legislation;
>
> It proposes an allocation of resources to serve national objectives, between the private and the public sectors, and within the public sector;

3. The most notable exclusions from the "comprehensive" budget were the monetary policy activities of the Federal Reserve and related international monetary transactions.

It embodies the fiscal policy of the Government for promoting high employment, price stability, healthy growth of the national economy, and equilibrium in the Nation's balance of payments;
It provides the basis for executive and agency management of Federal Government programs;
It gives the Treasury needed information for its management of cash resources and the public debt;
It provides the public with information about the national economy essential for private business, labor, agriculture, and other groups, and for an informed assessment by citizens of governmental stewardship of the public's money and resources.

It is sometimes suggested that to meet these different objectives, particularly the first three purposes listed above, different budgets are required. Indeed, the emergence of competing budget concepts in recent years—the administrative budget, the consolidated cash budget, and the national income accounts budget, plus several alternative tabulations on appropriations and other spending authority—are taken as evidence of the fact that no *one* budget can do all the jobs involved in the budgetary process.

This argument, however, runs head-on into the opposite argument—that different and competing budgets confuse public and congressional understanding and impede governmental decision-making.

Is there a way out of this dilemma? It is the Commission's belief that there is, and that a unified concept of the budget as described in this Report, and developed at length in Chapter 2, can provide an integrated and comprehensive statement of governmental accounts which will serve usefully the several different purposes required of the budget, while improving its clarity, consistency, and intelligibility.

In deciding whether it is possible to develop a unified budget, one must distinguish between *competing* budget concepts, which cause confusion, and *complementary* budget concepts, which actually aid in understanding the scope and economic impact of the Government.

The administrative budget, the consolidated cash budget, and the national income accounts budget have often been used as competing measures of the total scope of Federal financial activity; they are not unified and can be used together only with a fairly elaborate reconciliation that tends to confuse more than it enlightens.

The Commission believes that there should be a unified budget—with complementary components—which will put an end to competing measures. A statement of Government receipts and expenditures other than loans, with a resulting expenditure account surplus or deficit, is complementary to a statement of net lending—i.e., loan disbursements less loan

> repayments. Net lending is then added to the expenditure account surplus or deficit to yield the figure on the total budget surplus or deficit. More directly, this is the difference between budget receipts and total budget expenditures, which cover the full range of Government programs requiring congressional appropriations.
>
> . . . The Commission's recommendations, therefore, view the budget as a unified set of summary data. This approach is in contrast to the historic tendency to view the budget in terms of a single number—the surplus or deficit.
>
> This overconcentration on the surplus or deficit figure is responsible for much of the present proliferation of budget concepts. In turn, it has been a root cause of public confusion and has been responsible for accusations of "gimmickry." If the public is to view the budget more broadly, the executive branch, the Congress, and the press should exercise leadership and educational responsibilities. It is not possible for one number to portray the scope, character, and economic effects of the Government's financial plan. (1967, 2–3, 7)

Here is a strong, lucid argument: there are multiple goals for budgeting, different measures are most appropriate for different goals, and a well-designed budgetary accounting system can provide all of these measures. But this chapter will show that though the *principle* of the unified budget was generally accepted, none of the specific commission *proposals* were adopted without challenge or exception. Accrual accounting has yet to be adopted in full, credit and capital spending programs and offsetting spending programs were notable sources of budget gimmickry, and debt was created without being recognized as such. Even the comprehensiveness of the budget was challenged on numerous occasions.

There are several good explanations for this record. First, as good as the commission's work was, it was certainly not the last word. The commission compromised to co-opt potential opponents, leaving the unified budget system with a variety of loopholes that could be exploited. Second, the commission understood only imperfectly which information would be most useful. As experts recommended new approaches, the value of the commission's report was reduced (see Hartman 1984; Morse 1971).

Third, the commission's wish that budgetary elites wouldn't capitulate to the temptation to emphasize one measure in public debates was obviously optimistic. Since the public worries about granting excess power to budgetary elites, allowing elites to issue complex budgets with multiple summary measures will not foster confidence that these elites can be held accountable. Similarly, politicians who wish to generate blame or seek credit for budgetary actions find that a bottom line makes their position easier to communicate.

These pressures, along with a strong traditional belief in the ideal of the balanced budget, made the process emphasize one aggregate measure of budget results—the cash deficit (Savage 1988).

But the most important causes of budgetary accounting instability were the strategic actions of *both* advocates and controllers of spending. Consider first the opportunities for spending proponents. Chapter 2 described how two programs often received budgetary resources that far exceeded reported costs because the rules of budgetary accounting were neither comprehensive nor definitive. These free resources were not counted toward the deficit measure, so cutting them would not have helped decision makers reduce the reported deficit. Nor were unreported budgetary resources usually visible to the opponents of this spending. It might have been reported in bits and fragments, but the complexity of interpreting and collating sophisticated financial transactions over long periods of time was daunting to typical opponents.

These were the typical outcomes from fiscal illusions: decision makers were not expected to control unreported costs, and controllers of spending were less able to document these costs. Many spending advocates understandably responded to these incentives—they searched for tactical opportunities that they could exploit. Spending advocates weighed the possible gains from such end runs against the payoffs from other plays. They also had to consider the ability of the defense to counter these end runs—whether flagrant end runs might upset controllers, inviting extra attention to flaws in the budgetary decision standard. On the other hand, there were situations in which decision makers aided and abetted end runs around budgetary rules.

This chapter catalogs a wide range of accounting tactics used in federal budgeting, and partially identifies the conditions under which they were used, successfully or unsuccessfully. Table 4.1 displays the catalog's categories, which are grouped into three sections. The first describes tactics that affected how the scope of the budget was determined. The second section describes outlay tactics, and the third describes obligation and financing tactics.

Many of the situations described in this chapter were very complicated. I have tried to describe the essence of each accounting rule and the associated tactic but not overwhelm the reader with detail. Nevertheless, I fear that I won't be completely successful in this regard—some readers may find the length and complexity of the cases numbing. Many budgeting participants felt the same way through the 1980s, when accounting tactics were especially popular.

Accounting tactics are by no means unique to the federal government. They have counterparts in the major accounting controversies in state and local governments and the private sector. For example, the problem of scope—of determining which activities should be included in the budget and which should be excluded from it—resembles the generic accounting objective that the "reporting entity" be "defined." State and local governments have long

TABLE 4.1. Accounting Tactics

Determining the Scope of the Budget
Establish off-budget status
Create a "privately owned" government-sponsored enterprise
Spend through tax-preference mechanism
Accounting for Cash
Pay with unrecognized cash equivalents
Offset outlays with collections
Forgive expected repayments
Underestimate spendouts and change effective dates
Accounting for Commitments
Avoid the full-funding requirement
Lease instead of purchase
Use uncounted guarantees
Ignore other long-run costs

wrestled with the problem of to what degrees their budgets and financial statements should incorporate the finances of relatively independent public authorities. In some locations—New York being the extreme example—the process of manipulating the reporting entity or the scope of the budget has been central to budgetary strategies (Leigland 1988; Patton 1985). Similarly, outlay tactics and obligation and financing tactics take advantage of different conceptions of the proper "basis of accounting," which in the budgetary context means: when spending (and perhaps uncertain commitments to spend) should be recognized.[4]

Determining the Scope of the Budget

The President's Commission on Budget Concepts recommendation that the budget be comprehensive was its strongest. But despite the principled consensus about the desirability of the unified budget, the scope of the budget continued to be a major practical issue for nearly two decades after the

4. While this chapter covers a wide range of budgetary accounting tactics, it follows budgetary convention by ignoring resource allocation by regulations. Regulations are excluded from the budget because they do not cause a *direct* claim on the government's financial resources. On the other hand, regulations can be close substitutes for spending and may be adopted because they are treated as costless to the government by budgetary accounting—some controls on agricultural production are good examples. To the extent that the budget is viewed as a mechanism for rationing *society's* resources, as opposed to the *government's financial* resources, then this definition is less than comprehensive. For discussions of a "regulatory budget," see DeMuth 1980; Wood, Laws, and Breen 1981; and Litan and Nordhaus 1983, 133–58.

commission's report. Spending proponents employed three tactics to remove their programs from the budget. The first was to simply declare a program or its funding source to be off-budget. The second was to constitute a program as a government-sponsored enterprise, a privately owned organization that carries out governmental activities. The third tactic was to spend the government's financial resources through the tax-preference mechanism. These tax expenditures were traditionally considered to be nonbudgetary transactions.

Establish Off-Budget Status

What could be a better tactic to reduce the visibility of spending than to require that it be excluded from the budget? (Samuelson 1981). Here are some examples:

The Export-Import Bank was declared off-budget by Congress in 1971 at the request of President Nixon, who wished to expand its lending. Congress brought it back on-budget in 1976 after having difficulty conducting oversight.

The Section 202 Housing for Elderly and Handicapped program was placed off-budget by Congress in 1974 in response to a HUD-OMB proposal to terminate the program through impoundments. Section 202 was returned to the budget in 1978 as this threat receded in the Carter administration.

The Strategic Petroleum Reserve (SPRO) was declared off-budget in 1981. This tactic protected SPRO from a cut in spending that was threatened by the budget resolution. The resolution's initial projection of these savings was unrealistic, for it assumed that "oil bonds" would be sold to finance the purchase of the same amount of oil that would have been bought in the absence of a cut. When it became apparent that this plan wouldn't work (because of the high cost of selling oil bonds), the Reagan administration proposed that the purchase of oil for SPRO be placed off-budget, and this was accepted by the Congress.[5]

Most off-budget spending in the decade following the Congressional Budget Act relied on the off-budget status of the Federal Financing Bank,

5. Eight years later, GAO responded to the request from Representative Philip Sharp, the Democratic chair of the Subcommittee on Energy and Power, "that we examine alternative, nontraditional methods of acquiring oil for the Strategic Petroleum Reserve. You were concerned with the budget deficit and sought to reduce government outlays for the SPR. . . . We examined approximately 40 proposals in three broad categories that increase government revenues by selling financial instruments such as bonds . . . acquire oil by means other than outright purchase . . . [and] set up a separate SPR entity" (GAO 1989e, 1).

which was described in chapter 2. Yet the availability of the FFB as a source of fiscal illusion was initially unintentional. The FFB was instead supposed to reduce the cost of direct agency borrowing from the market by packaging these borrowings. To prevent double counting, the FFB was to be treated simply as a conduit from the Treasury to the agencies. But circumventions of accounting rules then allowed borrowing from the FFB to be counted as contributions from nongovernmental sources. Outlays financed by borrowing from the FFB understandably exploded, reaching a peak of $21 billion in 1981. In this year, the major borrowers from the FFB included Defense's foreign military sales program, HUD's low-rent public housing program, Tennessee Valley Authority's Seven States Energy Corporation, the Export-Import Bank, the U.S. Railway Association (Conrail), and the Postal Service. CBO reported that from 1974–81, use of the FFB led to an understatement of the deficit by $82.3 billion, which was 22 percent of the reported deficit over this period! (Shillingsburg 1982, 27).

The off-budget tactic was also used by proponents of the Social Security program. Like other trust funds, the Social Security trust funds were included in the budget in 1969, which meant that any reductions in Social Security benefits (or increases in payroll taxes) would be counted as deficit reductions. This did not greatly worry program advocates at first, but with the conjunction of the Reagan administration's conservative ideology and a solvency crisis for the funds, benefit reductions became more likely. The program's supporters then began to promote heavily the ideas that Social Security was a "self-financed" trust fund, that reductions were unnecessary and unfair, and that Social Security should be removed from the budget. The Social Security Commission in 1983 agreed, and Congress scheduled off-budget status for the program by 1993. Perceived continuing threats against the program led advocates to request accelerated off-budget status, which was granted in the Gramm-Rudman-Hollings Act in 1985 (Koitz 1985).

It may be that Social Security's proponents worked for off-budget status primarily to symbolically satisfy their constituents. One would think that Social Security would not need off-budget status, given the massive amount of political resources that its advocates controlled. One would also think that off-budget status would benefit Social Security less than it would any other program, as it was rather difficult to hide a quarter of the government's spending! Off-budget status did protect the program, however, because it created another procedural hurdle for those who would reduce the program's spending—first, they would have to bring it on-budget.

Other dedicated revenue trust funds—the highways, airports and airways, inland waterway, and unemployment insurance trust funds—would have benefited more from off-budget status. Frustrated with budget ceilings on these programs, their advocates tried again and again to escape the unified budget by proposing amendments to reconciliation, authorization, and appropriations bills. None were accepted, though there were close losses (Zuckman 1992).

Not all off-budget programs received their special status from statutes. Two programs were placed off-budget through the president's interpretation of the Budget and Accounting Act. The Postal Service was taken off-budget by President Nixon in 1974. This reduced reported outlays by over $300 million, but the action was rationalized as providing the service with a businesslike environment "independent" from political influence. A similar rationale has been advanced for the off-budget status of the Federal Reserve. Several presidents have considered including the administrative costs of the Fed in the budget, but have drawn back for fear of the Fed-bashing charges that would be raised (Meyers 1985).

OMB director David Stockman launched a counterattack on most off-budget programs in 1985. He proposed legislation to repeal their off-budget status, and following the traditional treatment of proposed legislation, included even these technically off-budget programs *in* the budget. This change was especially advantageous for Stockman, because he also proposed to cut dramatically spending by FFB-financed programs. By placing these programs on-budget, *he could now claim deficit savings* from these cuts. Later in the year, the Balanced Budget Act eliminated almost all off-budget protections.[6] Aside from Social Security, only the Postal Service has regained its off-budget status (Starobin 1989a).

In sum, the off-budget tactic relied on a radical misperception of the character of spending. When spending was off-budget, the fiscal illusion that resulted was total—spending had to be ignored. But when the tactic was not accepted, it also failed totally. After passage of the Balanced Budget Act, which reaffirmed acceptance of the unified-budget concept, the probability of success for a simple off-budget tactic became quite small (Healey 1993).

Create a "Privately Owned" Government Sponsored Enterprise

A more subtle tactic than a simple off-budget declaration is the creation of a government sponsored enterprise (GSE). A GSE is an organization that is privately owned, but that is also perceived to have quasi-governmental status. This quasi-governmental status usually results from the characteristics of the GSE that distinguishes it from other privately owned organizations. A GSE is established and chartered by an act of Congress, and is exempt from certain taxes and regulations. The owners of a GSE are those who purchase its stock. A

6. See Rauch 1985c; John M. Berry, "More Control Sought Over Off-Budget Costs," *Washington Post,* 1 January 1985, sec. A.

GSE has a line of credit with the Treasury and can also borrow money in the credit market. GSE borrowings are classified as agency debt by the credit market, even though the enabling statutes for GSEs typically include language that matches or resembles the following:

> No obligation which is insured, guaranteed, or otherwise backed by the corporation, shall be deemed to be an obligation which is guaranteed by the full faith and credit of the United States.

Agency debt trades at a very small premium above Treasury debt, signifying that the credit market considers agency debt to be only slightly more risky than the "risk-free" Treasury debt. This preferential treatment of GSE debt is based on the widespread perception that the Treasury will bail out holders of a GSE's debt should the GSE become insolvent, irrespective of the government's disclaimer of such responsibility.

The Commission on Budget Concepts decided that government-sponsored enterprises should be excluded from the budget, despite the close similarities between GSE and Treasury debt. This decision was based on the belief that the government's budget simply could not include the finances of privately-owned organizations. In its discussion of the issue, the commission asked,

> Who owns the agency? Who supplies its capital? Who selects its managers? Do the Congress and the President have control over the agency's program and budget, or are the agency's policies the responsibility of the Congress or the President in some broad ultimate sense? (President's Commission on Budget Concepts 1967, 25; see also Staats 1967, 187–95)

These were broad questions that implied that proper budgetary classification of a borderline organization could be reached only after a weighing of factors. The commission's practical response to the dilemma was a simple rule: if an organization was completely privately owned, it should be excluded from the budget. Accepting this rule was a close call. A commission member who was active in the deliberations told me,

> A lot of us thought there should be no gray area—it's either government or it's not, and if the federal government is involved, even if secondhand, we ought to be able to quantify it and show it in the budget. But the president's commission backed away from it, because they thought it would be too hard to quantify.

The commission's GSE rule placed organizations off-budget even if they were endowed with substantial governmental powers, *as long as* they were perceived to be privately owned. This created a continuing tactical opportunity for those who were sophisticated enough to design GSEs. One would have to convince the Congress to charter an organization, and then capitalize it by selling stock to private individuals, who would then become the legal owners of the organization. At the same time, however, this private organization would be granted special powers that allow it to borrow at near-risk-free rates, and in return would be constrained to pass this financing advantage on to a selected class of beneficiaries. The result: a government subsidy equivalent to appropriating funds out of the Treasury. In other words, it would be like dressing a government agency in drag.[7]

Some GSEs—the Farm Credit Banks and the Federal Home Loan Banks—were created prior to the Commission on Budget Concepts, and thus benefitted from the commission's decision. Others—such as the Federal National Mortgage Association (Fannie Mae)—were privatized or created soon after the commission's report. An undated OMB staff document describes FNMA's treatment:

> As a result of the report of the President's Commission on Budget Concepts, the secondary market activities of Fannie Mae, previously excluded from the budget, would soon be included—adding an estimated $2.5 billion to the budget in one step. The fear of adverse public and Congressional reaction worried the Johnson Administration.

and led the Bureau of the Budget to restructure FNMA as a private organization. The OMB document then quotes HUD secretary Weaver.

> The main reasons for transferring are two. First, it has been expected that the secondary market operation will ultimately become privately owned. Secondly, because the operations of the secondary market are now within the budget, the amount and the volume of the activity is influenced by the vagaries of the total budget situation.
>
> By putting the secondary market operations outside the government and, thereby, outside the budget, it would be possible for Fannie Mae to be more responsive to the needs, we believe, of the building and mortgage financing industries than it can now be.[8]

---

7. See Phaup 1985 for a general overview of GSEs.
8. See also U.S. Department of Housing and Urban Development 1986, chap. 2.

Another GSE—the Student Loan Marketing Association ("Sallie Mae")—was privatized in 1982.[9]

After the Balanced Budget Act foreclosed the straight off-budget opportunity in 1985, creating a GSE appeared to be an advantageous off-budget tactic. Examples of proposed GSEs in 1986–87 show the extent of diffusion of the tactic: for small business, the Corporation for Small Business Investment Corporations (COSBI); for airlines, the Airways Corporation, to replace the Federal Aviation Administration (FAA); for local governments, the National Public Works Corporation; for the elderly, the Federal National Long-Term Care Reinsurance Corporation, and several different GSE-style "corporations" to carry out uranium enrichment operations. In at least three of these cases, the proposals were designed by former budget agency or budget committee staffers, who had the comparative advantages of knowing that the GSE design was opportune and also were skilled enough to develop proposals for new GSEs that could pass review (see Haas 1988b).[10]

A notable example from this period was a new "subsidiary" of the Federal Savings and Loan Insurance Corporation. In 1985, to get around myopic appropriation limits on salaries, OMB approved the transfer of the regulatory staff of the on-budget Federal Home Loan Bank Board to the Federal Home Loan Banks, which were GSEs (see GAO 1987, 15–16). This showed how far the private ownership rule could be bent—a regulatory staff that could close insolvent thrifts using the sovereign powers of government *cannot* be private in any meaningful sense, but the budget world decided it would ignore that fact. Then, in 1986, the Administration proposed creation of the Federal Savings and Loan Insurance Corporation Financing Corporation (FICO). The Federal Savings and Loan Insurance Corporation (FSLIC) needed a large amount of cash to close insolvent thrifts, but the Gramm-Rudman ceiling on outlays would be violated if this cash were provided and thrifts were closed through the regular on-budget method. FICO was concocted to solve these problems. It would be owned by the "private" Federal Home Loan Banks, but would generate funds to close insolvent thrifts by borrowing with an implicit government guarantee. The guarantee was all the stronger because the Financing Corporation was granted the insurance premiums that were required by law to flow to the FSLIC if FICO did not exist. Such a patent fiscal illusion was designed by

9. Another example is Senator Proxmire's unsuccessful effort in 1979 to have the Central Liquidity Facility for credit unions declared off-budget on the grounds that the credit unions owned the "stock" of the facility.

10. An apparent requirement for new GSEs is a creative name, usually of feminine gender. Consider the proposal by Representative John LaFalce to create the "Venture Enhancement and Loan Development Administration for Smaller Undercapitalized Enterprises," or "Velda Sue" for short. LaFalce was also responsible for the aforementioned COSBI, which when considered by the Congress should have been described as the "Cosbi bill" (reverse the words).

technicians in the Treasury Department and OMB's Housing Branch, with the support of OMB's political leadership. Other technicians eventually acquiesced to FICO for two reasons: first, it was judged a minimally acceptable alternative to the failure to provide needed financing through regular appropriations, and second, because the political pressure to accept the Financing Corporation's design was intense.[11]

Another example was the 1986 creation of the College Construction Loan Insurance Association (CCLIA), which was brought to life by the Student Loan Marketing Association and higher education institutions.[12] CCLIA was designed to reduce the cost of financing higher education facilities by insuring the debt issued to finance these facilities. Even though many of the current debt obligations for this purpose were already exempt from federal taxation (as state government debt), CCLIA was projected to reduce the average interest rate on borrowing for this purpose by about 1 percent. Like the pseudo-GSE FICO, CCLIA was treated by OMB as a GSE even though it was still partially owned by the federal government. As a similar subsidy from appropriations had been cut and prospects for revival were not strong, this case shows that even the higher education coalition retained some budgetary skill during a period when it was not very successful (see GAO 1993; Starobin 1993b).

The GSE tactic illustrates the general phenomenon known as sector-blurring—there is no clear dividing line between the public and private sectors.[13] Because of this, any general rule that controllers could develop would invite creative responses. And when controllers gave into pressure and classified as off-budget those activities or organizations that belonged on-budget, the problem threatened to become worse. An example is provided by a letter sent by Senator Howard Metzenbaum to the CBO director on 16 November 1987. Metzenbaum, who often received publicity for opposing proposals that he considered to be raids on the Treasury, wrote:

> On November 20, the Labor Subcommittee will conduct a hearing on S. 1811, a bill to assist the steel industry to refinance certain pension costs.

---

11. This paragraph summarizes hundreds of pages of complex memos that I obtained. As the amount provided by FICO proved far too small, its creators followed by proposing another pseudo-GSE—the Resolution Financing Corporation, or REFCORP. The Resolution Trust Corporation was then created, a belated acknowledgment of the government's organizational responsibility for financing its deposit insurance liabilities. Almost all of the RTC's financial transactions were excluded from budget target calculations. However, the Congress continually failed to provide sufficient funds that would minimize the cost of the resolution, apparently for fear of being blamed for allocating these (off-budget but too large to hide) funds.

12. The initial nickname of "Cecilia" was replaced by "Connie Lee."

13. For a general discussion of the difficulty of deciding whether organizations are public or private, see Bozeman 1987. See also Leazes 1987; Burkhead 1956, chap. 16; Seidman 1988; Moe and Stanton 1989.

> The measure is intended to permit the government to facilitate private refinancing of certain pension costs. It is not intended to have federal budget consequences. I would appreciate receiving from you answers to the following questions:
>
> 1. What is the budget impact of the legislation?
> 2. If there are on-budget costs, what changes would be necessary to the proposal so that the intent of the authors is accomplished—that the measure not entail on-budget costs?
> 3. In light of the fact that CBO scored the FSLIC refinancing bill as an off-budget program, what differences exist between that measure and S. 1811 which could possibly explain any budget scoring differences?
> 4. Are there any differences between S. 1811 and S. 1665, the Farm Credit Amendments Act, which would cause one to be scored on-budget and one to be scored off-budget? Please explain.[14]

The request to please explain was grating to controllers, who were essentially being asked to provide the map to the hidden treasure, with the implicit understanding that failing to do so might lead to a walk down the gangplank. In this case, CBO's 19 November response was artful—it responded directly to the questions, and then suggested that "we are doubtful that changes can be made to S. 1811 that would negate any possible federal budget impact. The problem is that certain steel companies are not financially able to meet their pension obligations." Note that "doubtful" is not as strong a descriptor as, for example, "do not believe." Had Metzenbaum been more tenacious with follow-up letters, he could have received much more useful information. My confidence is based in part by considering the contemporaneous bailout of the Farm Credit System. This rescue provided over $4 billion, creating two GSEs—the Farm Credit System Financial Assistance Corporation (FCSFAC) and the Federal Agricultural Mortgage Corporation ("Farmer Mac"). Spending propo-

---

14. This letter was not at all extreme. Consider another letter to the director of CBO, which described a proposal to create an endowment for historic preservation programs. It would have granted $133 million to the new endowment with the provision that outlays not be scored unless the endowment's principal was used. In the description of the proposal that accompanied the letter, "This means that the grant establishing this endowment for the National Trust would not constitute an outlay nor would it increase budget deficits." The letter was intended to see if CBO would interpret the bill's language in the same way. The letter said in part:

> Before I take a position, I would appreciate your review and reaction of the attachments. I have been approached previously seeking support, but the language of the current proposal has a slightly different look that needs further review. Specifically, I would appreciate your review of the following questions:
>
> (1) How would you score budget authority and outlays associated with this proposal?
>
> (2) Are there precedents? Do you have examples?

nents, including some Agriculture Committee staff who had previously worked in budgeting positions in the Congress, repeatedly queried CBO, OMB, and the Treasury for rulings on the budgetary effects of proposals, until they designed a rescue that was sufficiently off-budget. The package required some direct and indirect contributions from borrowers to "capitalize" the GSEs (in order to create "private ownership" status), but the debt the new GSEs issued was essentially uncollateralized. This was possible because the capital needs of GSEs are minimal. Capital is generally required for financial intermediaries to reduce the apprehensions of those who would lend intermediaries money. The exception to this rule is the financial intermediary called the government, which needs no capital because it can tax, borrow, and create money with near impunity. For this reason, GSEs can leverage tremendous amounts of money on small capital contributions.[15]

Like the simple off-budget tactic described just in the previous section, there were many attempts to use the GSE tactic. Like the simple off-budget tactic, only some GSE attempts were successful, usually when decision makers who were erstwhile controllers bent to the persistence of spending advocates. Like the simple off-budget tactic, controllers sought to limit the use of the GSE tactic in legitimate fear of copycats of the FICO and FCSFAC successes. And as they argued against creating newly proposed GSEs, they disregarded earlier and contradictory arguments in support of GSEs like FICO and FCSFAC. For example, although George Gould, the undersecretary of the Treasury, wrote a letter on 10 June 1986 justifying the FICO plan, including a statement that "this transaction cannot be replicated easily," he wrote another letter on 24 February 1988 opposing the COSBI bill, *with all his previous arguments reversed*! Such hypocrisy was common in Washington, especially for political appointees who expected to play the game for only a few years. It was less attractive to the career-minded controllers who wanted to find appropriate methods for reducing the long-term budgetary costs of GSEs. They eventually succeeded in convincing the Congress to adopt a weak regulatory regime on Fannie Mae and Freddie Mac (CBO 1991; U.S. Department of Treasury 1990; Stanton 1990, 1991; Taylor 1992).

A few final observations about the GSE tactic. First, its form limited its function—GSEs can only be established when some small amount of capital is provided by beneficiaries. Government-sponsored enterprises are unlikely means for fighting a covert war on poverty. The form also demands some technical skill, which implies a level of political mobilization that can afford

15. A year after the Farm Credit bailout, borrowers attempted to cancel their obligations to put up the capital that was necessary to create GSE status. OMB then threatened to take away this status and put all of the Farm Credit borrowing and spending on-budget, which effectively enforced this minor cost of using the GSE tactic.

the technicians that specialize in such machinations. Yet the form, once established, aids in political mobilization. Since a GSE is "private," it may be more active politically. For example, FNMA has its own PAC.[16]

Spend with Tax Preferences

Preferences in the tax code that lower the tax liabilities of individuals and corporations, and thus lower government revenues, are called *tax expenditures.* Unlike regular spending, in which the government actually distributes funds, tax expenditures cannot be directly observed—they are funds that are *not* collected by the government. But despite this low visibility, tax expenditures reduce the government's wealth just as does regular spending. In fact, the magnitude of tax expenditures matches or even exceeds regular spending in certain areas of the budget. For example, the largest tax expenditure for housing in 1992 allocated roughly $42 billion to taxpayers who deducted mortgage interest. In the same year, the government spent only half of that amount (in outlays) for all regular spending for housing assistance.[17] Nevertheless, tax expenditures do not receive the same scrutiny in the budget documents that regular spending programs do. Tax expenditures are typically displayed in a less visible supplemental table, rather than being integrated with regular spending in the main budget document.

Structural tactics did not create the majority of recognized tax expenditures, and especially the majority of the largest tax expenditures. Instead, decision makers simply did not consider it proper to include these expenditures in the income base when the preferences were established during the first half of the twentieth century. As the consensus definition of economic income broadened, however, most beneficiaries of these tax expenditures tried to maintain their structural protections. In addition, some tax preferences *were* clearly designed as structurally favored substitutes for regular spending programs. Some good examples are the various alternative energy tax incentives enacted during the Carter administration and the low-income housing credit, which was adopted in the 1986 Tax Reform Act. CBO and Joint Committee on Taxation data show that the *number* of tax expenditures roughly quintupled from the mid-1960s to the early 1980s, which suggests tax expenditures became more

---

16. On the other hand, the absence of normal accountability controls on these organizations creates a potential for rent-seeking by GSE managers. The most publicized example was the extraordinary retirement package for David Maxwell, who was the head of FNMA during the 1980s. See Matlack 1990a.

17. Useful sources on the establishment and control of tax expenditures include Birnbaum and Murray 1987; Conlan, Wrightson, and Beam 1990; Eismeier 1982; Howard 1992; Steuerle 1992; Surrey and McDaniel 1980, 1985; and Witte 1985.

popular tactics through the period.[18] (This comparison slightly overstates the rate of growth because of the tendency of analysts to identify more tax provisions as expenditures during the latter part of the period. Yet all lists of tax expenditures exclude the many expenditures that favor specific beneficiaries; these are variously identified as "transition rules" and "Louis B. Mayer" amendments.)[19]

An example of the motivation for substituting tax expenditures for regular spending is provided by a 1985 debate over funding for three war memorials—for Korean War veterans, black Revolutionary War veterans, and women veterans. The Congress turned down initial proposals to fund these memorials directly through appropriations, substituting financing from tax-deductible charitable contributions. The government's cost for each taxpayer who deducted the cost of a contribution would be the contribution multiplied by the taxpayer's marginal tax rate.

> In a hearing Oct. 29 before the Senate Energy and Natural Resources Subcommittee on Public Lands, [Senator William] Armstrong noted that of the $10 million raised privately for the Vietnam War memorial, $3.5 million went toward construction; the rest went for administrative expenses.
>
> In addition, he noted that although the Vietnam War memorial was erected with private funds, it ended up costing the federal Treasury the same amount it would have cost to build it with government funds—$3.5 million—because of tax deductions from contributions. Thus, he proposed that the federal government provide money directly.
>
> "While the idea of privately organized fund raising is attractive," said Armstrong, "the costs can be high."
>
> But during House debate, Mary Rose Oakar, D-Ohio, chairman of the House Administration Task Force on Libraries and Memorials, said that while she personally could support using taxpayers' money the panel

---

18. Details on tax expenditures are provided in annual estimates published by the Joint Committee on Taxation and the Congressional Budget Office and in the *Budget of the U.S. Government.* In addition, the Senate Budget Committee periodically publishes a detailed report entitled *Tax Expenditures: Relationships to Spending Programs and Background Material on Individual Provisions.*

19. The revenue lost from tax expenditures roughly doubled over this period. However, this comparison is doubly suspect. First, interactions between individual expenditures make any aggregate estimate unreliable. More importantly, the cost of tax expenditures varies directly with marginal tax rates. Revenue losses increased during this period mostly because marginal tax rates increased.

> chose private financing to gain support from members reluctant to authorize federal funds for the project. (Rothman 1985, 2312)

Note that the true meaning of the term "taxpayers' money" is *highly visible funds appropriated out of the Treasury,* whereas the term "private financing" truly means *low visibility funds not collected by the Treasury.*

Another illustrative case is that of the Earned Income Tax Credit (EITC). As initially designed, the EITC offsets the Social Security payroll tax liabilities of low-income workers with dependent children. In many cases, the legal credit exceeds the income tax payments of workers, and the government then pays cash directly to the workers. In 1977, OMB decided to report these cash payments—called *refundable* credits—as outlays. The *nonrefundable* credits—the offsets to tax liability that did not require cash payments—continued to be treated as revenue losses. Labeling the EITC refundable credits as outlays increased the likelihood that someone would propose to reduce EITC benefits, because these payments were now counted as higher visibility spending. In response to this threat, Senator Russell Long, a supporter of the EITC, convinced OMB director Bert Lance that these payments should remain on the revenue side of the budget. The decision was reversed in 1978 after Budget Committee staff and others filled the void left by Lance's retirement.

What causes the structural protection of low visibility? Its main cause is the inherent difficulty of measuring tax expenditures. By definition, tax expenditures exist only when one can demonstrate that a provision of the tax code differs from some "normal" or "reference" tax base. The normal tax base has not yet been revealed by higher powers, however, leaving the designation of what is normal to mortal tax experts who differ in training and ideology. Consequently, there have been repeated disagreements about the normal methods, to pick some notable examples, for depreciating assets or taxing married couples relative to single individuals. An additional complication is the difficulty of accounting for funds that are *not* collected by the government. For these reasons, tax expenditures have not met the expectation that budgeting use definitive information for a decision standard.

Attacks on the concept of tax expenditures by spending advocates also protected their low visibility. When the tax-expenditure concept was first publicized in the 1960s, many conservatives claimed that it implied "that the government owned all income that it did not tax." This misleading rhetoric served to divert attention from the fact that many tax expenditures were politically inconceivable as regular spending because of their regressive effects. Then in 1982, the Reagan administration's Treasury Department ended its practice of reaching agreements with the Congressional Joint Committee on Taxation on the reference tax base. The administration eliminated from its list of tax expenditures a number of major preferences (such as the investment tax credit) that had been created or expanded in the previous year's Kemp-Roth Economic Recovery Tax Act. The administration justified its act by citing theoretical differences over how to conceive of the normal tax, but as important was the corporate conservatism of the Reaganites. These conservatives were opposed to all government spending in the abstract and cut many programs on the spending side of the budget. Yet they were much less bothered by spending through tax preferences because such spending benefited their core supporters—corporations and upper-income individuals.

The difficulty of measurement, and the attacks on the concept by spending advocates who benefited especially from tax expenditures, continued the general perception that spending took place only on the outlay side of the budget. This restriction of the scope of the budget was even reflected in the titles and procedures of budgetary organizations. For example, the *Budget* Analysis Division of CBO analyzed the spending—that is, non-tax—side of the budget. The Treasury's Office of Tax Analysis, which conducted most of the analysis of tax expenditures, did not regularly interact with programmatic divisions within OMB during budget preparation. Congressional budget procedures also failed to routinely compare tax expenditures to regular spending. Congressional budgetary controllers could only raise points of order against new tax preferences that would cause estimated revenues to fall below the budget resolution's revenue floor. They could not force trade-offs between proposed tax expenditures and related spending programs.

Although tax preferences *generally* were protected by their low visibility and exclusion from regular procedures, the 1986 Tax Reform Act shows that this protection was not constant. The act eliminated hundreds of billions of dollars of tax expenditures in exchange for dramatically lowered tax rates. Crucial to its enactment was the widespread distribution by public interest groups and the Treasury Department of reports that showed the costs of tax preferences to government and the redistributional effects among taxpayers. But by 1991, the passion for a horizontally equitable tax system had faded enough that I could write in an annual wrap-up for the journal *Public Budgeting and Finance* that

> a tax cut bidding war developed through the latter half of 1991. In part, the bidding followed convention, with Democrats emphasizing "middle-class tax cuts" (with the middle class operationally defined to include even families with incomes of $100,000). The Republicans promoted a long list of expanded investment preferences, in full abandonment of the philosophy of the Tax Reform Act of 1986. The "Gone Fishing" sign that Chairman Rostenkowski hung around his neck in 1986 was finally packed

away, and replaced through tax institutions in Washington with one declaring them "Open for Business." (Meyers 1992, 5–6)

Spending advocates had reacted to the tactical opportunity caused by the continuing low visibility of tax expenditures in routine budget documents.[20]

Accounting for Cash Payments

When the government disburses cash or its equivalent in order to liquidate an obligation, *outlays* are the result. As discussed above, outlays matter because the all-important deficit is calculated by subtracting the revenues of the government from its outlays. Everyone wants to know the answer to the question: "How much cash does the government need this year?"

It might seem that it would be devilishly difficult to manipulate accounting for outlays. In contrast to tax expenditures, which are dollars that are *not* collected, outlays are actual payments by the government. But if you think this treatment should make them impossible to manipulate, then think again. Though accounting for outlays *is* relatively straightforward by comparison to accounting for other financial transactions, there have been several popular outlay ploys. One tactic results from the difficulty of recognizing whether certain payments are the equivalent of cash. Another involves crediting receipts against gross outlays to reduce reported net outlays. A third relies on the forgiveness of scheduled payments from the public. A fourth tactic is to underestimate expected outlays for the budget year, and a fifth is to change the effective date of cash payments.

Pay with Unrecognized Cash Equivalents

The standard definition of outlays recognized two forms of payment in liquidation of an obligation—cash or its equivalent. The tactic of paying with unrecognized cash equivalents takes advantage of controllers' difficulty in drawing the line between cash equivalents and less-liquid forms of payment.

A classic case involved monetary credits, which federal land agencies like the Bureau of Land Management began using in 1911. Monetary credits were certificates given by the agencies to sellers of land to the government. The certificates could be used by the sellers to make payments to agencies for specified types of future transactions with the agencies, such as for mineral rights leases. Accounting rules generally did not require that outlays be

20. On the other hand, the "pay-as-you-go" regime introduced by the Budget Enforcement Act of 1990, which is discussed in the next chapter, created a procedural incentive for parasitic spending advocates to hunt for politically vulnerable tax preferences.

recorded when monetary credits were traded for land. A justification for this treatment was that a monetary credit looked like a barter payment rather than a more liquid cash payment. On the other hand, payment by monetary credit substituted for cash compensation of land owners for transferring title, and created an obligation of the government to deliver without further payment the leasing rights attached to other lands.

In the early 1980s, supporters of land purchases in Congress and the Reagan administration made the conditions for the future use of monetary credits much less restrictive. Bills authorized copycat certificates labeled "bidding rights," "bidding credits," and "certificates of value." In one case, legislation passed by the House would have the Interior Department give a seller monetary credits that could be used to buy surplus property from the General Services Administration (GSA), thereby raiding the GSA's budget. After the level of monetary credits proposed in lands legislation grew to nearly $500 million in 1985, budget controllers finally responded by deciding to score monetary credits as outlays.

Other examples of paying with unrecognized cash equivalents include negotiable promissory notes from the FDIC and FSLIC, military payments certificates from the Department of Defense (DOD), FHA debentures from HUD, and generic PIK (payment-in-kind) certificates from the Agriculture Department (Rapp 1986). In all of these cases, these forms of payment substituted for cash payments in order to evade budgetary controls, but their proponents argued that these payments should not (at least immediately) be recorded in the budget. The cash-like payments often angered budget controllers, not only because of their evasive use, but also because they were usually more costly than paying cash.[21]

The most extreme case of nonrecognition of cashlike payments is the sorry story of the FSLIC. FSLIC insured the deposit liabilities of thrift institutions, promising to pay off depositors when thrifts went bankrupt. The risk to the federal government from providing this guarantee increased during the 1970s because of a process called *financial disintermediation.* This term refers to the loss of deposits in thrifts, which were unable to pay interest rates that matched those offered by competitors such as money market funds. To maintain their market share, many thrifts offered higher interest rates on deposits, after having successfully lobbied for elimination of regulatory limits on these rates. But they also had to earn the additional income to pay these higher rates. Deregulation permitted thrifts to make riskier, potentially more profitable investments, but unfortunately, many thrifts invested poorly or fraudulently.

---

21. In the 1990 president's *Budget,* OMB recorded $477 million in negative outlays for food stamps that had been distributed in past years but had not been redeemed. This "savings" offset other spending.

While the magnitude of the resulting losses has shocked every observer, it is not true, as many politicians have claimed, that there was no warning of the financial risk faced by the federal government.[22] Rather, there were early signals that thrift regulation was ineffective and that deposit insurance premiums should be increased to cover the risk of heavy losses. But the thrift industry and its supporters lobbied for alternative financing. One approach was a tax preference—the All Savers Certificates of 1981—that actually ended up costing the thrift industry. Another approach was to provide cashlike financing—unrecognized as outlays—in the form of promissory notes. The Garn–St Germain Depository Institutions Act of 1982 authorized FSLIC to issue these promissory notes to thrifts in return for net worth certificates, which were pledges by the thrifts to pay back FSLIC out of their future earnings. FSLIC allowed the thrifts to count the notes as capital, which prevented FSLIC from needing to close down the thrifts and pay off the depositors with cash.[23]

Controllers argued unsuccessfully that these promissory notes should be simultaneously treated as cash-equivalent payments by FSLIC (promissory notes) and borrowing from the FSLIC (net worth certificates). They lost in part because of the widespread hope that the condition of the thrift industry would improve substantially, allowing the thrifts to pay back FSLIC. Though some of the thrifts did make it back to financial health, the general condition of the industry worsened. The outlay tactic postponed the day of reckoning and made the judgment—one for hundreds of billions of dollars—much worse.[24]

Offset Outlays with Collections

Another tactic reduced the amount of outlays recorded in the budget by netting collections against gross outlays. It was based on the fact that the government receives income in different ways—from taxes, user fees, proceeds from the sale of assets, and voluntary contributions (believe it or not!). The budgetary accounting problem was: how should these different receipts be presented in the budget? The President's Commission on Budget Concepts recommended that receipts that involve government compulsion (primarily from taxation) should be classified as *revenues* (on the taxes side of the budget) and receipts that come from business-type operations should be classified as *negative out-*

---

22. The best account is Kane 1989.

23. This regulatory leniency was rationalized with so-called Regulatory Accounting Principles, or RAP, used in contrast to the standard Generally Accepted Accounting Principles, or GAAP. Others called the rationale Creative Regulatory Accounting Principles, or CRAP.

24. See OMB Staff Paper, "Budgetary Treatment of FSLIC and FDIC Debt," 11 April 1988; Testimony of Frederick D. Wolf, Assistant Director, General Accounting Office, before the House Banking Committee, "The Federal Savings and Loan Insurance Corporation's Use of Notes and Assistance Guarantees," 8 September 1988.

lays (on the spending side of the budget). These negative outlays were classified into three categories: *offsetting collections* were netted against outlays at the account level, *offsetting receipts* at the agency or department level, and *undistributed offsetting receipts* against total outlays.

This rule allowed decision makers a good deal of latitude, for identifying what is compulsory is sometimes difficult. An example was the premium income received from participants in the Supplementary Medical Insurance program (SMI, also known as Part B of Medicare). When these funds were first included in the budget, they were classified as revenues because of the nearly universal participation in the program—the argument was that Part B was such a good deal that it was effectively compulsory, interpreting compulsory as meaning "compelling" rather than "coercive." This practice was deemed unfortunate by the Reagan administration because it made obtaining savings in this program more difficult—an increase in premiums would be counted as a tax increase, and the administration had pledged not to raise taxes. But if the premiums were instead classified as negative outlays, premiums could be increased without the administration risking being accused of having raised taxes. This reclassification was made unilaterally by OMB director Stockman in 1982. The change also reduced the level of total outlays, though of course this was offset by a comparable reduction in the level of total revenues. Consequently, the administration not only could avoid the charge that it raised taxes; it could also show that it was supposedly restraining spending.[25]

Most offsets of receipts against outlays had the opposite effect on a program's spending, in that they allowed a program to spend the same or greater amount after the offset. The most popular tactics were the prepayment of loans and the sale of loan assets. Both tactics accelerated receipt of future negative outlays.

Remember the Rural Electrification Administration, which was described in chapter 2. In 1985, when REA's main financing source, the FFB, was placed back on budget, REA faced a predicament. It had been lending for long terms at low interest rates and borrowing for short terms at high interest rates; as many bankers have discovered, this is one of the best methods ever invented for going broke. REA wanted to refinance its high-interest loans from the FFB, but could not do so unless it paid a prepayment penalty. OMB and the Treasury developed the prepayment penalty in order to protect the FFB from interest-rate risk—had borrowers from the FFB been able to pay back old loans without this penalty, they could have refinanced every time interest rates fell and kept loans when interest rates rose.

---

25. Simply offsetting revenues against outlays is not as important a tactic as capturing revenues by having them dedicated to a particular purpose, which is discussed in chapter 6.

In 1986, however, supporters of REA proposed to allow REA borrowers to repay loans from the FFB without penalty. Their amendment to a supplemental appropriations bill would have reduced outlays by $7 billion by offsetting repayment receipts against spending. In effect, the scheduled repayments from future years would be accelerated to the budget year. The prepayment was estimated to cost the government (and benefit REA borrowers) over $2 billion (on a present-value basis). Under threat of a veto, the Congress agreed to limit the co-ops' opportunities to prepay, and OMB interpreted the provisions very conservatively, reducing actual offsetting receipts from the projected $7 billion to about $2 billion. But REA borrowers kept proposing amendments to the continuing resolution and several other legislative vehicles, and the House and Senate agreed to more liberal prepayment terms, finding these "deficit reductions" were too good to pass up.[26]

This treatment of loan prepayments is a great example of the select application of a rule by decision makers, for what OMB strenuously opposed in the case of REA it embraced in the case of foreign military sales. Senator Exon, an advocate of REA, was quick to notice the inconsistency.

> Ironically, the administration which has repeatedly made an assault on the rural electrification administration and has thrown up every roadblock possible to REA financing is now advocating a prepayment and refinancing program for foreign military sales contracts similar to the policy advocated by Congress for the REA. . . . It is absolutely stunning and contradictory that the Reagan administration is so anxious to pass along the benefits of low-interest rates to foreign governments and so reluctant to pass similar benefits along to rural Americans.[27]

The proposal was rather complex, allowing relatively rich countries (like Israel) to pay back their loans without penalty and poor countries (like Egypt) to capitalize the interest payments on loans into a lump sum to be paid at the end of the loan. The prepayments were so large that they offset the forgone interest from the capitalization option, creating net savings in the first year of the plan. As a CBO analysis concluded, "This budgetary effect is remarkable and misleading. It appears to suggest that the U. S. Government can provide debt relief to other countries and at the same time improve its own financial condition in the short run."[28] The GAO calculated by August 1989 that the prepayments without penalty had cost the government about $2 billion (GAO 1989a).

---

26. See *Congressional Record,* 5 June 1986, S 6829–42; Helen Dewar, "Low-Cost Power Wins GOP Backing," *Washington Post,* 6 June 1986, sec. A.

27. Remarks of Senator Exon, *Congressional Record,* 6 March 1987, S 2813.

28. Statement of James L. Blum before the Subcommittee on Foreign Operations, Committee on Appropriations, U. S. House of Representatives, 6 May 1987, 2. See also Frederick Kempe,

A final variant of the tactic to offset outlays with collections was used by programs that collect fees that they are supposed to bank for future use. The Federal Housing Administration (FHA), for example, typically charged home purchasers up front for its insurance on low-downpayment mortgages. The program did not insure mortgages that exceeded a specified amount, with a higher permissible amount for designated high cost of housing areas. In 1989,

> desperate for some quick money, the Senate Appropriations Committee has voted to expand dramatically a home mortgage-insurance program that already has lost hundreds of millions of dollars—a move critics say could end up costing taxpayers lots more . . . the maximum single-family home mortgage insured by the Federal Housing Administration (FHA) would exceed $150,000 in some areas. In most high-cost areas, the maximum is now $101,250. While helping more families buy homes with low down payments, closing costs and interest rates, the measure eventually could increase the FHA's risk because it would be insuring more mortgages. In the short run, however, it is expected to yield added revenue. The FHA collects premiums from home buyers. The more loans made, the higher the revenues. (Kuntz 1989b, 2391)

Forgive Expected Repayments

The government makes many investments and loans with the general expectation of receiving repayment in full or in part. Spending advocates used the forgiveness tactic by convincing the government to not demand expected repayments. This forgiveness tactic was only available to those who already owed the government money. However, it was especially attractive for those who could claim to be suffering financial problems, and especially when the repayment provisions were not strictly required by the law.

Forgiveness has the advantage of being less visible than provision of a cash payment. Forgiveness was the functional equivalent of an outlay because it eliminated an expected negative outlay. (If you had to read the above sentence twice, you're not the only one to be confused by forgiveness.) To describe forgiveness with other words, instead of providing the public with a cash payment, the government failed to collect one due from the public. The effects on the government's financial resources were the same.

The first example of forgiveness involves loans made to the Department of Energy (DOE) (and its predecessor, the Atomic Energy Commission) by the

---

"U.S. Planning to Ease Terms on Loans to Allies under Military Sales Program," *Wall Street Journal,* 12 December 1986, 27; OMB White Paper, "President's Decision on Restructuring Loans under the Foreign Military Sales (FMS) Program" (no date).

Treasury for the uranium enrichment program. This program was established as a business-type program that would enrich uranium for private corporations at full-cost-recovery prices. The Treasury provided capital in the form of appropriations, and the enrichment program's managers repeatedly promised in testimony to charge purchasers for the full costs of enrichment. In principle, these prices and the repayments they enabled should have included imputed interest on the borrowing that financed the appropriations. However, the DOE was not *formally* required to make repayments to the Treasury, though this was the stated long-term objective of the Congress when it wrote the enabling legislation. Repayments were instead used to partially offset new appropriations when calculating the net government investment in the program. This accounting practice stimulated the DOE to invest in overcapacity.

During the early 1980s, DOE faced strong competition from two European firms providing similar services. DOE understandably wanted to lower its prices, and one way was to shrink the capital base it had to amortize. Therefore, in 1982 and 1984, the Department of Energy wrote off—with OMB's support—over $4 billion of unrecovered Treasury investments in the program. This action reduced the repayments to be made over the useful lives of the enrichment plants, with a loss on the government's investment of over $300 million a year (and a subsidy of a somewhat smaller amount to the nuclear industry).

Overinvestment and forgiveness were encouraged by the failure to write strict repayment provisions into the law. Full-cost-recovery repayments were not assumed in outlay accounting, and the failure to receive repayments was not recorded as a loss of negative outlays. No one was charged with spending by forgiveness.[29]

The Power Marketing Administrations (PMAs) of the Energy Department also used the tactic by deferring repayment of loans to the Treasury. For nearly fifty years the Bonneville Power Administration (BPA), the largest of the PMAs, claimed to have "never missed a payment" on these loans. In reality, changes in the 1960s and 1970s to the various statutes and regulations that governed BPA allowed it to indefinitely postpone principal payments until the fiftieth and last year of the loan! In addition, interest payments were subordinated to—that is, given a lower priority than—operating expenses and payments on loans from private lenders. These practices redefined when a payment was due. OMB director David Stockman described the result: "each and every repayment study shows that Bonneville is 'on schedule' in repaying its debt—

29. Civiak 1985; GAO 1984b; and Elizabeth Tucker, "U.S. Uranium Program Said Mismanaged," *Washington Post,* 11 March 1986, sec. A.

even when they actually repay nothing."[30] The value of this subsidy to Bonneville's ratepayers was estimated by OMB to exceed $900 million in 1986 (see Moore 1985).

This case differs from the uranium enrichment case in that over most of the period during which forgiveness was permitted the BPA was not suffering from financial problems. In contrast, power rates in the Northwest were far lower than in any other section of the country. A coalition of influential members of Congress, the energy-intensive aluminum industry, and public-power distributors were skillful enough to reduce the visibility of nonrepayment. By the 1980s, Stockman and members of Congress from regions not served by PMAs attacked these subsidies, but their timing was unlucky. With the default of the Washington Public Power Supply System in 1983, supporters of BPA were able to fight off OMB attempts to establish a full-cost-repayment schedule (Kleit and Stroup 1987).[31]

Underestimate Spendouts and Change Effective Dates

Generally, the timing of outlays is estimated rather than formally limited to specific time periods.[32] These estimates are usually prepared by calculating the historic relationship between the obligation and disbursement of funds in each account; the result are standard "outlay rates" for each account. But making outlay projections is much more difficult for some accounts than for others. For example, procurement programs that have long periods of production and that rely on untested technologies often suffer spending "slippage," making outlays occur much later than estimated. Also, a changed mix of programs can affect outlay rates for a department. In the Department of Defense, for example, there are quite different spendout rates for procurement (slow) and for operations and maintenance (fast). When the mix of budget authority provided for procurement and operations programs changes, departmental first-year outlays change as well.

Spending advocates have taken advantage of these uncertainties in projecting outlays. In 1985, seeking to protect the defense budget from cuts, the Reagan administration stopped using historical outlay rates. They claimed that outlays would be $11 billion smaller than would be predicted by historical experience, using the belabored argument that management reforms would

30. Testimony before the Committee on Interior and Insular Affairs, Subcommittee on General Oversight, Northwest Power and Forest Management, U. S. House of Representatives, 7 March 1985.

31. See also Guy Gugliotta, "Forget Oil; U.S. Rules Helium Market," *Washington Post,* 29 June 1993, sec. A.

32. For exceptions, see the House foreign assistance appropriations bill for fiscal year 1987; and General Accounting Office 1990.

lead to these savings. This tactic led to a budget-resolution compromise that protected defense spending. The resolution included Congress's budget-authority numbers and the administration's (lower) outlay numbers. Larger outlays would have precipitated cuts in budget authority. Experience then documented that the outlay rates were unchanged, and a technical reestimate in January 1986 returned the outlay rate to an analytically sound basis.

A related tactic of defense advocates was shifting the mix of programs during budget preparation toward slow-spending accounts, which reduced total outlays in the budget year. This caused ships to be bought without the fuel to steam them, however, leading to later pressure to provide more money for the fast-spending accounts. When this tactic was used successfully, supplemental appropriations were made for the fast-spending accounts, increasing the total amount spent on defense.

Cash payments can not only be misestimated; they can also be changed. The most recognized outlay tactic—it would be hard to find an area of the budget where it hasn't been attempted—changes effective dates. Effective dates are the dates on which payments are made or recorded. These dates can occur at the beginning or end of a fiscal year. To reduce reported outlays, effective dates are changed to eliminate the recording of outlays during the budget year. Examples are two effective date tactics used to help meet the Gramm-Rudman-Hollings target for fiscal year 1987. The first was a speed-up of the last general revenue-sharing payment to local governments, which was scheduled to occur in October 1986, at the beginning of the budget year. By instead making the payments in September, money was "saved." In actuality, the same amount was spent in the current year, but current-year spending was perceived as water over the dam. At the other end of this same budget year, the Defense Department was ordered by the Congress to change the pay date for military personnel from 30 September 1987 to 1 October 1987, "saving" $2.9 billion.

Another illustrative effective-date attempt was the appropriation by the House of $200 million in assistance for the Philippines on 18 September 1986, with the proviso that the funds be spent by 1 October. Chairman Whitten of the Appropriations Committee gave the rationale for the time limitation:

> if moneys were expended under the continuing resolution, they would be scorekeeped by CBO as actually having occurred in fiscal year 1987, and that would mean that we would breach the Gramm-Rudman ceiling for fiscal year 1987.
>
> So at the suggestion of a number of parties, what we are trying to do on a bipartisan basis is to respond to the moving and eloquent statement that Mrs. Aquino made this morning in a way which does not damage the

> commitment that I strenuously feel to abide by the budget ceilings for fiscal year 1987.
>
> As you know, there is a different set of rules which applies as far as Gramm-Rudman is concerned for fiscal year 1986. The technical ceiling for that year has already been breached, it has been breached a long time ago. So we really do not face that specific problem.[33]

The effective-date tactic was most useful for responding to short-term threats—after all, it is a rather obvious attempt at misperception. Because of this, one might think that it could be used only once for each program. However, it would have been possible to shift military pay back to fiscal year 1987 in the preparation of the fiscal year 1988 budget, thereby "saving" the same $2.9 billion again! This approach was used in the Medicare program in 1980 and 1981.[34]

After 1987, the patently gimmicky nature of effective-date changes proved embarrassing, leading to adoption of a provision that prohibited counting most effective-date changes against budget targets. But the inevitable loophole was created by the fact that many legitimate policy changes affect the timing of outlays in ways that are indistinguishable from tactical effective-date changes. Consequently, even proposals for effective-date changes began to include waivers of the following type.

> Any transfer of outlays, receipts, or revenues from one fiscal year to an adjacent fiscal year that occurs pursuant to any provision of this Act or any amendment made by this Act shall be considered a necessary (but secondary) result of a significant policy change as provided in section 202 (b) of the Balanced Budget and Emergency Deficit Control Reaffirmation Act of 1987.

Nor was control of effective-date tactics helped by the 1989 OMB approval of another proposed shift in military paydays, which stimulated advocates of domestic spending to propose similar shifts for their favored programs.[35]

Accounting for Commitments

If the main purpose of budgeting is to control use of the government's scarce financial resources, accurate accounting for commitments is absolutely neces-

33. *Congressional Record,* 18 September 1986, H 7216.

34. See also CBO 1987a, 116–17 for a description of two effective date gimmicks for Medicare.

35. *Congressional Record,* 20 July 1989, H 3960, 3978–79; 27 July 1989, H 4417–22; Dan Morgan, "Budget Plan for Agencies Includes Payday Shift," *Washington Post,* 18 July 1989, sec. A.

sary. In theory, a financial balance sheet for the government could provide the most definitive statement of commitments. The balance sheet would value all the government's assets and liabilities, and every proposed action would be evaluated for its effects on the balance sheet. Commitments would be recorded whenever decisions were made to give assets away or accept new liabilities.

Accounting for commitments does not meet this ideal; many question the applicability of this private-sector model of accounting to governments. In the private sector, one purpose of a balance sheet is to inform owners of the value of an organization should it be necessary to liquidate it. But the federal government is the ultimate going concern—if citizens can't imagine living without the government, why would they want to be informed of their hypothetical equity interest in it? Moreover, if one truly considers the government's constitutional responsibilities when constructing a balance sheet, the task clearly becomes impossible. What is the true value of the government's most valuable assets—the powers to tax, to create money, and to borrow? And how could one make tangible the government's largest commitments—to "provide for the common defense, promote the general welfare" and other charges of the Constitution? (Mautz 1991).

The practical alternative to full-scale commitments accounting has been the recording of *budget authority* (BA). There were three methods for recording BA. For some accounts, budget authority was recorded *when financing was provided* to programs. For other accounts, budget authority was recorded *when agencies were given permission to obligate funds.* For yet other agencies, BA was recorded *when agencies actually obligated funds.*

These various methods of recording budget authority were so confusing and inconsistent that many controllers thought the concept of budget authority was an accounting lemon. The flaws were so serious that the manufacturer even felt it necessary to advise buyers of the warranty limits—for years, OMB's *Historical Tables* warned users that

> because of its heterogeneity, budget authority does not always constitute a stream of resources closely related to an associated stream of spending (budget or off-budget outlays) . . . it is not additive—either across programs or agencies for a year or, in many cases, for an agency or program across series of years—in the same sense as budget receipts and budget outlays are additive. (Office of Management and Budget 1989, 94–95)

Why was the budget authority concept so imperfect? Technical difficulties certainly played a major role. The most vexing was the proper treatment of time, as in: "time is money." Because spending for different programs occurs over different time periods, and because money has different values over time, accurate comparisons of spending cannot be made without methods that reliably account for these differences. Discounting procedures, developed by economists and accountants, have long been available for converting different values over time to their present values (see Gramlich 1990, 92–114). But in the practical world of budgeting, spending advocates have restricted use of these methods.

Spending advocates also took advantage of another major technical difficulty: how to account for uncertain commitments. Obligations and financing are often affected by unknown conditions or future events. While this reality suggests range estimates would be most appropriate, the desire for a bottom line in budgeting created an insistence for point estimates. Spending advocates exploited this denial of uncertainty in a variety of ways.

This section begins by discussing two tactics that mostly involve budgeting for the purchase of physical assets—avoiding the full-funding requirement and leasing instead of purchasing. The discussion then turns to tactics involving financial transactions, particularly for guaranteed loan commitments. The fourth section moves to tactics for even more intangible costs—those for long-run benefit payments to individuals.

Avoid the Full-Funding Requirement

A major principle of budgetary accounting for commitments is that commitments should be fully recognized when made. The logic is simple. Budgetary commitments made by governments are generally irrevocable—few citizens want their governments to default on its bills. Therefore, when commitments come due, the government must have assets to finance them. Recognizing commitments up front can effectively reserve assets for eventual costs.

OMB's general rule for procurement of facilities and equipment was that the full costs should be estimated and recorded up front when a program is committing itself to purchase these goods. But this full-funding rule was often violated.[36] In the cases discussed below, proponents of spending were able to have only first-stage costs of the contract recorded, even though it was generally expected that future stages would be funded. They thereby had a competitive advantage over fully funded programs, because only portions of the true costs of the favored programs were visible.[37]

---

36. A GAO report found many procurement, research and development, and social programs that were not fully funded (1978c).

37. This tactic is the opposite of the capitalization tactic discussed in chapter 6. The tactic of capitalization gives programs their full funding up front because support for the spending is expected to fade. In contrast, those who use the tactic of avoiding the full-funding rule expect that support for the spending will continue once a project is started.

Water resources advocates used this accounting tactic to supplement the distributive policy designs and credit-claiming opportunities that are well known to most observers. Traditionally, each water resources project received appropriations not for the projected entire cost of the project, but rather in annual amounts for only the payments to be made in each year. In addition, under the Rivers and Harbors Act of 1922, the programs were excepted from the Anti-Deficiency Act, the act that prohibited the obligation of funds prior to receiving appropriations. The exception allowed the Corps of Engineers to use a continuing-contract provision, under which the Corps could obligate funds as long as a project was authorized, *even if* appropriations had not yet been provided. These accounting and financing methods were functional doubletalk: when appropriations were not provided for the full cost of the project, budgetary accounting didn't record the likely full costs because the commitment wasn't legally final, yet the expectation that the commitment was politically final allowed the Corps to obligate funds without risk.[38] This special advantage continued despite repeated opposition from OMB, according to a budget technician active in the 1960s.

> In those days, the Corps of Engineers didn't worry about OMB. That's less true now, when the budget is affected by general views and strategies. OMB tried two or three times to have the full-funding concept adopted for water resources. We found out that you really cannot affect procedural matters that reflect the views of Congress unless you have a lot of White House support. And nobody ever communicated the concept of full funding well.

Another tactic of failing to fully fund commitments was the manipulation of contract terms to underreport (or "lowball") total expected costs. This was a way of life in the Defense Department for decades. Advocates of defense spending regularly took advantage of the uncertainties in building high-tech armaments to provide less funding than would actually be required. Whistle-blowing Air Force cost analyst A. Ernest Fitzgerald succinctly summarized the tactic: "There are only two phases of a program. The first is 'It's too early to tell.' The second: 'It's too late to stop.'"[39]

An example is from the Trident submarine program. During the initial consideration of the program, the Navy assured Congress that the Tridents could be built quickly and at a unit cost of $1.35 billion each. As data on project costs became more reliable, however, it became clear that this estimate was

38. Comptroller General Decision B-187278 of March 28, 1977.

39. Molly Moore, "A. Ernest Fitzgerald: Analyst Who Knows the Price of Exposing Cost Overruns," *Washington Post,* 23 February 1987, sec. A. See also Fitzgerald 1989.

quite low. The Navy's tactical reaction was to negotiate a contract that set a target cost—the figure used to record budget authority of only $1.35 billion for each sub—and a ceiling price—the figure that the Navy actually expected to pay. In violation of the full-funding principle, the ceiling price was 147 percent of the target cost.[40]

Lease instead of Purchase

To the extent that the full-funding rule was enforced, an incentive was created to lease rather than purchase goods. This tactic was enabled by the flimsy rule on accounting for lease commitments. As long as the lease included a termination-for-convenience clause, obligations for a lease had only to be recorded in the budget *when payments were made* rather than *when the lease was signed.* This treatment was based on the determination that with a termination clause, a lease *could* be canceled, and if a lease *could* be canceled, then there was no long-term obligation. Therefore, the only budget authority that would be recorded in the budget year would be the budget year's lease payments and the costs of terminating the lease. This practice spread out costs over several decades that would otherwise be expensed (charged to the first year). But astute advocates also arranged for relatively high termination premiums, which gave a strong disincentive to cancel a lease. When this was done, a lease was truly a long-term commitment. Some of the technically cancelable leases actually included provisions at the end of the lease that conveyed ownership of the asset to the government (so-called lease-purchases). This accounting treatment presented programs with an opportunity to reduce reported costs by substituting leases—which were often purchases in fact—for explicit purchases.

Leasing was a time-honored tactic, particularly for objects of expense—buildings and computers—that did not receive much attention in the budget process.[41] Use of the tactic expanded throughout the 1980s. An interesting example was the expansion of the leasing of noncombatant ships and aircraft by the Pentagon (also described in Leonard 1986, 196–97). By the early 1980s, the Navy had outstanding over $1 billion in five- and ten-year leases for ships. In 1983, the Navy and the Air Force proposed a significant expansion of

40. Morton Mintz, "Depth Charge: Cost Overruns On New Trident Sub Leave a Muddied Wake," *Washington Post,* 4 October 1981, sec. A; Rick Atkinson and Fred Hiatt, "Contracting Conducted over Golden Safety Net," *Washington Post,* 31 March 1985, sec. A; Ruth Marcus, "Case against General Dynamics Tripped over Two Little Words," *Washington Post,* 30 July 1987, sec. A. For similar stories of lowballing of space and high-tech research and development spending, see Matlack and Marshutz 1987; Kuntz 1990b; Robert Smith 1989.

41. For buildings, see Armbrust, Isaacson, and Musell 1983.

leasing of ships and aircraft for sealift and airlift missions. The plan would have delayed the reporting of about $7 billion in lease payments (undiscounted) over the twenty- and twenty-five-year lives of the leases. In addition, additional costs would have been borne by the Treasury, because private lessors were able to capture tax advantages from accelerated depreciation.

Why was the leasing plan proposed and adopted? A GAO report stated,

> According to Navy and Air Force officials, at the Assistant Secretary level, the type of assets they plan to lease would not successfully compete with other higher priority programs for procurement funding. For that reason, their perception is that leasing is the only other alternative. (1983b)

Yet 1983 was not a bad year for the Pentagon's budget! In contrast to many cases discussed in this book, in which accounting tactics were used in response to threats, this leasing tactic was used *even though* the Pentagon had been hugely successful in acquiring appropriations for large procurement programs. The leases reduced the peak in reported defense obligations. A budget technician who felt burned by this tactic complained to me, "The DOD staff have gone to the best business schools, and they'll do anything they can to boost their budgetary resources and to hell with the economic analysis about the true cost."[42]

The new leasing proposals stimulated attempts to control leasing practices. The Deficit Reduction Act (DEFRA) of 1984 eliminated the ability of lessors to capture tax advantages from leases with the federal government. Yet, even without this major benefit, the leasing tactic still diffused, as attempts to adopt tighter budget accounting for leases foundered. The Army, for example, proposed to sign a $400 million mortgage to build a new base at Fort Drum.

> Army leaders . . . add that their plan to turn to private industry to finance, build and maintain Fort Drum's light-infantry complex would avoid putting a big bulge in the federal deficit and future army budgets.

---

42. Another leasing example was NASA's 1976 $786 million purchase of a satellite communications system from Western Union through a ten-year operating lease that was financed by the Federal Financing Bank. The lease was designed primarily by a NASA budget official who had previous experience with the Navy's earlier ship leasing program. NASA also proposed a major lease in 1986, and in 1989, proposed a variety of leases under the guise of promoting "commercialization of space." In both cases, NASA was facing tighter budgetary constraints than in previous years (Office of Management and Budget 1981, 63–64 and addendum E; no listed author, "Lawmakers Blast NASA Budget" 1989, 444–45.

> West [the Army's acting comptroller] said that soundings in the financial markets indicated that giant investment and construction companies stand ready to write a mortgage for the Army in which the federal government would be virtually guaranteeing repayment.[43]

Within the next several years, new leases were proposed and some enacted for prisons, Coast Guard icebreakers, family housing for Defense, long-term care facilities for the Veterans Administration, the Voice of America, office buildings for the Judiciary Branch, the National Archives, the Pennsylvania Avenue Development Corporation, and ten major office buildings to be under the control of the General Services Administration, including new headquarters for the EPA and Transportation Department.[44]

Controllers faced a dilemma over control of the leasing tactic. Since the costs of outright purchases were scored up front, many decision makers were reluctant to fund spending that had no immediate political payoff—constructing new buildings for Washington bureaucrats, for example. They were receptive to arguments that simple leases be used instead. However, lease-purchases could be much less expensive than these simple leases if designed to reduce the apprehensions of lenders. This was typically done by providing a federal guarantee of the borrowing by the lessor. Given the savings, controllers could therefore find it relatively attractive to allow lease-purchases—a little purity would be lost for the sake of cost savings (Blose and Martin 1989; GAO 1989b).

On the other hand, the risk of diffusion appeared to be great by the late 1980s. The proposals that tipped the balance were included in several fiscal year 1990 appropriation bills, including a NASA leasing plan for an advanced rocket motor, which would have been conveniently located in the district of Chair of the House Appropriations Committee, Jamie Whitten, a man who was not beloved in OMB or the White House.[45] OMB soon decided to propose that GSA's buildings be purchased with cash and expensed in the budget, and after negotiations with the Budget committees and CBO, developed a tighter accounting procedure for lease-purchases.[46]

---

43. George C. Wilson, "Army to Seek Mortgage to Construct N. Y. Base," *Washington Post,* 12 July 1985, sec. A. The proposed lease was eventually blocked by OMB.

44. See "Judiciary Office Building Development Act," *Congressional Record,* 7 June 1988, S 7315–18; Judith Havemann, "10 Area Federal Building Projects Approved," *Washington Post,* 30 September 1989, sec. A.

45. Helen Dewar, "Senator Hits Proposed Financing of NASA Plant in Rep. Whitten's District," *Washington Post,* 10 September 1989, sec. A.

46. Haas 1990; David Lindsey, " 'Pay Up Front' Plan Worries Lawmakers," *Washington Post,* 23 April 1990, sec. D; Meyers 1991.

Use Uncounted Guarantees

Guaranteed loans were specifically excluded from the concept of budget authority in the Congressional Budget Act. The rationale was that since a typical guarantee was only a *contingent* liability for which the government would probably not need to disburse cash, it would be misleading to count the full amount of the guarantee as requiring budget authority. The perceived costlessness of guarantees provided many programs with opportunities for rapid growth.[47] Some spending advocates simply expanded the use of existing guarantees, and others substituted guaranteed loans for existing direct loans.

An example of the first approach was the wreck of the Maritime Administration's (MarAd) Federal Ship Financing Fund.[48] The Merchant Marine Act of 1970 had expanded the federal ship mortgage insurance program in hope of stimulating the construction in the United States of three hundred ships (including oil rigs, tugs, and barges) over ten years. Title XI of the act authorized MarAd to guarantee loans that provided from 75 percent to 87.5 percent of the costs of construction. The guarantees typically allowed the owners to obtain twenty-five-year financing at prime corporate rates.[49]

By the early 1980s, MarAd had guaranteed over $8 billion in loans. No budget authority was recorded for the strong possibility that guaranteed borrowers would eventually default. But with the slumps in oceangoing shipping and oil-rig markets that occurred from fluctuations in energy prices, many guarantees did get called, and the Ship Financing Fund went broke in 1985.

MarAd had intentionally ignored these likely costs when it disregarded a GAO recommendation that it establish reserves for these projected losses. The *Washington Post* reported,

> "There was a drive to keep the shipyards operating without too much concern for whether the projects were sound," a former agency official said. "These ships were built on speculation, on very thin financial information."

---

47. Ippolito 1984; Leonard 1986; Bosworth, Carron, and Rhyne 1988; and various CBO reports have described many examples and documented the growth of loan guarantee totals.

48. The folksinger Gordon Lightfoot had a late 1970s hit about the wreck of the ore freighter *Edmund Fitzgerald* in Lake Superior. Truth stranger than fiction is the fact that during the wreck of MarAd the director of its Office of Trade Studies and Subsidy Contracts was named Edmond J. Fitzgerald!

49. The financially creative shipbuilders combined other unrecorded government costs with the Title XI guarantee. One such benefit was the off-budget Capital Construction Fund, administered by MarAd, which deferred taxes on ship construction income. See Anne Swardson, "In Fine Print of Tax Bill, Shipbuilders Find Safe Harbor for Their Subsidy," *Washington Post,* 21 November 1985, sec. A.

> The report that angered Biaggi [a New York Congressman] was a 1983 study by the Transportation Department estimating that $900 million in loans were at significant risk and that agency officials made loans to companies they knew were in "questionable financial condition." The agency helped produce a glut in offshore oil rigs while its analysts were warning that at least 100 such rigs had been idled by an oil industry slump, the report said.[50]

The guarantee losses and OMB's strong opposition eventually led to elimination of new guarantee commitments for this program.

Threatened budget cuts were common stimuli for the second guaranteed loan tactic—substitution of guarantees for direct loans. A lobbyist and former staffer for one of the Budget Committees described one mechanism for adopting this tactic.

> A trade association came to me—they wanted to continue funding of their program, though Reagan wanted to give it the ax. I recommended that they convert the loans to guaranteed loans. They never had thought of that!

An example of the substitution tactic—though with the threat coming from the Congress instead of from the administration—was the 1986 proposal to establish the I-Match (for interest match) program in the Export-Import Bank (Ex-Im). President Reagan proposed to eliminate $1.8 billion in direct loans and replace this amount with guaranteed loans, supplemented by $100 million in grants to make up the difference between the interest rates charged by Ex-Im and private lenders. The result would have been a "savings" of $1.7 billion and protection of the Ex-Im program from likely reductions. Although OMB technicians were forced to allow this subterfuge, CBO scored the guarantees as equivalent to direct loans and counted them as requiring budget authority. A hopeful, but unsuccessful countertactic was then dreamed up by the House Banking Committee. It authorized appropriations for the interest rate match *only if* CBO decided not to score the guarantees as budget authority.[51]

Another substitution approach was to partially fund the projected costs of guarantees up front, but then back off of this recognition. One example was the raid of the Defense Department's Guarantee Reserve Fund in the Foreign Military Sales program. During the 1970s, controllers fostered the practice of

---

50. Howard Kurtz and Michael Isikoff, "Finance Program Sinking with Fleet," 16 July 1986, sec. A.

51. See H. R. 5548, the Export-Import Bank Act Amendments of 1986, as of 22 September 1986, and statement by Rep. Stephen Neal, "Reauthorization of the Export-Import Bank," *Congressional Record,* 25 March 1986, H 1590–92.

appropriating 10 percent of total guarantee commitments into a reserve for losses; these funds were considered to be obligated balances. But the practice was discontinued in a squabble over Carter's fiscal year 1981 budget. Although there was a consensus to expand the program in light of the Camp David accord, fiscal pressure made it difficult to do so through direct loans. Guaranteed loans were used instead, and appropriations for reserves were eliminated.[52]

Substitution can cut both ways, helping controllers instead of spending advocates. As a budget technician said to me,

> Remember, substitution is usually an improvement because the interest rate is closer to the Treasury rate, you can add a coinsurance requirement, and the government doesn't bear the servicing. It's positive budget optics.

By this he meant that although substitutions reduce reported costs, they may also provide fewer benefits. For this reason, guaranteed loan substitutions have sometimes been opposed by program advocates. Another cause of opposition is suggested by a political appointee at OMB.

> The agencies preferred direct loans over guaranteed loans. In terms of budget tactics, it was crazy, but it kept them closer to their constituents. Direct loans were thought of as grants, they didn't care about repayments.

The loan-guarantee tactic was effectively eliminated by the 1990 adoption of *credit reform.* Credit reform required that the likely costs of guarantees and direct loans be recognized up front. Credit reform also severely constrained the direct loan variant of the "offset outlays with collections" tactic (Cuny 1991; Phaup 1984). The final chapter discusses the passage of credit reform in more detail.

Ignore Other Long-Run Costs

This section turns from tactics involving spending for physical or financial assets to tactics involving long-term payments for benefits to individuals. These payments range from retirement benefits for the government's employees through benefits "earned" from previous taxes paid to the government to benefits for those defined as being needy. In contrast to budgetary accounting for physical and financial-asset transactions, there are no generic rules that have been applied to the wide range of benefit programs.

In general, spending advocates have sought accounting practices that recognize obligations for benefit payments *only when* financing is needed. The

---

52. For another issue of questionable FMS accounting, see GAO 1978a.

goal is to recognize costs *not* when the obligations are created, but much later. Recognizing costs when entering into commitments risks opposition. If the costs are not recognized until later, however, spending advocates can use past promises about benefits to mobilize the political support that virtually guarantees financing.

Successful tactics of this type were used by advocates for VA medical care, disaster relief, deposit insurance, Social Security, and crop insurance, to pick a few examples. Instead of describing these cases, this section describes two cases in which the recognition of costs for long-run liabilities was *increased,* resulting in cuts or slower-than-expected growth of the programs. In both cases, controllers worked to recognize the full projected costs of commitments when the legal commitments were made, acting on the belief that the government would make fewer commitments to pay these benefits under the new procedure. These examples are the military retirement and subsidized-housing programs.

Military retirement began as a pay-as-you-go system, in which retirement payments were funded from taxes received shortly before payments were made. This type of system differs from a fully funded retirement plan, in which the expected costs of benefits to be paid in the future are accounted for and funded when the obligations to make benefit payments are undertaken—that is, each year when workers are employed. Because the federal government did not use the standard normal-cost method for determining the military pension obligations it was taking on, decision makers could more readily commit to providing generous benefits—including retirement at half pay after twenty years—and to expand these benefits. Opponents of generous benefits often sought to reduce them, but never were able to overcome the political strength of military personnel—*and* the fact that they wouldn't get any credit for budgetary savings if reductions in benefits were actually made.

In 1983, Representative Les Aspin employed a tactic that made cuts in these benefits more likely. He inserted a provision into an authorization bill that required the retirement system to be converted to the accrual accounting method. Although many participants didn't realize it at the time, this change would allow cuts in benefits for future retirees to be shown as savings in budget authority. Then in 1985, Aspin amended the authorization bill to cut by 16 percent the retirement benefits for soldiers hired after the bill was passed. Current employees were grandfathered from any changes. To ensure that the package would go through, Aspin took $1 billion in the savings (of twenty years later) and spent it in increases in benefits that were paid right then.[53]

53. This prepayment reduced the savings by about half on a present value basis. See Rauch 1985a; Towell 1986; M. Smith 1983; Singer 1984.

Another example of ignoring long-run costs is provided by the subsidized housing programs. Prior to the passage of the Congressional Budget Act, budget authority for housing programs was recorded only for the appropriations that were provided to make payments in the budget year. This practice substantially underrecorded long-run costs because the value of new housing assistance contracts was growing (Gleeson 1980; Levine 1979). An OMB housing analyst at the time recalled,

> We knew perfectly well that we were tying ourselves up to more spending in the future. I remember in the Director's Review one year, we put together a table with the outyears comparing HUD's program and ours. [OMB director] Schultze said, "Gee, that's interesting. The numbers really pile up ten years hence. That's beyond my political horizon."
>
> One of my theories of budgeting is that there is a discontinuity in the discount rate—it occurs at the next election.

The Congressional Budget Act gave the budget technicians an opportunity to eliminate this underreporting. OMB decided that the act's language on contract authority (a form of budget authority) required that the maximum potential payments over the term of the contracts be recorded as the program's cost. Budget authority was calculated by multiplying the number of housing units by the projected subsidies by the years of the contract. In succeeding years, no new budget authority would be needed—outlays were to flow out of old budget authority as monthly rentals were paid. The only new budget authority in a budget would be for the incremental units—the new commitments.[54] As another housing technician said, the effect was that

> the program went from $2 million to $80 million overnight. That exposed the program to the glare of daylight, and the inevitable result was that subsidized housing was more vulnerable to Hill pressure to cut it.[55]

Housing lobbyists understood what had happened and unsuccessfully attempted to have GAO reverse the OMB practice.[56] They also tried to make their case in the press.

> Dolbeare, Weiner, and others in the housing lobby go further and say the whole housing budget is unfair because of the way it included funds for the full term of federal involvement—from 15 to 40 years.

---

54. A notable complication ignored here is the difference between project-based and tenant-based assistance.

55. At the time, a contract could last for forty years, and $2 million times forty years equals $80 million.

56. See Opinion of the Comptroller General, 14 August 1975, B-1716630.16.

> "OMB, in the past, was responsible for developing a method for computing the run-out cost of the housing subsidy so as to prepare an aggravated and distorted view of its budgetary impact," the National Housing Conference contended in a Dec. 12 open letter to the President that generally decried the low level of housing assistance contemplated for the 1979 budget. (Stanfield 1978, 18)

There was some merit to their claim. OMB was recording contract authority for contracts of up to forty years duration, but was often allowing HUD to sign contracts for only twenty years.[57]

Budgetary accounting for subsidized housing then became even more complicated. Ignored at the time of the redefinition of budget authority for housing was the problem that poor people would likely need to remain in the units when contracts reached maturity. But by the latter 1980s and early 1990s, many long-term contracts began to expire. To keep the currently assisted poor in the units, the government would have to appropriate huge sums of new budget authority. Yet this would require large offsetting savings in other programs if the government was to honor the constraints established by Gramm-Rudman-Hollings.[58]

There was an interesting mix of reactions to this problem. Some were lackadaisical. They kept subsidized housing in a separate category in their minds, holding the attitude about budget authority that was quoted above from an OMB document: "it is not additive—either across programs or agencies for a year or, in many cases, for an agency or program across series of years."

> "To me, it's a non-issue," says an official at OMB, where the deficit is of paramount concern. "We all know that these commitments we entered into are going to be renewed ad infinitum. They become like an entitlement." (Kuntz 1989a, 1045)

Others were more creative. A 1991 report on a Senate appropriations bill recounted how shifting from a five-year contract term to a three-year term "saved" two years of budget authority.

57. In addition, the recording of costs was in constant dollars over the term of the contracts, whereas a discounted stream of payments would be a more accurate reflection of current costs of future spending. On the other hand, others were arguing that OMB's method underestimated likely costs because it did not take sufficient account of likely rent increases.

58. In addition, in an effort to reduce reported costs, some developers had been granted the right to put back their mortgages for subsidized projects to the federal government after twenty years, and to then sell or rent the projects at market prices. The cost of this right was not effectively recognized in the budget, but when developers began exercising it, the government responded with legally questionable limitations on the developers.

> Mikulski said she found $565 million in unused money within the housing department and believes she is likely to find more. Overall, HUD would receive $23.9 billion, which is $342.5 million less than the House and $351 million less than the administration's request.
>
> The committee took advantage of an accounting device that will save the government no money but frees up fiscal 1992 cash for other programs covered by the bill. In the short term, this accounting change may solve HUD's bookkeeping problems.
>
> The committee's report was extremely critical of HUD's efforts to figure out just how much money it needs for rental assistance contracts, citing a 1990 HUD inspector general report that said in some cases there is an error rate of 95 percent.
>
> Kemp called Mikulski the evening before her subcommittee marked up its bill to say that HUD needed another $1 billion to cover expiring rental subsidy contracts that need to be renewed. Those contracts provide payments to landlords for low-income housing.
>
> An aide to Mikulski said Kemp admitted: "We goofed."
>
> To address the accounting problem, the committee's plan would force HUD to shorten the contracts to three years from five years and harden its estimates of the money needed to provide the housing. Instead of giving Kemp the $1 billion to renew the five-year contracts, the committee instead cut $1.2 billion out of the $2.5 billion account that shores up ongoing rental contracts that have run out of money. The change to a three-year contract allows the panel to appropriate less money in fiscal 1992.
>
> The change has an added benefit: It would free up the $1.2 billion in budget authority for other programs in fiscal 1992. But the money is likely to come due for the rental contracts three years down the road. (Zuckman 1991b, 1890–91)

Senator Mikulski's shift of the "commitment" from five years to three was precedented, as contracts had earlier been shortened from forty to twenty years, from twenty to fifteen, and from fifteen to five. Perhaps the logical projection is a future shift to one year! Then the government would count all its subsidized housing commitments as discretionary, *technically* cancelable at the end of each fiscal year.

Summary

The desire for a definitive budgetary standard led decision makers to develop rules for budgetary accounting. These rules determined whether spending was to be considered budgetary, how cash flows were measured, and how obligations to spend and finance were recognized. In reaction, some spending advocates tried to ensure that these accounting rules reported fewer costs in the short term. This would reduce the visibility of a program's true costs for the period that concerned decision makers the most. When accounting tactics diffused, controllers usually reacted by developing stronger rules. As a former Appropriations Committee staffer turned lobbyist said to me, "It's an iterative system that sometimes goes off into crazy mistakes, but that often also gravitates to a good result in the end. Special interest groups cannot get away with stealing too much." After this chapter, it may be appropriate to qualify this assertion with the phrase "with the same tactic."

Accounting tactics were not the only structural tactics available to spending advocates. Though budgetary accounting measures only the costs of spending, decision makers were also concerned about the effects of spending. Chapter 7 describes how spending advocates and controllers debated these effects. The next two chapters relate how they tried to change budget decision procedures and policy designs.

Chapter 5

Tactics for Budgetary Decision Procedures

By now, even the appetites of the readers who *like* accounting are probably satiated. While this and the next chapter do return at times to accounting topics, they focus on tactics that seek to change *who* decides *how* money is spent, and *when* they decide. One way to describe these tactics is to divide them into *budgetary decision procedures* and *budgetary policy designs*. Budgetary decision procedures are the rules that determine who makes budgetary allocations and when they are made. Budgetary policy designs are the rules that guide how programs are financed and how they spend funds. This chapter covers decision procedures, and the next chapter covers policy designs.

By necessity, budgetary decision procedures vary substantially across the range of programs. For example, a social retirement program like Social Security simply would not work if it had to be reauthorized annually. The variety of budgetary decision procedures creates different *arenas* and decision time periods of different *frequencies*.

Arenas allow decision makers to decompose overly complex decisions into manageable ones. They affect budget outcomes for individual programs by delimiting the potential competitors and collaborators for each program. Programs should want to enter or stay in arenas in which existing programs tend to collaborate in search of budgetary resources, especially when these programs have the potential to succeed. They should want to avoid or escape arenas that are dominated by assertive programs that seek to capture the funds of other programs in the arena. But there is a drawback to advantageous positions in arenas. They invite parasitism by programs that are in less-favored positions. These programs seek to join the advantaged or to have some of the funds of advantaged programs transferred to them, potentially diluting the value of the arena to the original program.

Regarding frequencies, programs funded through the appropriations processes are considered annually, but most other programs are reviewed less frequently. By being subjected to an annual process like appropriations, programs gain opportunities to have their budgets increased when conditions favor such outcomes. Some annual decisions that must be made also serve as

TABLE 5.1. Budgetary Decision Procedure Tactics

Arenas
- Escape competitors
- Join collaborators
- Avoid macrobudgetary controls

Frequency
- Underfund in expectation of supplemental appropriations
- Spend last year's money
- Play with the baseline
- Exploit inflation estimates
- Change the schedule

vehicles for spending approval for programs that would otherwise not stand as good a chance for approval. On the other hand, annual decision procedures present annual risks that budgets will be reduced if conditions turn bad. Programs financed through annual processes must also clear more hurdles than programs that possess more permanent forms of financing. The more hurdles to be leapt, the more likely objections to spending will be raised.

Macrobudgetary limits are enforced by controlling the decisions made with these microbudgetary procedures. Effective macrobudgetary procedures increase the frequency of budgetary decisions for programs that are typically made only periodically, and they expand the arena for budgetary decisions by comparing different microarenas. Macrobudgetary limits may affect budgetary outcomes when they apply unevenly to different decision procedures. It has often been argued, for example, that the budget process has penalized annually appropriated programs more heavily than other forms of on-budget spending.

Table 5.1 lists some popular arena and frequency tactics. The following sections give examples of their use by advocates and the responses by controllers.

Arenas

Arena is defined by Webster's as "a sphere or field of conflict, interest, or activity." In actual arenas like the Roman Coliseum or the Rose Bowl, there are physical limits on the size of the playing field, and usually strict rules for the game that is being played. (Even the results are often highly predictable—the lion will eat the Christians, and the PAC-10 team will beat Michigan, which I note as a Michigan graduate.)

Although arenas are defined less strictly in politics, political scientists of various methodological persuasions have long used this concept. To pick a relatively recent body of work, public-choice scholars have suggested that a committee can exploit its exclusive jurisdiction over a policy area to limit the number of alternatives that will be seriously considered by its parent body. Moving only a bit back in time brings to mind Schattschneider's classic *The Semisovereign People,* in which he vividly described how political strategists often try to change the scope of conflict. One of his summary points was that "nearly all theories about politics have something to do with the question of who can get into the fight and who is to be excluded" (1960, 20).

In budgeting, the arenas can be defined as the group of actors that make budgetary decisions and as the units for these decisions. For example, budgetary arenas for the Bureau of Land Management include the Natural Resources Division at OMB and the Interior Appropriations bill.

I begin by describing two arena tactics that spending advocates employ to choose competitors and collaborators. I then turn to the macro level, in which the budgetary arenas are the different control processes used by the entire government—the final stages of budget preparation in the executive branch, budget-process points of order and reconciliation in the legislative branch, and sequestration. Spending advocates use macrobudgetary arena tactics to avoid the constraints promised by these control processes.

Escape Competitors

One popular arena-shifting tactic is to establish a separate account for a favored program in order to escape competitors for the program's funds. Wildavsky described this tactic in the original *Politics of the Budgetary Process* (using the cases of the National Institutes of Health and the Weather Bureau's programs) (1964, 70). A more recent example was how NASA's advocates set up a separate account for space flight in 1984 to prevent the space shuttle from drawing away funds from research.[1]

The Department of Defense accepted the tactic of separating competitors to protect the programs that built its nuclear warheads. Ever since passage of the Atomic Energy Act of 1946—which was intended to assure civilian control of nuclear energy—the program to build warheads was managed and funded by the Energy Department (and the Energy Department's ancestors). DOD avoided being directly responsible for the costs of the program—the appropriations for nuclear weapons were made in the pork-legendary Energy and Water appropriations bill rather than the major defense appropriations bill. (The

1. Continuing with the space theme, advocates of "Star Wars" tried to protect the Strategic Defense Initiative (SDI) program when it lost its strongest supporter—President Reagan. Some SDI programs were retitled and shifted to other Department of Defense accounts ($829 million in fiscal year 1991, according to a critic of the program). See D. Morrison 1990a.

program's costs counted as part of the defense function in the budget, however.) The *National Journal* reported that

> because the Pentagon is under little budgetary pressure to consider the cost trade-offs imposed by its requests for nuclear warheads, [Senator] Nunn argued during the June 1984 debate, "what we have right now is a system . . . that basically says, 'Step right up, folks, the nukes are free. Get as many of them as you want.'" The Pentagon, [Senator] Warner added, "sometimes specifies the most complex and, therefore, the most expensive warheads that [Energy] can make, [while Energy] justifies its expenditures based on [the Pentagon's] requirements. The system has build-in incentives to promote high costs." (D. Morrison 1986a, 2935)

On several occasions, controllers tried to make DOD ultimately responsible for the costs of the warheads program by proposing to bill DOD for the costs of Energy's programs. But knowing that this would increase budgetary competition between DOD and Energy, these agencies headed off this major reform by making minor changes in their procedures. (Another political barrier to the reform was that it would have disrupted congressional committee jurisdictions.)

Controllers sometimes try to use the opposite tactic of *forcing* programs to compete. For example, the Reagan administration attacked categorical grant programs by combining them into block grants in the 1981 reconciliation bill. Over ninety categorical grant programs were reorganized into seven block grants (four of which were pure block grants, with few strings on the application of the funds). The administration argued that more flexible block grants would maintain services even though funding was reduced; authorizations for the categorical grants were cut by double-digit amounts and were often below appropriated levels. But state government officials didn't accept the flexibility rationale for the funding cuts.

> Arizona Gov. Bruce E. Babbitt, a longtime advocate of block grants, has charged that "block grants are now a tactical weapon to cut the federal budget while deputizing the governors to hand out the bad news." (Stanfield 1981a, 1800)

A key administration political official at the time admitted as much in a later interview with me.

> In 1981, we wanted to zero out a lot of inappropriate grant programs, and force them to fight their way back into the budget if they could. We

> took advantage of block grants, which allowed us to zero them out without fessing up to it.[2]

Join Collaborators (Whether They Want You or Not)

Another arena tactic is to join arenas rather than escape them. The symbiotic form of this tactic is commonly known as *distributive* politics. A large number of programs are packaged together to increase the prospects of gaining majority support for the individual programs. As the literature on this tactic is extensive, no cases are developed here (see, for example, Shepsle and Weingast 1981; Ferejohn 1974; Rundquist 1980).

The parasitic form of this tactic is less well documented. The method is to join an arena that is well financed or is subject to few limits on its obligations and then draw funds away from the programs that are members of this preferred arena.

Parasitic arena tactics were used in 1973 by advocates of mass transit programs, who raided the highway trust fund by gaining transfers of funds for "unwanted" highway programs to mass transit programs. Then in 1982, they convinced decision makers to earmark a penny of highway excise taxes for mass transit programs. A staffer for a public works committee explained the tactic to me: "There was no hope in getting general revenues for mass transit, so we did as Willie Sutton did."[3]

Defense programs have been frequent hosts for parasitic programs. A classic story of symbolic parasitism is how higher education loans were called National Defense Student Loans in the defense-favored 1950s.[4] In 1982, when defense programs again enjoyed budgetary success, funding was proposed for job training and business subsidy programs in the guise of "revitalizing the defense industrial base of the United States." For example, in one version of the Defense Production Act, this arena shift was put into language that would require the Defense Department be charged for job training spending:

> Notwithstanding any other provision of this section, no funds are authorized to be appropriated to carry out this section unless all of such funds are attributed to a budget function or budget allocation other than

---

2. See Ellwood 1982. See also Demkovich 1984 for a story about a related tactic. The administration tried to cut spending for the low-income energy assistance program by substituting short-lived court judgments from oil-pricing cases for appropriations.

3. Sutton responded to a query about why he robbed banks by explaining, "That's where the money is."

4. The loan programs created by the National Defense Education Act of 1958 were administered by the U.S. Commissioner of Education.

> one affecting or relating to education or labor, the Department of Education or the Department of Labor, the Committee on Education and Labor of the House of Representatives or the Committee on Labor and Human Resources of the Senate, or any subcommittee of the Committee on Appropriations of either House primarily responsible for appropriations for education or labor.[5]

The Coast Guard was also a parasite of DOD's budget. The Coast Guard contributed personnel and boats for some defense operations, as it also did for the Treasury Department's Customs Bureau. But the Coast Guard was part of Transportation Department, and generally received its funds through the transportation budget. Advocates of the Coast Guard often relied on its relationship with defense programs to substitute for cuts in the transportation budget. For example, in 1982 and 1984, the Coast Guard was partially funded by the defense budget, and in 1985, according to a story in the *Washington Post,*

> The House yesterday heeded the Coast Guard's pleas and added $100 million to the Pentagon's appropriations bill for Coast Guard operations. "Nobody is going to argue about defense," said Rep. Silvio O. Conte (R-Mass.), sponsor of the amendment. "You put this in the Transportation bill, and you are competing with Amtrak and mass transit," added Conte, the senior Republican on the House Appropriations Committee.[6]

In the latter 1980s, some advocates of the Coast Guard proposed that it be transferred to the Treasury Department, with continued support from Representative Conte (the ranking minority member of the Appropriations Committee), who described the Coast Guard as a reincarnated poor relation.

> Alexander Hamilton founded the Coast Guard, and it was under the Secretary of the Treasury. They had a long distinguished history, but they always got the hand-me-downs. They were the orphans, and we turned that thing around.
>
> For a good period of time they got along fine. Then they were brought in with the Transportation Department. I was not happy at that time and I am not happy now. I wish they were back with the Treasury. I think that is where they belong, not in Transportation.
>
> They are vying and competing, ever since Gramm-Rudman, with mass transit, they are competing with the FAA, they are competing with a lot of

5. H.R. 5540, as reported by the House Committee on Education and Labor on 17 May 1982.

6. George C. Wilson, "Senate Cuts Coast Guard Budget, Empowers It to Fight in Drug War," *Washington Post,* 1 November 1985, sec. A.

other agencies that maybe have a little more wallop and a little more power and a little more pull in that committee.

However, no one listens to me. I have said it. I have told the Commandant many times, "Your best bet is to get the heck out of Transportation. Get over back in the Treasury and you will do a lot better."[7]

Another example of attempted parasitism is provided by the assets-forfeiture fund. This fund received profits from the sale of confiscated property, and these moneys financed operations to control drug trafficking and payments to informants. In 1986, the Anti-Drug Abuse Act repealed the requirement to return the fund's unobligated balances to the Treasury at the end of each fiscal year. This change was justified by a projected increase in drug-control operations. However, the balances built up much faster than expected, and this attracted parasites. For example, some proposed the funds be made available for "emergency" prison construction, rather than eventually spending more on drug operations. Labeled as "a new source of funding" and adopted in the continuing resolution, the unobligated balances would be automatically transferred to the prison construction account at the end of the fiscal year.[8]

The appropriations-forcing authorization is another form of parasitism. Congressional committees are organizationally redundant; legislative and appropriations committees with similar jurisdictions sequentially approve budgets for all discretionary programs. First, the legislative committee authorizes a program (for either one or multiple years), and then the appropriations committee provides it with funds. During the 1960s and 1970s, spending advocates were often frustrated when ambitious authorizations were not matched by appropriations. They sometimes responded to these spending gaps by writing appropriations-forcing authorizations. An appropriation-forcing authorization conditions authorization of *all* programs on full appropriations for the programs at risk of receiving lower appropriations than desired by the authorizing committee. This tactic was used to protect funding for the National Aerospace Plane during the 1980s; it also was featured in conflicts between defense authorization and appropriation committees (Cloud 1989a).

7. *Congressional Record,* 3 August 1989, H 5038.

8. See *Congressional Record,* 10 April 1987, S 5180. Another interesting arena is the Federal Housing Administration account, which commingles a number of subsidy-providing FHA programs with the large and, for most of its history, extremely profitable Mutual Mortgage Insurance Fund, the basic FHA program. This commingling allowed profits from the basic program to be transferred to the subsidized programs. Though the subsidized programs were subject to obligation limitations, they looked less costly because they were funded by the basic program's profits.

Leave or Stay?

Unfortunately for spending advocates, the tactics of escaping competitors and joining collaborators are not easy to pull off. A major barrier is receiving permission to move—from one committee jurisdiction to another or from one agency to another. Agency heads typically oppose escape attempts so as to prevent a reputation for not caring about agency turf; members of Congress have this consideration as well as seniority rights that constrain possible reorganizations. Another barrier is the difficulty of calculating the relative values of leaving or staying in an arena—whether the competition within a prospective arena would be stiffer or looser than in a program's current arena.

A good illustration of the complexity of arena tactics is provided by the House Appropriations Subcommittee on Veterans, Housing, and Independent Agencies. The committee's jurisdiction originally encompassed "independent" agencies that lacked departmental status, some of which later grew up into departments: the VA, HUD, EPA, NASA, the National Science Foundation, the Federal Emergency Management Agency, and a number of smaller agencies like the Consumer Product Safety Commission and the Selective Service System. The arena's heterogeneity would seem to invite escape attempts; many of the agencies could reasonably be placed in other arenas that were focused on one governmental function (for example, Selective Service to defense, Veterans split between health, defense, and income security, Consumer Product Safety Commission to health, and so on). Escape attempts might also be expected because of the high degree of conflict within the arena. Over the past decade, its major programs in the arena had different advocates—science and space spending were most strongly supported by Republicans, and the housing programs by Democrats. Added to this volatile mix were spending pressures—big projects like the space station, expiring housing contracts, growing numbers of homeless, and a generation of aging veterans who were entitled to high-cost health care from the VA.

Advocates for the programs both collaborated and competed. They began by collaborating to gain a larger budget-resolution allocation (302b) of spending authority for the subcommittee. " 'Instead of competing with each other, we try energetically to expand the pot,' said Gordon C. Cavanaugh, general counsel to the Council of Large Public Housing Authorities" (Zuckman 1991a, 145). But after the subcommittee received its allocation, programs often became voracious competitors. Cavanaugh was then quoted as saying, "It's really difficult to see how all of us can sit in the boat. Somebody or their luggage is going to get thrown overboard" (Zuckman and Rubin 1991, 1578).

Regardless of the metaphor for arenas—pots, the more traditional pies, or boats—advocates for the different programs searched for ways to make both the first stage of collaboration and the second stage of competition benefit them. In 1987, for example, the Senate housing subcommittee was chaired by the legendary controller Senator William Proxmire. Because of his fiscally conservative ideology and his maverick operating style, Proxmire did not argue for a large (302b) allocation to the subcommittee in the meeting of subcommittee chairs, and the resulting lack of funds led the subcommittee to cancel the space station. But then the advocates of the programs in this arena got together under the leadership of Senators Bennett Johnston and Lawton Chiles, the chair of the Budget Committee. Chiles announced the Budget Committee would allocate some additional spending authority to the committee (derived from his timely manipulation of scorekeeping rules) and then amended the bill to add funds for the space station and a variety of other programs (Elving 1987).

Several years later, tighter fiscal constraints caused the House subcommittee to zero out funding for the space station. To save the station, the administration asked for a freeze on other space programs and for housing cuts. But supporters of unmanned space science projects felt this would take too much funding away from them, and they lobbied to cut the space station (Rubin and Zuckman 1991). The counterreaction from the administration's representative, who normally advocated block grants and other forms of budgetary arena competition, was as follows.

> Darman, testifying in defense of the space station at a House hearing just before the showdown, said the project is "a defining test of our civilization." He decried what he called "factional cannibalism" and said scientists opposing the space station are "politically naive" if they think money saved by killing it would go to their programs.
>
> When the Appropriations subcommittee voted to cancel the space station, Darman pointed out, it gave the bulk of the savings to social programs, not space scientists.
>
> Thomas Donahue, a professor of planetary sciences at the University of Michigan and former chairman of the Space Sciences Board of the National Academy of Sciences, said last week that the defeated scientists will not press their opposition to the space station in the Senate.
>
> "It is clear to me it would not be productive for us in the space sciences to wage a battle against the space station at this stage."
>
> He noted that key senators, such as Barbara A. Mikulski (D-Md.), who chairs the subcommittee that funds NASA, have declared support for the space station. That means the fight would be even tougher than in the House.
>
> But Donahue said he blames NASA for starting the fight. "It's not as though we decided to make war against the space station. It was the other way around."

> Not even in the days when the developing shuttle program was "eating our lunch" did the tensions escalate to today's level, he said. NASA—with its penchant for big engineering projects involving humans—and the space sciences are "unnatural partners. . . . I think we are in grave danger if we remain" a part of the space agency. He said he favors creation of a separate agency dedicated to the space sciences.[9]

With such conflict in the arena, most of its inhabitants tried to use the politically unassailable veterans for procedural protection. For example, a bill reported by the subcommittee in 1987 was potentially subject to a point of order for violating limits set in the budget resolution. *Congressional Quarterly* reported on the chairman of the subcommittee:

> Boland said he may ask the Rules Committee for a ban on amendments to exempt VA spending from across-the-board cuts. If such a rule is granted, lawmakers might approve the bill as is rather than be recorded as voting against veterans' spending. (Starobin 1987a, 1379)

That is, the rule would prevent amendments that would cut funding for space and housing, but not vets. Controllers would then have to specify cuts in individual projects, for which they could be blamed, or cut spending (including veterans spending) across the board. The reaction of veterans' advocates to such tactics?

> Rep. Gerald B. H. Solomon, R-N.Y., has introduced legislation to create a new appropriations subcommittee devoted solely to veterans. This group, he says, should not have to compete within the VA-HUD pie. "It's more important than the homeless, more important than the environment, more important than anything," says Solomon.
>
> But Solomon's is a lonely voice unlikely to win sympathy or votes from most members, particularly appropriators. Traxler and Mikulski would not want to give up any turf on their subcommittees. And veterans' programs are something that most members like to vote for—making a spending bill that includes controversial programs for the poor more palatable to lawmakers. (Zuckman 1991a, 146)

---

9. Kathy Sawyer, "Space Budget Battle: Humans 1, Robots 0," *Washington Post*, 19 June 1991, sec. A. There were similar attacks on the superconducting super collider by other members of the scientific research community.

Avoid Macrobudgetary Controls

Microbudgetary arenas are used to define how programs compete for initial budget allocations. Macrobudgetary arenas are used to restrain the sum of microbudgetary allocations to an acceptable total. Microbudgetary allocations are subjected to a series of macrobudgetary arenas—comprehensive budget review by OMB, the congressional budget resolution, and various enforcement procedures (points of order, reconciliation, pay-as-you go requirements, and sequestration). Spending advocates generally want to avoid being forced to compete in each of these macrobudgetary arenas. They make a variety of arguments to avoid macrobudgetary controls, such as:

The program is *too important* to be affected by short-term budgetary pressures.

The program is managed by *businesslike* administrators that wouldn't think of wasting money.

The program is *self-supporting* from nonappropriated funds.

When these arguments are accepted, programs reduce their exposure to cuts.[10]

Not many agencies have gained statutory exemptions from OMB's budget review. Exceptions include the regulators of depository institutions—the FDIC, the Comptroller of the Currency, and the Federal Reserve—who used all of the above arguments to convince the Congress to require presidents to include these agencies' budget requests in the budget without making any changes. In contrast, the regulator of savings and loans—the Federal Home Loan Bank Board—suffered from executive budget review; its budget grew less than the exempt regulators (and its insurance losses mounted more quickly, in part because of an underfunded program for monitoring bank management). As I mentioned in chapter 4, by 1985, both the Bank Board and OMB wised up, and the board shifted many of its expenses to the Federal Home Loan Banks. It then lobbied successfully for an end to apportionment of its remaining appropriations financing.[11]

Historically, the backdoor-spending tactic was the most important tactic for avoiding legislative macrobudgetary controls. Backdoor spending was slang for programs that had permanent authority to spend funds, meaning that

10. Some related examples were already described in the section of chapter 4 that detailed how programs were declared off-budget. Here the emphasis is on process rather than on accounting recognition.

11. A functional equivalent of being statutorily excluded from budget review is to have "a friend in the White House." In the Reagan administration, Ed Meese effectively prevented any critical budget analysis of plans to increase spending for criminal-justice programs.

existing laws provided funds on a continuing basis rather than requiring these programs to receive appropriations each year (through the implicit front door).[12] But controllers substantially limited opportunities to create backdoor spending by provisions in the Congressional Budget Act. New borrowing and contract authority had to be appropriated or was subject to a point of order, and bills containing new entitlement authority had to be sequentially referred to the Appropriations committees.

Though these controls generally prevented the establishment of new entitlement programs, some spending advocates attempted to avoid the controls. For example, in 1991 members of the House Public Works Committee wanted to increase the gasoline tax by "A Nickel for America," but were afraid that the Appropriations committees would not appropriate all of the new receipts. Committee leaders convinced the House Budget Committee that *if* the authorization bill passed *after* the appropriation bill (contrary to the regular schedule), the authorizing committee's spending total should be mandatory even if the appropriations bill allowed less spending. Widespread congressional reluctance to raise taxes—even just a "nickel for America"—never tested the endgame for this backdoor tactic (M. Mills 1991).

Unfortunately for controllers, not all legislative macrobudgetary controls were self-enforcing. Consider points of order against bills that exceeded committee targets for budget authority and outlays. These targets were known over the years first as 302a allocations, and then as 602a allocations, after the relevant sections of the Congressional Budget Act. The allocations were to be made when the budget resolution was agreed to, so that as spending bills were considered they could be compared to the budget resolution. But in 1987, at the request of spending advocates on the Appropriations Committee, the House permitted appropriations bills to be considered without having made the 302a allocations, ostensibly to give the Budget Committee's staff time to carefully calculate the proper allocations. Representative Trent Lott, the minority whip, appraised the situation:

> this provision permits the Appropriations Committee to go forward with some six or seven bills which may exceed the suballocations that are later filed. There is no explanation in the conference report as to why this provision is included. One can only assume that it was done for the convenience of the Appropriations Committee which has gone forward with its work. But it is a major loophole through which one can drive billions in excess spending.[13]

---

12. Discussions of "backdoor spending" may be found in Fisher 1980; and Schick 1975, 1980.

13. *Congressional Record,* 23 June 1987, H 5399–5400.

Spending advocates for mandatory programs avoided the reconciliation process more frequently. Reconciliation was set in motion by the budget resolution. The resolution directed committees to save specific amounts in the direct-spending programs that they controlled; these savings were then to be packaged in a reconciliation bill. Each Budget committee made assumptions in its report about ways of saving funds in specific programs, usually after negotiations between the Budget Committee and the spending committees. On occasion, however, the Budget Committee effectively ordered cuts, for if a spending committee had jurisdiction over only a few programs, a reconciliation savings target could most likely be met by accepting the illustrative programmatic budget cut outlined by the Budget Committee.

In 1987, the House Merchant Marine Committee responded creatively to such a directive in order to protect the boating lobby. Forced with a Budget Committee "suggestion" to save $94 million by adopting user fees for Coast Guard services, the committee decided instead to charge foreign oil tankers that had recently accepted protection from the Navy in the Persian Gulf, though there was great doubt that the committee had the jurisdiction to do this. Yet a member of the committee, Representative Mario Biaggi, recognized the value of this opportunity by saying, "We should just thank God this situation has developed" in the gulf (Starobin 1987b, 2507). Though the user fee was not adopted, the proposal bought enough time that the committee looked as if it had complied with the call for reconciliation savings.

Symbolic compliance with the budget resolution was possible because there was no formal penalty on the Congress if assumed reconciliation savings were not produced. In contrast to appropriations bills, reconciliation bills need not be passed for the government to keep operating. On the other hand, widespread stonewalling of reconciliation allowed presidential criticism of congressional inaction, and congressional leadership responded by jawboning committees. In 1990, the Budget Committee again recommended Coast Guard user fees, and the Merchant Marine and Fisheries Committee responded by proposing to increase a variety of other fees, including the tonnage tax levied on foreign vessels entering U.S. ports. But this time, the Merchant Marine Committee could not withstand greater pressure from the leadership, and the Coast Guard user fees were included in the 1990 legislation. In 1991, the committee tried to reverse the previous year's decision, proposing to repeal the new user fee by establishing access charges to computerized data on shipping tariffs (which raised opposition from supporters of free access to government information—marketing firms, the press, librarians). Congress adopted the proposal in 1992.[14]

14. Brent Mitchell, "Government Information as Revenue Source," *Washington Post,* 25 June 1991, sec. A; Newlin 1991; Davis 1992.

Another flaw of reconciliation for controllers was that it provided a procedural opportunity to *increase* spending. Though some committees resisted reconciliation directives, members of Congress generally wanted to pass a reconciliation bill so they could claim they acted in a fiscally responsible way. But many of them apparently calculated that this claim might be accepted even if the reconciliation bill included dubious savings *and* authorized new spending.[15] Much of this new spending was rationalized as adjustments made necessary by savings in other areas of the reconciliation bill. For example,

> An end-of-the-year scramble to curb the federal budget deficit might seem like an inauspicious time for a congressman to secure hundreds of millions of dollars in increased funding for a Great Society program.
>
> As his colleagues raced to complete budget-cutting and tax-raising bills in time to adjourn for Christmas, Waxman was fighting to preserve provisions that would enlarge Medicaid, the federal health program for the poor. His efforts provoked outraged opposition from the Reagan administration. "Right in the middle of budget reduction," exclaimed one White House official, "this guy is pushing one of the biggest expansions ever of a social welfare program!"
>
> In the end, Waxman, settled for provisions that would add an estimated $600 million to Medicaid over three years. That was about one-fourth of what he had sought. But a quarter of a loaf is considerably more than most other members of Congress can obtain for their favorite programs these days.
>
> "We didn't get all of what we wanted," Waxman said. "We didn't lose it all either." One result is that Medicaid will start covering thousands of low-income pregnant women and infants who do not now qualify for benefits because their family incomes exceed the poverty line.[16]

Three years later,

> Hailing from Kentucky, Sen. Wendell H. Ford knows it's better to have more than one horse in the race if you want to win the derby.
>
> As the 101st Congress comes to a close, the wily Democrat is forcing action on a number of his top legislative priorities by attaching them to a must-pass deficit-reduction package (HR 5835). Frustrated that many had

15. The omnibus character of reconciliation bills enabled slipping spending increases into them, for bills running into thousands of pages are hard to scan for objectionable provisions. See Steven S. Smith, *Call to Order* (Washington: Brookings, 1989): 52.

16. See Paul Blustein, "Waxman: Breadwinner For Medicaid Recipients," *Washington Post,* 23 December 1987, sec. A.

> stalled, Ford wants to push at least some across the finish line before Congress adjourns.
>
> If Ford has his way, this year's historic package of spending cuts and tax increases will also help preserve 1,500 federal jobs in his home state, slash the price of government-produced uranium for the nuclear industry and include a plate full of aviation law changes sought by various airline industry players.
>
> "You have to look at what's available to you," Ford says. "I've been thinking about this for some time." (Kuntz 1990a, 3485)

Beginning in 1985, controllers developed procedural limits on so-called extraneous provisions that could be included in reconciliation bills, but as these examples show, the controls were weak (see Keith and Davis 1993).

Gramm-Rudman-Hollings was in part adopted because of the failure to effectively enforce budget resolutions through points of order and reconciliation. Its leading remedy was sequestration. In the original conception, sequestration would have reduced spending for all programs to close the gap between the budget-resolution target and any higher enacted amounts. But the revisions of the sequestration process during consideration of Gramm-Rudman-Hollings shows how spending advocates can obtain exemptions from macrobudgetary controls before they are routine. Several months of backroom negotiations went on to determine which programs would be covered by the process. What began as an across-the-board procedure turned into a much narrower process, with numerous programs exempted or subject to special rules that limited cuts. Then after passage of Gramm-Rudman-Hollings, numerous spending advocates proposed that their programs be exempted from the new process. Most failed (the Coast Guard, Drug Enforcement Administration, Federal Aviation Administration, Immigration and Naturalization Service, Customs, selected veteran's programs, the Library of Congress, higher education student assistance programs, and so on), but some succeeded (COLAs for federal employee retirement programs, depository institution regulators).[17]

Sequestration also failed because of the low likelihood that politicians can jointly bind themselves to do something they don't want to do. Following the first pro forma sequester of March 1986, spending advocates found several ways to avoid sequestration. They relied first on accounting gimmicks like the loan-asset sales and effective-date changes described in earlier chapters. Then,

---

17. Exemption was also possible when a macrobudgetary procedure process was thought to have recently overreached its purpose. In 1982 and 1983, for example, some programs avoided the reconciliation process in part because of the discontent over the 1981 bill placing a ceiling on authorizations.

when the savings targets were far exceeded by projected spending levels, they increased the targets. This was the only reasonable course—to do otherwise would have eviscerated all discretionary programs—but it showed that the threat of sequestration was an empty one.

This scenario threatened to be repeated in 1990. However, controllers had gained ground, and a significant deficit-reduction package was adopted instead. Part of this legislation was the Budget Enforcement Act (BEA), which replaced the empty threat of sequestration with new procedures. Fixed deficit targets were dropped in favor of deficit-reduction targets that were tied to projected spending levels. Second, four macro arenas were established. Three were for discretionary programs, grouped into categories of defense, international, and nondefense. Procedural fire walls were built between these programs, which prohibited transfers from one category to another. Spending caps were also created for each arena. The fourth arena joined mandatory spending programs and revenues. This part of the budget was to be controlled by a pay-as-you-go process. Deficit increases from new spending or tax preferences would have to be offset by spending cuts or tax increases (Doyle and McCaffery 1991).

Many controllers disapproved of some of the Budget Enforcement Act's provisions. For example, they thought the levels set for discretionary spending caps unnecessarily accommodated spending advocates, and projected that loopholes for emergency spending would be exploited. But the controllers were pleasantly surprised over the BEA's first two years, for in general, the act withstood most challenges. Few emergencies were declared, and, more important, the fire walls didn't come tumbling down. The walls had been built on the insistence of spending advocates for defense and international programs. They complained that absent fire walls, spending advocates for domestic programs would convince appropriators to abandon the budget resolution's allocations among the three categories, shifting money away from defense and international programs. Even after the dissolution of the Soviet Union strengthened the position of domestic-spending advocates who wanted to raid defense, most of their attempted invasions failed. Proposals to allow large transfers were voted down by a coalition of deficit hawks (who wanted to protect the discipline created by the BEA) and defense-spending advocates (Hager 1992). Domestic-spending advocates then attempted minor incursions to test arena boundaries. A good example was Senator Harkin's successful attempt to fund $210 million in breast cancer research out of the Pentagon's budget. However, the Office of Management and Budget counted this spending as part of the domestic arena (Towell 1992).

Competition was also produced by the pay-as-you-go requirement. Pay as you go had informally been applied to tax policy since a revenue-neutral norm developed during consideration of the Tax Reform Act of 1986 (for example, see Matlack 1990b). For consideration of two tax bills in 1991–92, most spending advocates felt obliged to cover the costs of proposed tax expenditures by suggesting offsetting reductions in other tax expenditures. Ironically, President Bush vetoed both bills that passed the Congress for fear of being charged with supporting the tax increases from these offsetting tax-expenditure reductions, which might be viewed as hypocritical since he claimed his opponent would favor tax increases.

Competition in the pay-as-you-go arena was attenuated, however, by several flaws in the pay-as-you-go controls. For example, the controls covered only spending from legislation; new spending from administrative actions were not covered. In 1992, the tax committee chairmen Bentsen and Rostenkowski took advantage of this provision, convincing the Treasury to administratively extend an expiring preference for research and development by multinational corporations.[18] Bentsen also tried to exploit a more serious flaw of pay as you go—the fact that it applied only to the five-year budget window. Bentsen's proposal offset *only* the first five years of the huge cost of long-term tax breaks for individual retirement accounts (IRAs), using temporary provisions that would bring funds to the government *only* for the five years for which pay as you go applied. As Viveca Novak of *National Journal* put it, "The budget window is made from a peculiar glass that fogs up when questioning observers peer too far ahead" (1992, 2610). Both of these tactics tried to exploit scorekeeping rules, which are covered in the next section.

Frequency

To repeat from chapter 3, though a routine schedule is one of the defining characteristics of the budgetary process, this schedule is often violated. Frequency tactics are the means. In many cases, these tactics manipulate scorekeeping decisions, in order to avoid controls that are triggered by scorekeeping decisions. Scorekeeping is the process of comparing budget actions to targets. By keeping a running total of budget actions, performance in meeting budget targets can be assessed, so that performance or targets can be adjusted if necessary.

Until recently, scorekeeping principles were infrequently printed and rarely analyzed. (In the 1990 Budget Enforcement Act, scorekeeping principles were set out in detail.) Almost all budgeting participants deferred to scorekeeping experts because of the process' technical complexity—it required knowledge not only of the routine schedule for each program, but also of committee jurisdictions and accounting rules. But the assistant director for

18. David S. Hilzenrath, "Wriggling Out of Budget Constraints," *Washington Post,* 9 January 1993, sec. A.

budget analysis of CBO explained that complexity was not the only reason scorekeeping was so arcane.

> The major reason why CBO and the Senate do not have a written set of scorekeeping rules is that they change slightly from year to year. Enforcing a budget resolution is a political process, not a technical one, and compromises are often needed to keep the process going. . . . In conclusion, then, what we follow in Congressional scorekeeping could be called *G*enerally *A*ccepted *S*corekeeping *P*ractices. All you acronym bugs can quickly translate this phrase into a meaningful word that captures the essence of the process. (Blum 1987)[19]

In both legislative and executive scorekeeping, political decision makers had the final say. For example, CBO made initial scorekeeping decisions, but the House and Senate Budget committees retained the authority to change CBO recommendations. Consequently, the different politics in the House, Senate, and the executive branch produced different scorekeeping rules for each institution over the period studied. However, when the Balanced Budget Act shifted final scorekeeping authority for sequestration to OMB, these institutions negotiated frequently to develop relatively common scorekeeping practices.

The first four frequency tactics forced scorekeepers to ignore new spending. The first tactic was to underfund programs in expectation of supplemental appropriations. The second tactic was to spend previously appropriated money for a different purpose without having it counted as a budget year expenditure. The third tactic was to play with the baseline and the fourth to exploit inflation uncertainties. The last frequency tactic changed the timing of budget decisions.

Underfund in Expectation of Supplemental Appropriations

For many years the distinction between discretionary and mandatory programs was unclear for some programs. The programs in doubt were known as *appropriated entitlements* or as *pro forma appropriations.* Although these programs were nominally funded by appropriations, the true practice was to pay the cost for all who demanded access, so they were in essence mandatory programs. This treatment was appreciated by spending advocates. For example, a late 1985 internal OMB document stated with evident frustration that

---

19. Other useful discussions of scorekeeping prior to the BEA can be found in a memo from Assistant Director Carey P. Modlin of the OMB to congressional spending committees (1986); and in the House Budget Committee's *Staff Manual on Scorekeeping Rules and Enforcement Procedures,* which is periodically published.

> perhaps the most egregious example of congressional masking of spending is found in the Agriculture Appropriations Bill. Virtually every budgetary gimmick in the book has been tried, nearly all initiating with the House Appropriations Subcommittee and Committee.

According to this memo, from fiscal year 1984 through the recent fiscal year 1986 appropriations, over $1.7 billion was provided to the USDA through the intentional underfunding of appropriated entitlements and pro forma appropriations.

Intentional underfunding worked because it was relatively easy to enact supplementals to make up for the underfunding. As stated in chapter 4, supplementals were perceived as the proverbial water over the dam—spending in budget years received more attention than spending in current years. Supplementals also acted as a vehicle for funding other programs, thereby providing coalition support to the underfunded program. Of these vehicles, the Commodity Credit Corporation was the turbocharged, eighteen-wheeler version. Its underfunding was even institutionalized, for the CCC was traditionally funded in a regular spring supplemental. This timing was followed ostensibly to respond to crop-year timing, but the real reason was that the timing conveyed a political advantage. Its urgency allowed other projects to gain consideration and sometimes passage.

Scorekeeping controllers didn't want to record savings that resulted from underfunding appropriated entitlements or pro forma appropriations. But on occasion, given the difficulty of accurately projecting spending needs, controllers did not recognize underfunding. On other occasions, decision makers made scorekeepers look the other way, allowing favored programs to avoid the enforcement rules that were intended to prevent underfunding.

The internal OMB document quoted above gives examples of this tactic.

> Some programs are required by law to be reimbursed for prior year losses. For example, the Commodity Credit Corporation incurs losses for mandatory payments to farmers. Often Congress fails to appropriate part or all of the requested funds to cover these losses. By not reimbursing the CCC for outlays already made, the appropriations committee claims "savings" (when compared with the President's request) that it then uses to fund discretionary programs in the Agriculture bill such as the Soil Conservation Service. . . .
>
> In 1986, the House Appropriations Committee is understating the amount of Child Nutrition funding needed by $686 million. The bill permits the availability of an added $665 million, not scored with the bill, contingent upon a later supplemental request. HAC also assumes the availability of an additional $21 million for the program from unscored

> transfers, instead of providing a direct appropriations. In 1984 and 1985, HAC proposed only partial year funding in Food Stamps, artificially understating spending by $769 million in 1984 and $374 in 1985. In each year, later supplementals made up the shortfall. In 1986, funding is short by $24 million.

In the latter cases, this tactic increased funding for the Extension Service, for administration of crop programs, and for other purposes. Controllers attempted to prevent use of this tactic by converting the CCC to a more automatic appropriation.[20]

Another example of intentional underfunding that led to supplementals was budgeting for disaster relief. Since disasters are largely unpredictable, appropriators can apparently save money by not appropriating any funds for disasters, risking the chance that disasters actually occur. When disasters inevitably occur, the pressure for supplementals is irresistible (see Goodisman 1983; Oppenheim 1983). Paradoxically, controllers may cooperate with this tactic. Controllers fear that if appropriators set aside funds equal to the average annual costs of previous disasters, and then losses from disasters are low, spending advocates will press for more declarations of less-disastrous disasters—and funding will be available.

This willingness to enact supplemental appropriations for disasters was used by tacticians for other programs. In January 1987, only four months into the fiscal year, before there was any way to project the amount that would be needed for disasters, $50 million in disaster relief funds were transferred to the Emergency Food and Shelter program, which provided grants to states for the care of the homeless. This money would have been required for disaster assistance if the program experienced average losses, for as Senator Gramm said in the debate, "We are transferring money out of an emergency fund for disaster relief, without any guarantee from the Lord that there is going to be a commensurate reduction in disasters."[21]

The food stamp program provides a variant of the intentional underfunding tactic. Beginning in 1977, the program was capped in the appropriations process. This cap technically deprived food stamps of entitlement status, be-

---

20. See debate in the *Congressional Record,* 30 June 1987, S 8978–92; and Rapp 1987a. OMB also used a bargaining countertactic. It proposed program changes to the appropriated entitlements, which meant that these programs needed fewer appropriations. When the Congress didn't go along with the program changes, OMB refused to accept higher appropriations for the subcommittee, which would force cuts in discretionary programs.

21. *Congressional Record,* 29 January 1987, S 1366–74. Though the Budget Committee leadership accommodated this strategy, they tried to limit its spread by including in scorekeeping reports a projection of $57 million in "mandatory items requiring further appropriation action" ($57 million instead of $50 million to account for differences in outlay rates). This upset the Appropriations Committee, which noted that disaster relief funding was provided by discretionary appropriations, was not mandatory, and should not be counted as requiring further action.

cause appropriations had to be received before benefits could be paid to those who applied. According to the law, when USDA expected that funds would be insufficient, it was supposed to reduce benefit payments.

The cap was originally proposed by conservatives, who believed that ceilings could serve as effective constraints on spending. But the caps were not strongly opposed by some program advocates, who successfully gambled that the caps would be ineffective. They thought it unlikely that a mechanism could be developed to reduce benefits during a funding crisis, and expected that all those who applied for payments would eventually receive them, as in other entitlement programs. During the 1979, 1980, and 1981 fiscal years, supplementals were adopted to make up for funding shortfalls, as "it was argued that it was too late in the fiscal year to revise the program sufficiently to achieve needed savings" (Richardson 1981; Rhyne 1980). The underfunding tactic thus reduced the need during budget preparation to adopt real cuts in program spending—making food stamps discretionary gave only the appearance of control.

A related tactic is *over*funding and then shifting funds elsewhere. This tactic takes advantage of overestimates of the funding needs of recognized mandatory programs. Such overestimates are rarely intentional, for they trigger interest in reducing a program's costs. But once the unintentional overestimate is recognized, spending advocates may claim that the reduced funding requirements represent savings, and use these savings to finance new spending elsewhere. This tactic was used in favor of commodity programs

> The main provision . . . would achieve more than $900 million in budget "savings."
>
> It would require corn and wheat farmers to idle a higher percentage of their land if grain surpluses exceed certain limits in the 1988 crop year. Theoretically, the government would save money by not having to purchase and store the surplus grain that would have been produced on the idled land.
>
> The acreage-reduction triggers were set at 6 billion bushes of surplus corn and 1.9 billion bushels of surplus wheat, levels the Congressional Budget Office (CBO) earlier this year had predicted the crops would exceed. CBO has since revised those estimates downward, which means the acreage set-asides are unlikely to go into effect.
>
> Nevertheless, Congress' rules for reconciliation require CBO to "score" the savings of the new provision on the basis of the original surplus estimates, giving the agriculture budget credit for savings that won't really occur. (Rapp 1987c, 2619; see also Rapp 1987d)[22]

22. On similar gambits with energy programs, see Haas 1987, 2681–82.

Both tactics—underfunding in expectation of supplementals, and using windfalls from overfunding—are now much more difficult to carry out. Controls on supplementals adopted from 1985 on, and in particular, in the Budget Enforcement Act of 1990, allow only supplementals for declared emergencies (absent offsetting cuts or new revenues). Emergencies differ in the eyes of various beholders, of course, and 1991 featured a variety of attempts to classify spending proposals as responding to emergencies. For example, a supplemental appropriation for the war against Iraq included emergency subsidy increases for GI bill education benefits and life insurance (Fessler 1991). In general, however, controllers have been much more successful in limiting use of this potential loophole than most observers expected.

Spend Last Year's Money

Underfunding tactics are based on inconsistent scorekeeping within a budget year; in contrast, the tactic described here distorts scorekeeping from year to year. The trick was to spend last year's money while making it look as if you were not. The tactic features reappropriations. A reappropriation is an extension of the availability of previously appropriated but still unused budget authority. Without an extension, this budget authority will lapse. For many years, the Congress scored reappropriations as *not* providing funding to a program in the budget year. The executive branch, in contrast, typically counted it as such, letting the old budget authority lapse and charging a program for use of new budget authority.[23]

The internal OMB document quoted above noted that the Congress used its scoring principle to the advantage of the programs that receive reappropriated funds.

> Balances of funds appropriated in earlier years but not targeted for immediate use or not needed for their original purpose can be retargeted for other purposes, permitting the committees to fund new or expanded programs without showing new budget authority. In the case of funds no longer needed, normal budget procedures would call for lapsing (canceling) the unused funds and appropriating new budget authority. By transferring balances from one purpose to another, often from a long-term project to a short-term one, the Congress can change program priorities and ultimate spending totals without increasing recorded budget authority for the recipient account.

Another version of this tactic was to rescind unobligated balances. The unobligated balance is the budget authority provided to an agency that has not been committed by the agency. The Congress scored savings from rescissions

23. A history of the reappropriations strategy may be found in Fisher 1975, 130–33.

of such balances to the budget year, which offset the costs of new spending. In contrast, the executive branch scored rescissions of unobligated balances as savings for the (past) year in which budget authority had been provided (too late to offset spending).

When funds that were reappropriated or rescinded were not going to be spent for their intended purposes, then the claims of savings made by the Congress were false.[24] Controllers typically complained, for example, over rescissions of subsidized housing programs to finance other spending.[25] After OMB unsuccessfully argued for years that the Congress should agree to adopt OMB's practices, the tactic was effectively limited by new scorekeeping principles.

Play with the Baseline

The budget *baseline* projected spending as "if programs and activities of the United States government were carried on during the year at the same level as the current fiscal year without a change in policy," to use the statutory language in place in 1989. Unfortunately, for many programs, "the same level" and "without a change in policy" were inherently contradictory. Consider Social Security, an entitlement program that has more eligible beneficiaries year after year. To pay Social Security benefits "without a change in policy" (paying all eligible beneficiaries), the "same level" of financing (last year's spending) would be insufficient.

In practice, the baseline was normally calculated as follows:

1. For discretionary programs:

    Begin with the appropriated amount for the current year, or for some programs, the maximum obligations allowed by law.
    Multiply this amount by expected inflation.
    Add the two. The total is the amount needed to finance the current policy level for the budget year.

2. For mandatory programs:

    Estimate the budget year demand for the program in number of units (beneficiaries, for example).
    Multiply estimated units times the expected unit costs.

---

24. OMB also manipulated rescission and reappropriation rules during this period to cut spending. Illustrative examples can be seen in the budgets for the National Institutes of Health and the Corporation For Public Broadcasting from 1987 to 1990.

25. Statement of Harry S. Havens, "Use and Impact of Rescission Procedures," General Accounting Office, testimony before the Subcommittee on Legislative Process, Committee on Rules, House of Representatives, 25 September 1992.

This is the amount needed to finance the budget-year demand. These different methods implicitly resolved the inherent contradiction in the baseline definition by emphasizing "same level" for discretionary programs, and "without a change in policy" for mandatory programs. For example, the baseline for the mandatory Medicaid program grew at a rate far exceeding general inflation, because more people became eligible for Medicaid and because medical costs increased at a much faster rate than general inflation. In contrast, the baseline for the discretionary programs did not grow in response to demographic increases. For example, the Head Start baseline was adjusted only for inflation, and not for the increased number of poor, preschool children.[26]

Some controllers argued that these practices created pressure for spending. Since the baseline accounted for demographic and cost increases in mandatory programs, their rapid spending growth appeared natural. For example, controllers suggested that a 15 percent annual rate of growth in health programs was in fact "a change in policy." They also suggested that discretionary programs should not receive inflation adjustments. Director Darman forced OMB to use a without inflation baseline for discretionary programs shortly after the Bush administration took office, in hopes of putting some substance into the flexible-freeze nostrum that candidate Bush prescribed during his 1988 campaign. In return, spending advocates argued that inflation adjustments reduced funding disparities between discretionary and mandatory programs. If the baseline for discretionary programs was not adjusted for changes in prices, these programs would effectively be cut by the rate of inflation, while mandatory programs could automatically spend more in response to cost *and* demand changes.

The Reagan administration used baseline tactics in the early 1980s to foster and protect the defense buildup. In 1981, the budget resolution included the goal of increasing defense spending by 5 percent above inflation in each of the following five years. Then, in 1982, the administration convinced the Congress to discard the regular method for constructing the baseline for defense spending, almost all of which was discretionary—the baseline was to include the standard inflation adjustment *and* the 5 percent planned increases. This tactic radically changed perceptions of the amount of funds the Defense Department was acquiring. Even though the real financial resources spent on defense were increased far above the rate of inflation, small reductions below the 5 percent real-growth total were called "cuts." As one of my informants said, this was like saying "Gee, that hurts, and pass the salt!" In contrast, when

---

26. Explanations of baseline calculations may be found in Congressional Budget Office 1989, appendix B; in the President's *Budget,* annually, in the section on "Baseline Estimates," and General Accounting Office 1986.

other discretionary programs were cut below the baseline, they received less funding than the amount necessary to compensate for inflation.

By 1983, opponents of defense spending began to argue that this practice gave an unfair advantage to the Pentagon.[27] They partially succeeded in changing perceptions, as by 1984 popular press accounts routinely added quotation marks to the phrase: *"cuts" in defense spending* (e.g., "Numbers" 1984). In addition, the House military committees refused to fund defense programs at the 5 percent real growth target in 1984. Spending advocates then turned to an additional manipulation, which came to be called the Rose Garden baseline. Senate Republicans and President Reagan held a news conference in the Rose Garden to announce that they would calculate the real-growth baseline from the previous year's budget-resolution target for defense rather than from the actual appropriations. The *Washington Post* reported that in the 1985 appropriations,

> Congress wound up cutting way back on Reagan's defense spending request, but some argue that use of the higher "Rose Garden" baseline for defense helped prevent even deeper cuts.
>
> "It helped, no doubt about it," said House Armed Service Committee Chairman Les Aspin (D-Wis.). "It had a lot of effect last year," said Rep. Dick Cheney (R-Wyo.), chairman of the Republican Policy Committee.[28]

Many budget technicians were uncomfortable with the baseline tactic, but were unable to oppose it. After passage of the Gramm-Rudman-Hollings Act, however, they recognized that the 1981 policy decision of real growth had been reversed by the freeze provisions of this act, and they convinced the Congress to revert to a no-real-growth baseline in 1986.[29]

Like many of the tactics described above, the directed-baseline tactic diffused. Spending advocates for agriculture, for example, attempted to use it on several occasions during the late 1980s. Here is an example from 1989:

> Privately, according to several congressional sources, they are arguing that this year's congressional budget resolution should assume target prices will remain steady at their 1990 levels, not continue to decline as they have been over the past three years. The effect would be to increase the agriculture baseline for price and income supports from fiscal 1991

27. See, for example, Joint Economic Committee, Senate Report 98–15 (1983): 101.

28. Helen Dewar, "Defense Budget's Elastic Logic," *Washington Post,* 10 February 1986, sec. A.

29. See also George C. Wilson, "Administration Debating Which Base to Use for Defense Budget Requests," *Washington Post,* 13 November 1986, sec. A.

> through 1994. The baseline sets the amount in the budget from which the Agriculture panels will be expected to make future cuts.
>
> The bottom line: A higher level from which to cut leaves more to spend. (Cloud 1989b, 319)

So did the Ways and Means Committee on behalf of Medicare. House Budget Committee chair Panetta argued that same year,

> The Medicare provisions in Title X of this bill include a number of reforms. One reform would set rather stringent outlay caps on payments for physician services, though these caps won't begin to bite hard for a few years. Unfortunately, the bill also contains a provision that basically directs CBO and OMB to ignore the caps when they compute their baselines. As a result, their Gramm-Rudman estimates will be too high, their budget baselines will be too high, and the scoring of subsequent Medicare legislation will be misleading.[30]

Medicare advocates also took advantage of another practical problem in developing the baseline. This problem was how to deal with expiring provisions—provisions of law that were scheduled to become ineffective on a certain date. If the baseline was supposed to show how much spending would be required without a change in policy, then perhaps the baseline should have zeroed out any financing for expiring provisions. This would force spending advocates to justify anew any spending for programs whose authorizations had just expired. However, spending advocates learned that they could take advantage of this practice by terminating *savings* after one year. For example, savings were produced by cutting scheduled reimbursements to hospitals for capital costs. However, the law required these savings for only one year, after which reimbursements would return to the previous, higher rate. The baseline would then show increased spending for capital reimbursements in the next year. But if the hospitals perceived that their reimbursements had been permanently reduced, the Ways and Means Committee could "reduce" the reimbursements each year. By doing this, they gained credit for savings that could offset spending increases in other programs. This expiring-provisions tactic might be called the "energized baseline," after the ubiquitous "Energizer Rabbit—it keeps going, and going, and going."[31]

A further complication regarding expiring provisions was that a small group of dedicated revenue programs (primarily for transportation) were treated differently in the baseline—their receipts and outlays were routinely

30. *Congressional Record,* 26 September 1989, H 5955.

31. Timothy J. Muris made a concerted attack on baseline practices, with special emphasis on health spending (1989).

assumed to be continued even though they were not yet extended in law. This advantaged spending advocates for these programs, who did not have to re-justify spending as authorizations expired. But this wasn't enough for aviation advocates, who were frustrated with appropriations limits on spending aviation user fees. In an attempt to force additional spending, the 1987 authorization law established a trigger-tax reduction, which was a large tax *decrease* scheduled for 1990 if appropriations in the two prior years didn't meet a certain percentage of authorized levels. Aviation advocates projected that the required increase in appropriations would be cheaper than the halving of receipts, and hoped that their threat would be taken seriously enough to force the baseline to show the deficit increase from the trigger-tax reduction. The administration didn't take the bait, however, refusing to assume the trigger-tax reduction would go into law (Starobin 1989b).

Exploit Inflation Estimates

Prior to the 1970s, despite the full-funding principle and the long-term nature of many procurement obligations, budget estimates did not include additional funding to cover the costs of price changes in the outyears—inflation was generally low. With the escalation of inflation in the 1970s, OMB allowed the Pentagon to add expected inflation to contracts and budgets, with the proviso that the adjustment should be consistent with the GNP deflator (GAO 1978b; Thomas 1986, 9; Stubbing and Mendel 1986, 85–86; McNaught and Ratner 1987). But unfortunately for the Pentagon, inflation was significantly underestimated for defense budgets prepared during the 1970s. From fiscal years 1978 to 1981, for example, prices for operations and maintenance purchases were budgeted to increase by 21 percent but actually increased by 40 percent. Though Congress passed supplementals in each year to cover many of these expenses, CBO calculated in 1986 that the supplementals fell $7 billion short of budgeted levels (Thomas 1986, 2, though see also 48).

The Pentagon responded to this loss of real funding by successfully petitioning OMB for clearance to apply a special deflator for major weapons systems. To develop this deflator, Deputy Secretary of Defense Carlucci ordered an analysis of changes in prices for weapons systems inputs from the high-inflation period, and it showed that these prices increased at double the rate of increase for the GNP deflator. After bargaining between OMB and DOD, OMB approved a special deflator of 30 percent above the GNP deflator for the fiscal year 1983 budget under the guise of "more realistic budgeting."

In reality, there were reasons to suspect that this special deflator would overestimate price changes and provide more money than the Pentagon actually needed, and this was exactly what happened.[32] In addition to this overfunding, the general rate of inflation was overestimated from 1982 to 1985. The range of estimates of the windfall ran from $23.2 to $49 billion, with at least $9 billion due to the special deflator. Yet as Senator Pryor complained,

> Reaping the benefit and being no fool, the Defense Department did not come up regularly and tell us we had given them too much money for inflation. I do not recall any reverse-supplementals the Defense Department asked Congress to enact.
>
> Instead, some mysterious things started to happen. Rather than asking for an annual balancing of the books, from time to time—actually whenever Congress seemed about to reduce the defense budget by too large a margin—we would be informed that some extra money had been found from previous budgets. Just lying around in an old shoe box. We were told we could move this money from previous budgets to the new one and thereby soften the blow of congressional budget cuts.[33]

Two uses of the tactic that miffed Pryor were the 1983 B-1 bomber reprogramming and the missing $4 billion of 1985. The Senate Armed Services Committee was intending to cut multiyear procurement funding for the B-1 to comply with the budget resolution targets.

> But just hours before the scheduled vote, Chairman John G. Tower (R-Tex.) came up with a letter from Office of Management and Budget Director David A. Stockman saying new inflation estimates had cut next year's estimated defense costs by $2.1 billion.
>
> Tower quickly moved to accept the reestimates, then to earmark $888.7 million of the dividend to finance several years of B1 production in advance.[34]

The tactic was repeated in 1985. GAO reported,

> Shortly after the Senate Budget Committee passed a budget resolution calling for zero growth in the FY 1986 military appropriation, the Secre-

---

32. These reasons are described in ibid and in GAO 1985c. Another argument for the special deflator might have been that the rapid increase in defense spending would lead to demand-pull inflation for weapons inputs, but this argument was not put forward by defense spending advocates, probably because it could have led to procurement stretch-outs.

33. *Congressional Record,* 22 October 1985, S 13726–27.

34. George C. Wilson, "OMB, Pentagon 'Find' Funding for B1 Bomber," *Washington Post,* 29 June 1983, sec. A. See also Helen Dewar, "Defense Bill Snags in Senate Debate," *Washington Post,* 12 July 1983, sec. A; Gordon 1983; and *Congressional Record,* 11 July 1983, S 9637–51, and 13 July 1983, S 9863–68.

> tary of Defense requested that Congress "recognize early" the $4 billion in what he called his "regular inflation savings" so that DOD "could meet the spending limits of the resolution and minimize the impact on national security. . . ." The $4 billion budget offer was not intended to be a further reduction to the Senate budget resolution. Instead, it was to be used to offset the effect of the budget resolution. This would require that the Congress direct DOD to reprogram the money to purposes that were not funded in the fiscal year 1986 budget. Thus, the total available authority (includes new and old budget authority and reimbursements) to the DOD would increase without increasing estimates of future outlays of the deficit. Other surpluses could be reapplied in a similar way to further mitigate the effect of a funding freeze. (GAO 1985c, app. 5, 1)

The Pentagon's tactical successes stimulated opponents of military spending to press for reforms to inflation budgeting.[35] Use of the special deflator was discontinued.[36]

Change the Schedule

Incremental budgeting theory maintains that annual decisions on a program's budget benefits the program. Short periodicity is likely to build knowledge about the program and foster trust in its managers by decision makers. But some spending advocates disregard this advice and try to change the schedule for making budget decisions for their programs. On several occasions, spending advocates for transportation and agriculture, programs that are authorized on multiyear schedules, changed these schedules so the Congress would consider legislation in the most favorable political climate. At other times, just a slight delay in a schedule proved useful. Under the Gramm-Rudman-Hollings sequestration procedures, for example, bills enacted after the sequestration deadline passed were exempt from future cuts. Understandably, in the week after the October 1988 deadline passed, $500 million in spending was enacted into law. (GAO 1988)

Another example was when spending advocates for defense proposed a conversion to biennial budgeting (Meyers 1988). This reform was proposed by the Senate Armed Services Committee, embraced by conservative advocates

---

35. Les Aspin, "Inflation Budgeting: On and under the Rocks," *Congressional Record,* 8 July 1985, E 3140–43.

36. Exploiting inflation estimates led to a failure to recognize financing when it was received. A counterpart tactic is to recognize financing *before* it is received. An example was the so-called normalization of Social Security receipts. This procedure—worth about $2 billion—credited Social Security on the first day of the month with funds that were projected to be received over the rest of the month. See T. Clark 1983.

like the Heritage Foundation, and endorsed by the Defense Department. The reform could have improved the efficiency of the Pentagon's procurement, and advocates also hoped, probably mistakenly, that Congressional micromanagement would decline. Another motive, though, was to lock in higher spending levels than those the Pentagon was expected to receive through two annual appropriations bills.[37] One reason the tactic foundered for the Defense Department, and for other agencies that copied it (including the Social Security Administration and the Veterans Administration), was that this motive became widely known (see also Michaelis 1993).

Summary

Frequency and arena tactics are related to the unfulfilled expectations that the budget process follow a routine schedule and demonstrate responsive control. Frequency tactics become opportune when there is uncertainty about the proper schedule for making budgetary decisions. Arena tactics are attractive when there is uncertainty about how controllers should group programs.

Over the past few decades, controllers responded vigorously to spending advocates' tactics that exploited budgetary decision procedures. To a large extent, controllers substantially limited the tactical opportunities of spending advocates. But they did so only after some of the many attempts by innovative spending advocates to exploit existing flaws in decision procedures succeeded and then diffused to other skillful spending advocates. As with accounting tactics, the budgetary decision procedure tactics of spending advocates contributed to the development of massive deficits.

Although controllers developed relatively effective controls on most budgetary decision procedures and accounting tactics, they were less successful in controlling tactics for budgetary policy designs and for arguments about the effects of spending. I cover these tactics sequentially in the next two chapters.

---

37. Hurry-up spending and advance appropriations work on the same principle: make the decision to spend now because future approval of spending might be more difficult. Hurry-up spending is money spent in the last quarter of a fiscal year that could not be legally spent after the end of this fiscal year. Advance appropriations are provided for fiscal years beyond the fiscal year for which the appropriation act is passed.

Chapter 6

Tactics for Budgetary Policy Designs

A budgetary policy design defines the permissible sources of *financing* for a program and guides how a program may *obligate* itself to spend funds. Tactics are available for both the financing and obligation aspects of budgetary policy design. Financing tactics guarantee financing each year without requiring political decision makers to approve this financing each year. By providing continuing financing, spending advocates can lock in high levels of political support, lowering the risk that reduced political support will lead to less money.

On the obligation side of budgetary policy design, programs whose enabling legislation or published regulations establish few prior conditions for obligations are likely to show high levels of spending. Decisions to spend can be made quickly, and spending advocates will pressure agencies to do this. Similarly, programs that are automatically responsive to economic and demographic changes—through indexation or open-ended beneficiary eligibility—will devote increased resources to increased "needs" much faster than the typical discretionary program. Spending advocates try to gain these advantages for programs whose purposes suggest an automatically responsive design.

As in budgetary accounting, perhaps the most important aspect of a program's policy design is the *complexity* of its obligations and financing. Few decision makers possess relatively complete information about a complex program; the others rely on cue givers or their own muddled impressions to make these decisions. When the attention spans of cue takers are limited, controllers find it difficult to convey information about the true operation of complex programs. The natural response of decision makers is to throw up their hands and call the program "uncontrollable."

Table 6.1 lists some popular budgetary policy design tactics. The following sections give examples of their use by advocates and the responses by controllers.

Financing

Financing tactics protect programs from the attacks of controllers by assuring permanency of financing. This section describes three types of financing

TABLE 6.1. Tactics for Budgetary Policy Designs

Financing
Dedicate funds
Capitalize high levels of support
Diversify financing sources
Obligations
Increase spending automatically
Adjust administrative discretion

tactics. Dedication tactics, which make revenues automatically available to programs, remove the need to obtain appropriations each year. Capitalization tactics provide financing before obligations must be made, which protects spending even if political support for it weakens in the future. Diversity tactics grant programs several sources of financing, providing protection when one source is limited.

Dedicate Funds

About half of all the federal government's receipts from the public are dedicated by law to specific programs. Approximately two-thirds of the dedicated receipts are from payroll taxes for retirement and disability, medical, and unemployment insurance. Included in the wide range of other dedicated funds are those for reforestation, wool production, coal-mining reclamation, immigration control, and restitution of crime victims.

For controllers, the tactic of dedicating revenues can be a method of imposing market incentives on programs. For spending advocates, dedicating revenues is usually part of a minimax—for "minimize the maximum regret"—strategy. The maximum regret is the most distasteful outcome that could occur; in budgeting, it is a large reduction in funding. Dedication protects against such losses because dedicated funds are not part of the general fund that receives most scrutiny. Yet dedication also ties the budgetary prospects of a program to the ability of a revenue source to keep producing income. Revenues can decline or fluctuate cyclically, leaving unfulfilled the appetites of program advocates for growth. In the 1970s, for example, highway spending from the Highway Trust Fund was constrained because increased gasoline prices reduced consumption, which lowered excise tax receipts. Because of this downside to the tactic, dedication is perhaps of most use when prolonged fiscal stress is expected.

Many dedications were carried out by statutorily describing a program as a *trust fund,* a symbolically important label (Derthick 1979, 228–51). This tactic played on the common belief that government trust funds were fiduciary in character, containing funds that couldn't be used for any other purpose. But the fiduciary implication of the trust label was a gross fiction. Only a small percentage of trust fund receipts were dedicated by court decisions or negotiated agreements; the great bulk were dedicated by statutes that could be amended or repealed. Another symbolic effect of the trust fund label was that it suggested that trust funds were self-financing, needing no augmentation from general revenues. This perception was also false, as only about three-quarters of trust fund outlays were financed by dedicated taxes.[1]

Beyond these perceptions, another reason that trust funds were advantaged in budgetary competition was procedural. As I mentioned in chapter 4, prior to the adoption of the unified budget in 1969, trust funds were excluded from the regular budget. This status was a partial stimulus for the creation of the Highway Trust Fund.[2] Although trust funds were included in the budget in 1969, they continued to enjoy other procedural protections. John Cogan has argued that the primary protection was jurisdictional.

> Establishing tax-financed trust funds and placing jurisdiction over them primarily in the tax writing committees created a revenue bias in favor of trust fund taxes and against general fund taxes. Faced with the choice of raising trust fund revenues or general fund revenues, the tax writing committees would naturally favor the former. The proceeds of trust fund taxes were directly tied to well-identified benefits, while the proceeds of general fund taxes were, by their very nature, spread among a diffuse array of programs, not all of which share the same degree of popularity. Moreover, since the tax writing committees had jurisdiction over trust fund expenditures, they would determine how the trust fund tax proceeds would be spent. Decisions regarding the expenditure of general revenues, on the other hand, would be made primarily by other Congressional committees. Responding to the incentives provided by the jurisdictional assignment, the tax writing committees substituted trust fund revenues for general fund revenues. (1988, 5)

The Congressional Budget Act exempted most trust funds from the backdoor spending controls that required other proposed mandatory spending to be referred to the Appropriations committees. Trust funds were also protected from permanent sequestration by the Gramm-Rudman-Hollings Act—trust funds had to temporarily delay some obligations, but these sequestered moneys

1. For a succinct review of budgetary reality for trust funds, see Congressional Budget Office 1990a, 47–53.

2. A useful history is provided by Wheeler 1978. See also Mudge 1982.

remained in the balances of trust funds. In contrast, sequestered moneys from federal funds (that is, nontrust funds) were permanently canceled.[3]

Trust funds were also privileged because they were often allowed to earn interest on the unspent portion of the balances in the funds.[4] These balances were lent to the Treasury, which reduced the need of the Treasury to borrow from the public. Laws that created funds required the Treasury to pay interest on these borrowings. Not only did this practice provide additional financing for trust funds, it also penalized controllers who caused extended delays in obligating a trust fund's balances. Accumulating interest on larger balances generally meant that in following years there would be more money available for obligation. (On the other hand, should the balances become so large that they couldn't be effectively spent over a reasonable short period, then the trust fund might be susceptible to a raid.)[5]

From a political perspective, dedicated revenues help spending advocates economically use their political resources. They need not lobby each year just to maintain an acceptable level of appropriations. In contrast, with astute timing, dedicated financing may protect a program that would otherwise suffer from variations in political support. This logic was used by labor organizations in 1987 when trade deficits were high. Advocates attached a provision to a trade bill that would have dedicated up to 1 percent of an import's value to a fund that would finance relocation and training programs for workers displaced by foreign competition (see Cooper 1986, 88).

Another example of trying to take advantage of a generally favorable political climate was when the IRS attempted to create a trust fund for its administrative expenses. The fund would have been financed by penalties and interest from taxpayers and was proposed by the IRS during consideration of the Tax Reform Act of 1986, one goal of which was to increase the fairness of the tax code. Deficit pressures also suggested the tactic, for when the IRS hired more auditors, revenues often increased by much more than the additional administrative expenses. Although the Senate agreed to the proposal, the House refused, because of the well-publicized failures in Philadelphia in which employees dumped tens of thousands of returns in the trash *before* they were processed.[6]

---

3. The use of the trust fund label reached an absurd point with the late General Revenue Sharing program (GRS). This account, which was financed *entirely* out of general revenues, was labeled a trust fund to prevent the Nixon administration from impounding GRS funds.

4. This is the only characteristic that differentiates trust funds from "special" funds.

5. A sophisticated version of this tactic is to require the Treasury to pay interest to the trust fund at a rate that exceeds the Treasury's marginal cost of borrowing from the public.

6. "The I.R.S. as a Self-Financing Operation?" *New York Times*, 1 July 1986, sec. A.

The large number of dedicated funds is evidence that this tactic diffused widely. An example of how diffusion can occur is provided by the history of programs that were associated with Gerald Mossinghoff, who was the head of the Patent and Trademark Office (PTO) in the early 1980s. At the time, the PTO was processing patent applications quite slowly. To reduce these pendency periods, the PTO needed to upgrade its computers, but pressure on appropriation bills made this hard to accomplish. With the support of inventors, Mosinghoff convinced the Congress to write precise language into law in 1984 that increased fees and dedicated them to the PTO account. Subsequently, Mosinghoff became a lobbyist for the pharmaceutical companies. Lo and behold, the companies supported user fees to pay part of the operating costs of the Food and Drug Administration (FDA), as long as these funds speeded reviews of new drug applications. Initially, this fee increase and dedication was blocked by the House Appropriations Committee. The committee didn't like the precedent it would have set for agriculture inspection programs, which were considered in the same appropriation bills as the FDA. In addition, the Reagan and Bush administrations wanted a portion of the fees to go to the Treasury rather than to the FDA, which caused the pharmaceutical companies to oppose these proposals. When the Bush administration finally agreed to fully dedicate the funds, dedication was passed in 1992 (Rovner 1992).

The dedication tactic was much less advantageous when controllers countered by subjecting dedicated funds to annual obligation controls. The contrasting experiences in the 1980s of the Land and Water Conservation Fund and eight other dedicated funds for wildlife and recreational programs provides a good example. One of the latter programs provided grants to the states for sport fishing programs and was known popularly as the Wallop-Breaux fund. It was financed by excise taxes on fishing equipment and motorboat supplies, and these revenues were permanently available for obligation. The value of this dedication was increased by a 1984 provision that increased these taxes and converted the fund from a special fund into a trust fund, allowing the fund to earn interest on its unobligated balances.

The Land and Water Conservation Fund (LWCF) provided funds for land acquisition by the National Park Service and other agencies. Established in 1965, it was financed from user fees and proceeds from land sales. In response to slow revenue growth, spending advocates convinced the Congress to dedicate a portion of Outer Continental Shelf (OCS) lease receipts to the fund. In 1976, Congress further required that more OCS receipts be made available if appropriations fell below a specified level.

There was a reasonable rationale for dedicating funds to both programs: fees paid by those depleting natural resources would be used to create or save other natural resources. However, the LWCF's dedication was much less advantageous than that of the Wallop-Breaux fund. The difference was that the LWCF was subject to the obligation limits included in annual appropriation bills, and the Wallop-Breaux fund was not. This constraint caused the LWCF's balances to appreciate to over $5.1 billion by fiscal year 1987, with appropriations out of the LWCF in that year amounting to only $211 million. Discontent with these results led the House Interior Committee to propose that the obligation limitation for LWCF be repealed (the House did not agree) and a presidential outdoor recreation commission to suggest that the program become a "true" trust fund (that is, not subject to obligation limits). But administration controllers opposed these changes and proposed as well that the funds going into the Wallop-Breaux fund be undedicated (Corn 1986; Glicksman and Coggins 1984; President's Commission on the American Outdoors 1986, 194–96).

Although an appropriation limitation on dedicated funds can be constraining, it may also create an opportunity for a shell game. This was the case for the aviation trust fund, which was financed by ticket and fuel taxes and interest from the Treasury. Because of obligation limitations enacted in annual appropriations bills, the fund accumulated a balance of over $5 billion by 1987. Aviation spending advocates complained that this balance violated what they believed was the principle of trust fund budgeting—taxes were supposed to be quickly used for improving airports and airways. They maintained that OMB was sitting on the aviation trust fund balances in order to artificially lower the deficit, rather than delaying funds to assure efficient purchases by the FAA, as OMB claimed.

While there was probably *some* truth to this accusation, aviation advocates were largely perpetuating an illusion, for the excise taxes they had paid were not the only sources of financing for airports and airways. Over the years, the Congress provided general revenues to pay the salaries of air traffic controllers, rather than paying them out of trust fund receipts. These appropriations were forced by a provision in the authorizing law designed by aviation advocates. When appropriations for grants to airports and for equipment purchases fell below specified floors, the law limited the amount of trust fund financing for FAA operating costs. The floors were set at artificially high levels—ones that might satisfy a Congress with strong pork-barrel preferences but that a typical president would find veto bait. Consequently, general revenues would have to be appropriated to keep the FAA operating, and the trust fund "balance" could grow to a level sufficient to justify moaning and groaning about the "skyway robbery" of the aviation trust fund.[7]

---

7. See, for example, Extensions of Remarks of Rep. Glenn M. Anderson, "Nation's Aviation Industry Opposes Trust Fund Diversion," *Congressional Record,* 31 July 1989, E 2736. For a detailed review of this shell game, see CBO 1988.

Capitalize High Levels of Support

Capitalization provides more financing than needed to cover obligations in the budget year. The tactic is based on, yet also degrades, the full-funding accounting principle. A program has a long-term goal, and to reach this goal, its advocates freely acknowledge that the cost will be huge. Since the goal is so important, it makes sense not only to project these huge costs, but also to appropriate all of the absolutely necessary funds up front. Typically with capitalization of this type, confidence runs out of bounds. Ignored is the truth that grand plans rarely work as planned, as is the usually preferable option of providing financing over a series of milestones. Capitalization disturbs budgeting's routine schedule.

Once capitalized, a program can obligate funds at times of its choosing. In the absence of capitalization, decreasing political support might be expected to cause a decline in a program's annual appropriation. But with capitalization, a positive action—a rescission—is *required* to reduce the program's financing. And as observers of American politics know well, inaction is more likely than action.

Like dedication, capitalization may be accompanied by other exemptions from budgetary accountability. When administrators of capitalized programs make poor decisions, they are not checked by the annual appropriations process, and this is a good recipe for scandal. (Remember the incrementalist's mantra that "frequent interaction builds confidence and trust"?) The tactic of capitalization, therefore, is likely to be more successful in the long run if programs are administered by an organization with a culture that fosters responsible spending.

A great example of the capitalization tactic and its associated risk is provided by the Synthetic Fuels Corporation (SFC). This quasi-governmental corporation was authorized in the Energy Security Act in 1980, in response to the OPEC-induced price squeeze of the latter 1970s. The SFC was organizationally separated from the Department of Energy, exempted from government pay scales and other routine controls, and provided with a lump sum appropriation of over $17 billion.

One reason the SFC was given this independence was the desire to bring experienced financial and energy experts into an organization that was relatively free of the bureaucratic procedures that frequently complicate public administration. The other cause was political. Playing on the short-term favorable political environment—the energy crisis—its sponsors advocated capitalization for the SFC. Capitalization would protect the program when support from the program declined—that is, after OPEC broke up, as cartels eventually do. An opponent of SFC remarked,

> People like Dan Dreyfuss [a staffer for the Senate Environmental Committee] have told me that they never believed that the goals they proposed would be met. They just wanted to make sure that when oil prices declined and the program started to lose favor, they'd have 500 million barrels of capacity, and the government couldn't turn its back on it.

An OMB technician described the process through which SFC was designed.

> We "used" budget concepts on that one because the White House had a mission. . . . We originally thought we'd set it up as a trust fund because of the import charge revenues. But then they said they wanted it to be a business-type enterprise that would get all of their money up front. When we found out that the White House wanted no salary ceilings and no OMB review, well, then *we* hit the ceiling. [A top OMB staffer] thought we'd at least show the effect in the budget, so we invented the reserve account in the Treasury, which became the parking lot for all of this dough. Still, there's no apportionment, and Synfuels set up a zero-balance checking account with Riggs [a local bank]. That way the Treasury can't say that Synfuels couldn't allow an obligation to occur. In retrospect, we did too good of a job.

Shortly after the SFC began operation, OPEC's solidarity broke and energy prices declined, and the SFC's management also committed horrendous operational errors. Political support for the program predictably declined as well. But with $17 billion already appropriated to the SFC, most of the budgetary debate turned on *how* instead of *whether* these funds would be obligated. It wasn't until 1984, when dissatisfaction with the program's management apparently crossed a threshold, that the Congress cut back the program's unobligated budget authority by 45 percent. In 1985, in the face of congressional pressure to rescind additional funds, the SFC successfully rushed to obligate a large portion of the targeted monies.[8] Capitalization thus enabled SFC to maintain spending in the face of strong opposition.[9]

---

8. Robert E. Taylor, "Synfuels Agency Is Moving to Commit Over $3 Billion before Congress Shuts It," *Wall Street Journal,* 15 August 1985, 54. Another example of capitalization, comparable in the long run of its saga, is that of the mandatory funding for timber production activities in the Tongass National Forest. See debate in the *Congressional Record,* 13 July 1989, H 3685–3718.

9. At the end of 1985, opposition to the SFC grew to be too great, and a decision was made to eliminate the program. But as part of the deal to abolish the SFC, a "new" program was created with a related purpose: the Clean Coal Technology Program. In a repeat of the advance capitalization strategy, $400 million of unobligated SFC funds were transferred to this program, and made available as an advance appropriation for fiscal years 1986–88. See statements in the

A variant of the capitalization tactic affects when appropriations are received by programs. Most programs are subject to the apportionment process, in which portions of an appropriation are doled out by OMB during the fiscal year. The Corporation for Public Broadcasting (CPB) arranged to receive special treatment. Established in 1967 as a quasi-governmental organization, it was granted a two-year advance appropriation—that is, in fiscal year one, appropriations were provided for fiscal years two and three. A number of rationales were advanced for this special procedure: it would make planning easier, the advance appropriations could be used as seed money from private fund-raising, and it would insulate CPB from short-run political pressures on its programming decisions (this latter goal has not been fully met). Despite this protection, CPB, like most domestic spending, suffered from the first year of the Reagan budget cuts, as the reconciliation act in 1981 cut its authorization of appropriations roughly in half. But CPB saved some of its special advantage in the midst of this bad situation. It successfully lobbied for language that required that the CPB receive all of its appropriations by 1 October of the fiscal year. Quick apportionment made rescissions or impoundments impossible, and also prevented CPB funds from being sequestered in 1987.[10]

Another advantage to the CPB of the rapid transfer of its appropriations was that it earned interest on the funds. Grantees often reaped similar profits by arranging to receive grants early and investing funds until they were needed. (The federal government also did the opposite—paying bills late—but on balance the government lost money from the timing of payments and receipts.) For much of the 1980s, OMB unsuccessfully tried to reduce this spending (even though larger state and local government profits from arbitrage investments on tax-exempt bond proceeds were restricted). Attempts by spending advocates to use the tactic continued even after OMB stepped up its campaign for additional restrictions. For example, early in 1987, the Congress passed the Clean Water Act over the President's veto, including a program in which the federal government would help capitalize state revolving funds for water-treatment facilities. Later that year, EPA decided that it would provide letters of credit to states in lieu of actually transferring cash, as language in the act apparently allowed them to do. These letters of credit wouldn't allow the state governments to earn interest, unlike cash that was transferred and could be invested; this was all the more important because the obligation of funds for the program was extremely slow. Senator Moynihan, a strong spending advocate

---

Congressional Record of Senators Domenici and Byrd 10 December 1985, S 17318–23 and the House debate 31 July 1985, H 6991–7006.

10. Other, often less successful examples of this advance appropriation strategy can be found in education grant programs. See listing of "Advance appropriations, advance funding, and forward funding" in the president's *Budget,* and CBO 1977.

for the program, responded by proposing an amendment that would have forced EPA to transfer cash beginning in 1989. The amendment was turned down only because of OMB's insistence that it would count higher outlays under the cash plan (Gurwitt 1989). In 1990, the Congress and the president wrote into law the Cash Management Improvement Act, which should prevent premature drawdowns of funds.[11]

Like funds with large balances of dedicated revenues, capitalized programs may attract attention from parasites. This was the fate of state legalization impact assistance grants. In 1986, when the federal government eased the legalization of resident aliens, it responded to heavy lobbying from states with many immigrants by providing grants to fund English and civics courses and other assistance. A permanent appropriations of $1 billion a year was provided for four years. After two years, much of the first two years' funds had not been spent, and advocates of helping emigrants from the Soviet Union proposed to transfer $200 of these funds to their cause. This attention helped the administration rescind much of the capitalizing appropriations over the next two years (Kirschten 1989).

Diversify Financing

A program that has more than one financing source has diversified, in much the same way that an investor can hold a broad portfolio or a business can produce a variety of products. In government, diversified financing sources include transfers from other accounts, voluntary contributions, the proceeds of one-time asset sales, and third-party payers for benefit programs.

Businesses use diversification to reduce risk, and so can government programs. Most important is that diversification can protect against the risk of elimination—when one source of financing is cut, there will still be financing from another source. Diversity may also allow an end run around restrictions on financing that are intended to serve as controls on policy. In these cases, appropriators may prohibit an agency from spending *appropriated* funds on particular projects, but agencies substitute *nonappropriated* funds to get around such limitations. Allen Schick once called this tactic "multipocket budgeting," citing its use by the Smithsonian Institution, which receives substantial funding from the private sector to supplement its appropriation (1978). But perhaps the tactic should be renamed as "the Ollie," in light of the Iran-contra case.

Diversity in financing can also be used to exceed ceilings on spending. The history of the stock and industrial funds of the Department of Defense show how. Stock funds purchased and maintained inventories of goods (fuel,

11. P.L. 101–453; House Report. 101–696, 13 September 1990. Though see GAO 1992b.

uniforms, etc.) for resale to their customers, appropriated accounts in DOD (for example, the Navy account for operation and maintenance). Industrial funds provided services (transportation, printing, etc.) to the same customers. The stock and industrial funds were working capital funds, and unlike other accounts in the DOD were not subject to annual appropriation limitations. Controllers gave this flexibility to the working capital funds to allow fund managers to make cost-effective bulk purchases for the stock funds and to operate the industrial activities efficiently.

An effect unintended by controllers was that the capital funds increased the financing flexibility of appropriated funds.[12] For example, in 1968, the capital funds apparently were used to avoid budgetary limitations. The Department of Defense changed the recognition of obligations by the appropriations accounts of their purchases from capital funds from *when orders were placed* to *when purchased goods or services were taken out of inventory.* For goods or services that took time to deliver, this allowed the appropriated accounts to delay the recognition of obligations for at least a fiscal year, thus serving the appropriated accounts as a short-term supplemental source of financing. The folk wisdom about this change was that it was made to help DOD finance the Vietnam War in a year when fiscal stress was high. After this date, DOD was inconsistent in its recognition of obligations. It sometimes selectively recorded obligations upon the placement of orders when doing so would effectively prevent appropriations from lapsing. GAO found that over $250 million in appropriations were improperly extended through use of this technique for fiscal year 1982 alone. As an OMB analyst responsible for overseeing DOD complained, with frustrated exaggeration, "They've effectively eliminated one-year appropriations."[13]

Another example was the use of the General Service Administration's Federal Buildings Fund as a source of financing by agencies. This variant of the diversification tactic will be familiar to those who know how depreciation can be used as a handy source of cash. The fund owns many buildings occupied by agencies, for which the agencies pay rent out of appropriated funds. If GSA didn't receive rent payments, it would be stuck with operating losses unless it reduced the building services provided to the agencies. Yet agencies were able to obtain appropriations language that ordered the agencies to reduce their payments to GSA, but which at the same time ordered GSA to provide the same square footage to these agencies. This supplemented agency financing by raiding GSA's capital. In 1991, GAO calculated that such rent restrictions cost

12. Perhaps this should have been expected given the well-known difficulty of allocating indirect costs.

13. See Maroni and White 1986; GAO 1983a, 1984a, 1989d; D. Morrison 1987c, 1992b; Twight 1989.

the FBF about $4 billion from 1975–89 (in 1989 dollars). (This estimate was too low, for on occasion agencies even failed to forward all of their appropriations for rent to GSA.) Scorekeeping practices were changed in 1990 to charge the Appropriations Committees for these raids.[14]

Even the professional financiers at the Treasury Department used the diversification tactic. In the 1960s and 1970s, the department supplemented its appropriations for salaries and expenses by raiding the Exchange Stabilization Fund—an off-budget fund that traded foreign currencies. And the Bureau of Public Debt on numerous occasions made up for appropriations shortfalls by reducing the compensation paid to the Federal Reserve Banks for fiscal agent services. (The Fed covered its costs by reducing the amount of its profits returned to the Treasury, but these receipts of the Treasury were counted as revenues.)

At times, the desire for diversification can lead to the development of proposals that many consider ludicrous. Consider the most recent "war on drugs." Like other government efforts of this type, this war featured extremely ambitious goals and required long, multitheater campaigns. Because many members of Congress were not eager to pay the cost of a full-scale war, some searched for alternative financing. The silly season started with a proposal from Chairman Whitten that the financing for the proposed Supplemental Appropriations Act for the Unfunded Authorization to Fight the War on Drugs (H.R. 2347)

> shall be derived from new receipts to the Treasury resulting from criminal fines collected pursuant to the plea agreement in the criminal case United States V. Drexel, Burnham, Lambert Inc.

The Administration's "drug czar" and two groups of senators then followed with proposals to sell

> $4 billion in small-denomination drug bonds that would mature within 12 years and pay annual yields of up to 4 percent. The money would go into a newly created "Drug War Trust Fund" with the proceeds earmarked for new prison construction, more federal prosecutors, drug treatment and other anti-drug programs. . . .
>
> The search for new ways to fund the drug war has become increasingly critical in recent weeks as Bennett puts final touches on his national "anti-drug" strategy due for release Sept. 5. Bennett confirmed that his plan is

---

14. See Armbrust, Isaacson, and Musell 1983; testimony of L. Nye Stevens, General Accounting Office, "Long-Term Neglect of Federal Building Needs," before the Senate Committee on Environment and Public Works," 1 August 1991.

"going to cost more money," which might have to come out of other government programs.

But the ambitious scope of Bennett's agenda—expected to include substantial increases in aid to state and local governments—already is running up against President Bush's pledge not to raise taxes. Bennett appeared to hint at that yesterday after a meeting with a delegation of U.S. mayors.

"I'll go on record: Crack is worse than taxes," Bennett told reporters after the meeting. But he quickly added that, while tax increases may be needed "down the road," there were other budget-cutting proposals that should be looked at first, such as cutting congressional "pork."

The drug war bond idea seems at first one way to avoid any of these tough choices. . . . To pay off the bonds when they mature and avoid adding to the deficit, proponents have recommended a new "check-off" line be included on federal income tax forms. Taxpayers could designate that a portion of their refunds go for the drug program.[15]

Obligations

Obligation tactics limit the ability of controllers to prevent agencies from obligating funds. These tactics succeed because financing requests *must* be approved after obligations are made; the unacceptable alternative would be that the government violate its promises.

This section begins with the obligation tactic of indexing. Indexing allows programs to automatically increase obligations in line with cost increases. The other major obligation tactic described here adjusts the discretion held by administrators to obligate funds. Spending advocates can reduce the influence of controllers who want to be active overseers of administrators by limiting administrative discretion. In contrast, when controllers are not active, then spending advocates can convince agencies to take advantage of their discretion.[16]

Increase Spending Automatically

Indexing provisions force automatic increases in obligations based on annual changes in measured indices of prices, costs, or wages. The most common

15. Michael Isikoff, "'War Bonds' Considered for Bennett Drug Battle," *Washington Post,* 25 July 1989, sec. A; Introductory Statements for S. 1380 and S. 1389, *Congressional Record,* 24 July 1989, S 8612–14, S 8625–28.

16. Another obligation strategy, mentioned in the previous chapter, is to convert from discretionary to mandatory status. This requires spending on all eligible beneficiaries rather than allowing rationing of benefits among the potentially eligible.

form of indexation is the cost-of-living adjustment or COLA, which increases benefit payments by the rate of change over the previous year in a price index. In contrast, many health programs are indexed directly, in that reimbursements to health care providers cover cost increases. (In the 1980s, some health programs were partially deindexed by caps on reimbursement.)

Indexation provisions were approved in waves—mostly for retirement programs in the mid-1960s, and then in the 1970s for many other programs, including payments to wool producers, the Presidential election campaign fund, and special benefits for disabled coal miners. As of the late 1980s, over thirty programs were indexed, comprising about a third of federal spending. For those readers who are interested in the full details, R. Kent Weaver's wonderful book on indexing fully describes the dynamics of indexing politics.[17]

Indexing was a beneficial tactic for a number of reasons. The main benefit is almost too obvious to mention—indexing eliminated the need to annually use political resources to support bills that would provide increases to compensate for inflation.[18] The indexing tactic was used both by groups rich in political resources (dairy farmers, for example, who were major campaign contributors) and by groups much poorer in the currency of political influence (coal miners with black lung, for example). Another benefit was that the automatic nature of a COLA conveyed the image that a program's beneficiaries had a *right* to a steady level of benefits, an effect that is discussed more broadly in the next chapter. A final benefit of COLA indexing was that it made programs eligible to participate in a coalition with advocates of the Social Security program. During the 1980s, proposals to reduce COLAs for a broad range of programs were opposed successfully in part because of the lobbying by powerful Social Security advocates against changes in *any* COLAs (see, e.g., Rauch 1985b).

One program that was not formally indexed was the veterans compensation program. A COLA was provided annually for this program, *but not automatically;* rather, the Congress annually authorized the COLA through *discretionary* action. There were three reasons for this failure to seize an apparent tactical opportunity, all of which are linked to the extraordinarily strong political support enjoyed by veterans. First, the discretionary COLA procedure gave the Veterans committees annual opportunities to claim credit.

---

17. Additional discussion of indexation may be found in Congressional Research Service 1981; and DeMilner 1981, chap. 4.

18. See also Derthick 1979. A popular story in Washington is that indexing of Social Security was intended to end the partisan bidding wars that produced large discretionary benefit increases. Derthick makes clear in chap. 17 that advocates of the program thought that indexing was a great idea *when added to* a large discretionary increase in benefits.

Second, the "must-pass" COLA bills provided legislative vehicles for additional spending proposals. Third, some veterans advocates hoped that they could enact a COLA that would be larger than would be provided by the automatic calculation.

This discretionary procedure presented a risk under Gramm-Rudman-Hollings, for the law protected only automatic COLAs from sequestration. When the first sequestration order went into effect in March 1986, the veterans compensation COLA was de facto exempt; it had been provided the past December. Yet, the second sequester would have occurred prior to the next COLA, making the COLA subject to cancelation. The response of veterans spending advocates was to amend Gramm-Rudman-Hollings to require the assumption of an automatic increase for veterans in the Gramm-Rudman-Hollings baseline, *even though the increase was to be provided by discretionary action.* This was an exception that proves the importance of rules—veterans had the political resources to make indexing generally unnecessary, but they still needed to "index" their program to avoid the budgetary control of sequestration. Another risk of the tactic was shown in 1990, when a dispute over benefits for Agent Orange victims delayed passage of the veterans COLA provision by the time COLAs were automatically provided to other benefit programs.[19]

Federal government civil servants also attempted an indexing tactic, but were less successful because the indexing procedure could be ignored. The Federal Pay Comparability Act of 1970 established a procedure that could have led to a rough equalization of public- and private-sector pay. A board was established to survey private-sector salaries, compare them to federal salaries, and then determine the federal pay raises that would make private and federal salaries comparable.[20] However, the act also established an alternative procedure, in which the president could recommend smaller pay increases. (The Congress could overturn the plan with a one-house veto, but after the *Chahda* decision, this procedure became unconstitutional.) The alternative plan option was used by the president in each year after 1978, causing federal workers to be paid less than they would be under the comparability procedure (Hartman 1983; House Committee on Post Office n.d.).

A program with even weaker political support was the Aid to Families with Dependent Children program (AFDC). Like Social Security and other indexed benefit programs, AFDC grew by leaps and bounds through categori-

---

19. Bill McAllister, "Hill Dispute Killed Vets' Benefit Bill," *Washington Post,* 30 October 1990, sec. A.

20. While this procedure differs in some respects from the typical procedure for indexing by COLA, it resembled it by enabling automatic spending increases following comparisons to representative values.

cal changes in the late 1960s and early 1970s. But AFDC was not protected by indexing from the inflation of the late 1970s and 1980s, and the average benefit declined in real terms over this period. The failure of spending advocates to convince the government to adopt indexation was partially due to a program-specific barrier. Unlike Food Stamps and most other indexed programs, AFDC benefit levels were set by the states. Adoption of indexing for AFDC would have required a significant redesign of this program (see Weaver 1988, 111–15).

Adjust Agency Discretion

In the classic iron-triangle model, agencies cooperate with client interest groups and solicitous congressional committees to direct funds to favored programs, with no controllers involved. This model once may have been a good description of the pattern of influence for many programs, but it surely is no longer. Controllers usually reduce agency discretion to obligate funds for preferred objects of expense and at preferred paces.

Most discussions of agency budgetary discretion have focused on the trade-off between accountability and efficiency. Elected officials often reduce agency discretion because agencies abused the flexibility they were initially granted.[21] Unfortunately, accountability controls are often used to adversely micromanage programs. As important as is the trade-off between accountability and efficiency, there is another way to understand the level of budgetary discretion allowed agencies. The degree of discretion granted to agencies does not simply reflect the level of trust decision makers have that agencies will spend money properly.[22] It is also determined by the tactical actions of spending advocates and controllers.[23] For example, when spending advocates can't count on controllers being inactive, they often attempt to *limit* the discretion granted to agencies. This tactical approach may seem paradoxical at first, because limits generally imply controls on spending. However, this tactic actually *prevents* controllers from interfering with agencies.

Consider how spending advocates can react to one way that controllers obstruct agency spending plans: controlling *when* obligations are created. At the extreme, controllers may force an agency to stop creating obligations until financing lapses, or until obligations are thought to be no longer necessary or

21. The best discussion of budgetary discretion is by I. Rubin 1993, 234–52.

22. An interesting recent example was the controversy over how foreign contributions for the Desert Storm war would be treated. The administration's proposal to place the funds in a National Defense Gift Fund, a trust fund exempt from appropriations controls, enraged the Congress. See Doherty 1990.

23. A fascinating historical discussion of tactics that adjust discretion may be found in Fisher 1975, chaps. 3–5. See also Pitsvada 1983, 83–101.

even feasible. Spending advocates can respond by mandating speedy obligations. An example is provided by a 1987 law (P. L. 100–11) that required the "timely issuance" of grants to school districts for cleaning up asbestos. Although the Congress had previously appropriated $50 million for this purpose, the administration quickly proposed to rescind almost all of the funds and backed up its intent by not distributing grant applications to the school districts. Their hope was that by postponing the process of grant review, they would push receipt of grants beyond the summer, practically the only period when most schools could remove asbestos. Congress responded by passing a law that forced the administration to obligate the grants by March.[24]

Controllers can also review the purposes of spending, looking for programs to cut. A tactic to prevent such cuts is to specify the purposes for which funds must be spent. This approach is commonly called earmarking. During the nineteenth century, earmarks often were placed in the law. After the adoption of the Budget and Accounting Act of 1921, most earmarks were included in legislative reports. Even though these reports usually didn't have the force of law, spending advocates in the Congress could expect that agencies would respect these congressional requests—after all, the agencies would have to return to Congress for a budget in the following year, when they could be penalized if they ignored earmarks.

The earmarking tactic was recently imported to bills funding academy-based research. Prior to the 1980s, lump-sum appropriations were provided to funding agencies, which allocated research grants through the peer review process. This process produced merit allocations heavily weighted in favor of the large, prestigious research universities. During the 1980s, small colleges and less-prestigious universities reacted to their failures in competitions by gaining numerous earmarks in appropriations bills.[25] Some were aided in this process by a Washington lobbying firm, Cassidy and Associates, that specialized in gaining earmarks. Cassidy turned the revolving door, hiring as lobbyists former congressional staffers with experience in writing earmarks.[26] The firm's activities were chronicled in a fascinating series by *Washington Post* reporter Dan Morgan.

> Until 1985, the National Defense Stockpile Fund was a little-known entity in the federal bureaucracy that bought and sold scarce commodities such as chrome and titanium for the country's strategic needs. . . .

24. *Congressional Record,* 24 February 1987, H 759–63.

25. An excellent historical review can be found in Boseman and Rose 1988; see also Savage 1991.

26. Incidentally, the firm's spokesman was named Roy C. Meyers—not me.

> Cassidy . . . persuaded the appropriators to pass millions of dollars through the Stockpile Fund to finance the construction of "strategic material research centers" at universities in their home states and districts.
>
> The Stockpile Fund story illustrates how a successful lobbying idea can mushroom from a brainstorming session in a downtown Washington office into a multimillion-dollar spending program. As Cassidy's president and chief operating officer, James P. Fabiani, recalled the story, it involved a little luck.
>
> A client, the University of Massachusetts at Amherst, was losing scientists and urgently needed new ideas, he said. Cassidy officials learned that the scientists specialized in work on plastic-like materials that could substitute for rare metals such as titanium. Using computerized compilations of appropriations laws, researchers matched up the word "titanium" with the National Defense Stockpile Transaction Fund, and a strategy was born, according to Fabiani.
>
> It was a natural fit. Rep. Silvio O. Conte, the ranking Republican on the powerful House Appropriations Committee, represented the town of Amherst, and had been Fabiani's boss on Capitol Hill until 1982. Fabiani held an education degree from the university.
>
> As ranking minority member of the full committee, Conte is a member of the subcommittee that originated spending legislation for GSA and the stockpile. Cassidy had contributed $500 to Conte's campaign in 1984, and Fabiani had given $1000.
>
> The idea was for Amherst to create a "strategic and critical materials research facility" and have money passed through the Stockpile Fund to finance its construction. Conte had $9.5 million inserted in the House subcommittee's version. To balance it, then-Sen. Paul Laxalt (R-Nev.) put in the same amount on the Senate side for a similar center at the University of Nevada in Reno.[27]

Senator Nunn of Georgia led one reaction to this explosion of earmarks, when the Senate Armed Services Committee deauthorized some earmarks and required the Defense Department to prevent obligation of other earmarks until after it had notified the Congress—a so-called report-and-wait provision (Matlack 1988). Senator Byrd reacted differently to a presentation by West Virginia University officials in support of a "materials research center."

> When a staff member told him that several present were lobbyists, Byrd directed them to wait outside while he met with his constituents.

27. Dan Morgan, "As Federal Funding Tightens, Lobbyists Find a Surer Way," *Washington Post,* 18 June 1989, sec. A.

> "I then began to express to the university people my indignation and anger," Byrd recalled. "I asked them: Why do you think you have to employ a lobbyist? I said I was for anything that benefits West Virginia, and that I was always going to be supportive. I'm on the Appropriations Committee—if I can't do it, nobody can."

Byrd then canceled his support for *this* earmark (he became known as the king of earmarks after he took over the chair of the Appropriations Committee) and convinced the Congress to write into law a requirement that grantees report the names and compensation of consultants and lobbyists that helped them seek the grants.[28]

Earmarking tactics have some drawbacks. Controllers regard earmarks as flagrant violations of the goal that funds be allocated to maximize effectiveness, so they target earmarks for cuts. In addition, since earmarks are specific, the media and auditors can use them to demonstrate wasteful spending and embarrass decision makers. One example was the 1991 proposed earmark to buy a Gulfstream executive jet for the Speaker of the House and other leadership members. (Gulfstream jets are produced in Georgia, which apparently changed Senator Nunn's attitude about the appropriateness of earmarks.) The inevitable labeling of the proposal as "Air Foley," following the "Air Sununu" scandal, proved fatal for the purchase of this plane.[29] On the other hand, though Presidents Bush and Reagan challenged the Congress to rescind many similar earmarks by highlighting supposedly unnecessary projects like research on blueberries and weed control, they largely failed. Many members of Congress learn to bear the criticism because they believe that their constituents expect them to seek earmarks (Starobin 1993a).

If, when controllers are active, spending advocates try to require speedy obligations for preferred purposes, what obligation tactics do they use when controllers are less active? They convince agencies to take advantage of their discretion. Perhaps the best example in the literature is Derthick's captivating story of the loss of control of spending for social service grants. States reclassified expenditures as social services to qualify for federal funding, and program spending more than quadrupled in only three years (Derthick 1975).[30]

This tactic was used by states beginning in the mid-1980s to effectively raise the federal match for Medicaid. The states were stressed by rapid growth

28. Dan Morgan, "Byrd Drops Home-State Effort in Anger over Lobbyists' Role," *Washington Post,* 31 July 1989, sec. A.

29. This was only a temporary setback for Gulfstream. See Steven Pearlstein, "Gulfstream Aerospace: Master Player in Capitol Hill Appropriations Game," *Washington Post,* 9 June 1991, sec. A.

30. A similar explosion in spending occurred during the latter 1980s in the programs providing assistance to states for foster care programs.

in Medicaid, much of it for long-term care. Faced other spending pressures, and then with a recession, the states had to consider serious cuts in Medicaid. Spending advocates in many states came up with an alternative. They convinced the states to encourage Medicaid providers to make "contributions" to states, which qualified for federal matching funds. Providers were also taxed, which boosted the bills they sent to the states; this also increased federal contributions. Once the states received the matching funds, they reimbursed providers for their contributions and tax payments. An example of this approach from Pennsylvania:

> In 1990, a federal court ruled that the state had been underpaying acute care hospitals that treat an unusually high volume of patients eligible for government assistance, and ordered a substantial increase in rates.
>
> Faced with the need to raise Medicaid reimbursements by about $340 million a year, the state found out a way to have the federal government cover the added costs.
>
> Some 170 hospitals receiving Medicaid benefits formed a foundation, borrowed some $365 million for a bank and donated the money to the state treasury. The amount qualified the state for enough federal matching money to pay for the rate increases without resorting to new state taxes. The facilities were quickly reimbursed—sometimes within 24 hours, according to a hospital source.
>
> Former HCFA administrator Gail Wilensky, testifying in a congressional hearing in 1991, called it a "cute trick."[31]

Control of these gimmicks began in 1991, when the Health Care Financing Administration issued draft regulations banning their use. This stimulated negotiations between OMB and the governors and then congressional legislation, which generally restricted use of the gimmicks, albeit with some states grandfathered through 1994. But the Clinton administration, soon after taking office, agreed to renegotiate these limits and released some withheld funds to the states.[32]

Agencies sometimes enjoy discretion because controllers have been lulled to sleep. By showing receipts from its operations, an agency can appear to be well managed or businesslike. A CBO colleague once half-seriously remarked to me that budget officers tend to avert their eyes from such programs because they fear that if they examined the programs they'd find that the receipts were a mistake! This factor probably aided for years the beneficiaries

31. Dan Morgan, "Medicaid Loopholes Closing for Strapped States," *Washington Post,* 7 February 1993, sec. A.

32. Rapp 1992; Rovner 1991; Dan Morgan, "Medicaid Payments Raise Deficit Fear," *Washington Post,* 13 February 1993, sec. A.

of Interior programs that failed to charge market-based fees for grazing and mineral rights. After opponents of these subsidies brought more attention to the issue, they were defeated by the dominance of the "Sagebrush rebellion" within the Reagan administration.[33] With the advent of the Clinton administration, grazing subsidies again became a major issue. Initially, Clinton proposed legislation mandating higher grazing fees, but he withdrew this proposal after opposition from western Democratic Senators. Then, Interior Secretary Babbitt administratively proposed smaller increases in fees, which dissatisfied both environmentalists and subsidized ranchers. Both sides reacted by proposing bills that would reduce administrative discretion. For example,

> "We want to codify any change in the grazing fee system. That codification gives us stability," said Bill Myers, executive director of the Public Lands Council and a director of the National Cattlemen's Association. "We don't want the administrative solution." (Camia 1993, 2150)

Spending advocates from the West also plundered the Interior Department's oil and gas leasing programs during the 1980s. Before 1981, Interior placed individual tracts up for lease and calculated the "fair market value" for the tracts from reasonable models that combined geologic and economic information. After the entrance of Secretary Watt, Interior used its discretion to lease whole areas of tracts. GAO concluded this practice led to decreased competition for the leases, lower government revenues, and higher profits for the lessees. Throughout the process of adopting areawide leasing, Interior claimed that the practice would *increase* government revenues, but there was little data to support this claim (GAO 1981, 1985a; Durant 1992, chap. 8).

Congressional controllers could respond to Watt's spending tactic only by passing a bill; in this case, they would have to pass a bill over President Reagan's veto. In contrast, controllers in the executive branch have a wide range of procedural opportunities to reduce administrative discretion—budget review, apportionment, procurement, and regulatory review processes. Congressional controllers are even more disadvantaged if they do not sit on committees with jurisdiction because oversight of proposed shifts of funds is largely done by committees. Spending advocates usually only need to convince the Appropriations subcommittees to quietly approve the shift.

---

33. *Washington Post,* "Watt Turns Out to Be a Generous Landlord," (1 June 1982, sec. A; J. Davis 1985; T. R. Reid, "Western Grazing Fees Slip Out of Budget Noose," *Washington Post,* 2 February 1986, sec. A; P. Davis 1991.

Summary

Policy-design tactics take advantage of the common fear that controllers will be too strong. Controllers have been most successful in dealing with automatic spending increases, as there have been few new indexations and entitlements since passage of the Congressional Budget Act. On the other hand, spending for the indexed programs and entitlements existing at that time has grown with relatively little constraint. Financing tactics remain especially available for exploitation.

Chapter 7

Tactics for Portraying the Effects of Spending: "It's Worth It"

This chapter explores the use of policy argumentation in budgeting. Policy argumentation is the process by which conditions are identified as problems, and proposed solutions are evaluated for likely success.[1] Policy argumentation in budgeting examines whether proposed spending can help solve publicly defined problems.

Understanding and describing budgetary policy argumentation is relatively difficult. In contrast to budgetary accounting and decision processes, there are no rules for policy argumentation. No rhetorical judges disallow invalid arguments about the supposed effects of spending.[2] Decision makers receive information from a great number of governmental and societal sources and are free to interpret arguments about the effects of spending in the ways that they choose.

The most important within-government sources of information about the effects of spending are the agencies, who defend their requests to the Appropriations committees with "justification books." These documents are aptly named, including interpretations of why programs need requested funds. The agencies also produce evaluation studies, often used in an attempt to resolve disputes about the effects of a program.

Information about the effects of spending also comes from OMB. For most of the 1980s, the administration produced a *Major Themes* volume that accompanied its budget request. Originated by Director James Lynn of the OMB during the Ford administration and expanded during the Stockman years, this volume added detailed arguments for the administration's budget proposals that would not fit in the regular budget documents. In the Bush administration, OMB director Darman integrated this interpretative material fully into the budget's main text.

1. Useful sources include Richard Smith 1984, 44–63; Whiteman 1985, 294–311; Meltsner 1987; Majone 1989; D. Stone 1989, 281–300; Schulman 1988, 263–91; and Schneider and Ingram 1990, 510–29.

2. I use the terms *justifications, arguments, rationales, interpretations,* and *rhetoric* interchangeably in this chapter.

Within the Congress, support agencies and caucuses like the Democratic Study Group and the (Republican) Wednesday Group produce relatively even-handed analyses of the perceived effects of spending. In addition, the "Dear Colleague" letters that are sent from one member of Congress to another are an especially important source of rationales. A staff director for a House Budget Committee member told me that his office received twenty to fifty "Dear Colleagues" a day, and about half of these letters included analysis that was relevant to budgeting.

The term *analysis* is used here with its broadest connotation. Certainly many decision makers have carefully considered how spending will affect agency performance. In addition, though President Johnson's initiative to have all agencies adopt the Planning-Programming-Budgeting System (PPBS) form of program budgeting failed, many agencies now use modifications of PPBS to jointly consider the costs and benefits of spending.[3] But much of what is labeled analysis in the budgetary process does not hold up to the quality standards of professional analysts, particularly the information that comes from outside the government. Many arguments about the effects of spending are simple and emotional; this style is especially prevalent when the method of argumentation is oral—floor debates, committee hearings, and lobbying sessions.

Given the variable quality and many sources of arguments, one might doubt whether there is any structure to the argumentation process. Are there characteristics of budgetary argumentation that shape behaviors, and that can be exploited by budgetary tacticians? I will argue below that there are. First, however, I describe some important arguments made by spending advocates and controllers about the effects of spending. Table 7.1 lists these arguments. While this list is by no means exhaustive, I believe it contains some of the most popular and influential arguments.

Common Arguments about the Effects of Spending

Investments

Perhaps the most common rationale for spending is to claim that spending is an investment. The popularity of this rationale greatly preceded President Clinton's reliance on it.

Investment in the private sector usually means that money is being spent on a project that is expected to return income in the future. For most private investments, an expected yield, or return on investment, is calculated. In gov-

---

3. For reviews of PPBS, see D. Axelrod 1988, 259–308; Wildavsky 1975, part 4; and Schick 1973. For current budget "systems," see Jones 1991, 15–27; Sample 1992, 339–46; GAO 1992a.

TABLE 7.1. Popular Spending Rationales

Investments
Spinoffs
Earned rights
The truly needy
Merit goods
Macroeconomic effects
Federal responsibility
Leveraging
Spending gaps
Disastrous consequences
The level playing field

ernment, the basic meaning of the term investment is the same—spend now for future benefits—but the implications are often different. Rather than the hope of profits, a government investment often signifies that spending in the present will allow the government to *avoid* larger costs in the future. For example, the Department of Labor estimates how job training programs reduce future costs for unemployment compensation, delinquency, incarceration, and welfare dependency.

Investment arguments are effective because they rebut the impression that budgetary accounting creates—accounting depicts spending as "costly," but investment arguments uses the same metric to portray it as "cheap." The argument takes the following form: "Yes, dollars are spent now, but the real cost is much lower because dollars will be coming back in future years. If you can afford to wait for a bit, then this spending will actually save you money."

In addition, investment arguments are consistent with one purpose of budgetary control, which is to reduce the deficit (government dissaving) in order to stimulate investment and economic growth. The current practice of national income accounting complicates attainment of this goal, for all government spending, even spending that most likely produces long-term benefits, is counted as consumption. Spending advocates can criticize this accounting practice and suggest that cuts in their programs would be false savings, ones that would reduce the reported deficit but also reduce total investment.[4]

Another important distinction between private and public uses of the investment label is that yields from public investments are often difficult, if not impossible, to quantify. Many government goods and services are given away for free to increase social equity, or because there is no efficient way of charging for or restricting access to them. But the inability to cite specific yields has not deterred some advocates from using the investment argument.

4. For discussions of this issue, see Congressional Budget Office 1990b, 1987b; Rauch 1989.

Consider the following from the Corporation for Public Broadcasting's 1987 *Annual Report:*

> In FY 1987, the American people through their Congressional appropriation to the Corporation for Public Broadcasting, invested $200 million in public broadcasting.
>
> What was the return on that investment?
>
> Unlike a commercial broadcasting investment, the return didn't come in dollars. Nor could the performance of this unique not-for-profit national enterprise be measured in terms of the familiar bottom line.
>
> But public broadcasting had, nevertheless, a very real bottom line, a very real return on investment. Its 1987 bottom line was—as in the two decades since the Broadcasting Act of 1967—the priceless enrichment it brought to American society. It was a bottom line of expanded public awareness, stimulating learning, engaging cultural experience, and innovative action to tackle social problems. It was a bottom line shared by Americans at large as well as by the diverse subgroups that make us up: children, adult learners, ethnic and racial minorities, the physically challenged. (32)

This rhetoric began by accepting the logic of the investment argument but then challenged decision makers to be charitable with a program for which it was hard to demonstrate effects. It transformed an unknown quantity to the infinitely valuable "priceless enrichment."

One of the best uses of the investment logic was found in the campaign for increased spending on social service programs. For an example of the argument, the Children's Defense Fund justified its proposed Children's Survival Bill as follows

> The Bill is based on a sound and simple premise: an investment of scarce resource in our nation's children will protect our nation's future.
>
> Children are the country's future workers and taxpayers, its future leaders, artists, teachers, and scientists. Today's children must shoulder the national debt, finance our Social Security system, and lead this country into the twenty-first century. All Americans have a stake in helping healthy and educated children become self-sufficient, creative, and productive adults.
>
> Wise investment in children now is sound national and economic policy in a time of budget crisis. Research proves that children's programs that provide services like prenatal care and immunization save us more money than we spend on them. It costs about $10 to provide a baby with a series of immunizations, compared with hundreds of thousands of dollars

> for a lifetime of care for a child with severe disabilities caused by preventable sickness. Every dollar spent on comprehensive prenatal care save more than $3 in health care in the first year of an infant's life alone. (Children's Defense Fund 1986)

To be able to make such claims, advocates of spending for social services marketed studies of the investment-type character of their programs. For example, the House Select Committee on Children, Youth, and Families produced annual reports entitled *Opportunities for Success: Cost-Effective Programs for Children,* with information drawn from agency studies.

It might be somewhat surprising that spending advocates felt they had to document investment returns; appeals to the heartstrings might be sufficient. Advocates of the programs always used such emotional arguments but found they needed to balance the negative impacts of a tight fiscal environment and the children's lack of political resources. In addition, earlier advocates had suffered from conservative criticism that the programs had not been proven effective—the appeals to the heartstrings were turned into the "bleeding heart" criticism. After studies showed convincingly that some programs were effective, no wonder the investment argument was used.[5] It is now in danger of overuse, however, as President Clinton seems to employ it for all of his favored programs, only some of which will be able to document investment returns.

Spinoffs

Programs often seek to show that there are benefits to spending besides meeting a program's primary goals. These indirect effects are often described as *spinoffs* or *spillovers.* The tactic is often used by advocates for spending on research and development, and the leading case is that of NASA. As part of this effort, NASA annually published a glossy report filled with articles showing new products that manufacturers claim were aided by NASA-supported research.

> An estimated 30,000 secondary applications of aerospace technology have emerged in the 27 years of NASA's existence. These "spinoffs" span so broad a range of public needs and conveniences that it is difficult to find an area of everyday life they have not pervaded. Collectively, they add up to significant gain in terms of human welfare, industrial productivity and

5. Rauch 1984; Rovner 1988; Spencer Rich, "Aiding Children Now, Saving Money Later," *Washington Post,* 4 April 1988, sec. A; Kosterlitz 1988b; Paul Taylor, "Corporate Chiefs Promote Infant Care," *Washington Post,* 7 March 1991, sec. A; Haas 1991a; Kellam 1992. For a critique of the cost-effectiveness evidence, see Graham 1991.

> economic value, dividends on the national investment in aerospace research. (1985, 3)

Reports from the mid-1980s included such advances as fiberglass roofs for shopping malls, computer imagery for cosmetics sales, and a "relaxation system" one large step removed from the Orgasmatron of Woody Allen's *Sleeper.* But most of the claimed spinoff products were more mainstream high-technology improvements.

During its early years, NASA relied on images that were heroic (man in space) and competitive (the space race with the Russians) to justify its spending. The motivational power of these goals weakened after we reached the moon. The spinoffs argument was an attempt to supplement the basic rationale for spending on space and thus broaden its supporting constituency, for few people beside NASA employees directly benefited from its programs (McDougall 1985, 436–49).

Because the spinoffs argument was made so forcefully, researchers of "knowledge utilization" sought to specify the magnitude of indirect benefits from NASA spending. Most found the effects to be quite small (Office of Technology Assessment 1986a, 22–24). Yet the spillover argument remained potent. Consider a 1991 *National Journal* report on the House debate over the space station.

> "Space research in bone-calcium loss may lead to a cure for osteoporosis," Tom D. DeLay, R-Texas, predicted. "Scientists can also tackle hypertension and other cardiovascular diseases and conduct studies of cancer and immunological disorders," Mary Rose Oakar, D-Ohio, added. "America's youth is already disinterested in science and math," Gregory H. Laughlin, D-Texas argued. "Cutting the space station will solidify this decline."
>
> Rep. Jim Bacchus, D-Fla. chose an even more sweeping canvas upon which to paint his vision. "The space station will be useful to the advancement of democracy," he proclaimed.
>
> "The debate was mind-boggling because the House was basically voting in favor of a station that would cause the blind to see and the lame to walk," John E. Pike, space policy director for the Federation of American Scientists, said. "After listening to that debate, I was embarrassed for the company I was keeping. It was painful. It was deceptive."[6]

---

6. D. Morrison 1991a, 1672. See also A. Rubin 1991. As spending pressures forced two "downsizes" of the station, these dubious claims lost any persuasiveness. The spending rationale then changed (M. Mills 1993).

Earned Rights

Many observers have commented that over recent decades the budget has been transformed from one that largely purchased goods and services to one that largely transfers income from taxpayers to beneficiaries. Understandably, then, a lot of effort has gone into trying to prove that people and organizations deserve their benefits. This section and the following two describe three types of arguments about the worthiness to receive benefits—that the benefits are earned rights, that they are provided only to the truly needy, or that they are for merit goods (see also Schneider and Ingram 1993).

Earned-right arguments seek to create the perception that people or organizations have contributed in some way to the government and are entitled in turn to certain benefits (Straussman 1988). Sometimes financial contributions are claimed—Social Security is the prime example. Given the low correlation between contributions and benefits in this program, the earned-right argument is not very accurate, but it has proved persuasive (Derthick 1979, 224–27).

Implicit contracts are another source of earned-right perceptions. Native Americans claimed that there was a federal duty to spend on their welfare because the United States had violated treaties. Veterans often said that "some vets made the supreme sacrifice for our country" and that surviving vets deserved to be fully compensated for their risk taking. Retired federal employees tried to protect their generous pension benefits by claiming that they accepted lower pay than available to their counterparts in the private sector in return for expected higher-than-average retirement benefits.[7]

Once the earned-right argument is accepted, the debate is almost over. The natural conclusion is that the government would be acting inequitably if it retroactively reduced benefits that people had earned or had to depend on because of government advice (but see Eule 1987). The argument's power is illustrated by the common grandfather design of cuts in earned-right programs. These cuts protect current beneficiaries (the grandfathers) from cuts, shifting the burden of reductions to future beneficiaries (see, e.g., Rotherham 1985).

The Truly Needy

Our society owes a debt to Director David Stockman of the OMB for popularizing the phrase *truly needy* (we also owe debts *because of* David Stockman).[8] His use of this term was an attempt to limit government spending for benefit programs by distinguishing the near-poor from the poor. The difficulty

---

7. On Native Americans, see House Committee on the Interior 1983; on veterans, see Senate Veterans Affairs Committee 1981, 123–61; and Kosterlitz 1988a.

8. At various points in the Reagan administration, "safety net" and "social contract programs" were used in its place.

is that there is no absolute standard for defining poverty. This is a familiar problem to policy analysts, who have long debated the appropriateness of the Census Bureau's poverty thresholds and the OMB-HHS poverty guidelines (e.g., see Ruggles 1990).

Political arguments about how to define and measure poverty take different forms. One approach is to show the number of people unable to afford basic services—who's hungry and who's homeless. These descriptions of the truly needy in classes suggest categorical program designs to aid them. Another approach is to argue that the income of the truly needy is an unacceptably small percentage of the better-off, or that the percentage hasn't narrowed over a period of time, which reveals lack of progress in the fight against poverty. A third approach is to project a dim future for the truly needy because of their current status, because of their reduced chances of finding good jobs, or a dim future for the country, because of the lower-quality labor pool.

Cultural predispositions often affect the success of arguments about who is truly needy. For example, it is extremely unlikely that the full-employment concept of truly needy will be accepted in our country. The culture's work ethic disdains shirkers; lingering racism may also prevent a guarantee of employment.[9] In contrast, the culture symbolically reveres children, which helps arguments for children's programs (though there's certainly room for spending more on these programs) (Steiner 1976). Another cultural impact on the truly needy argument results from the amorphous political definition of the middle class. Numerous programs of the federal government provide subsidies to people who earn many times the poverty line, but when income-related payment limitations are suggested for these programs, their advocates deny that these people are in any way rich (Reischauer 1982; Barnes 1990; DeMott 1990).

The controller's response to the truly needy argument is the simple counterclaim that the beneficiaries are really richer than is commonly thought. An example of how this argument is made—and how it can backfire—is provided by Robert Greenstein, a leading opponent of the Reagan administration's budget policy for welfare programs

> Specifically, he [Stockman] contends that in 1981, 42 percent of all benefits in these programs went to families over 150 percent of the poverty line, and that 150 percent of the poverty line for a family of four that year was $13,390—or 92 percent of the median annual income for employed workers.
>
> The misuse of statistics is particularly striking here. First, Stockman has compared 150 percent of the poverty line for a *family of four*

---

9. This argument is made by, among others, Wildavsky and Cavala 1970.

> ($13,390) to the median income for an *individual* worker. Sorry, but you can't do that. The real numbers go like so: The median income for a family of four in 1981 exceeded $26,000—not $13,390—and 150 percent of the poverty line is about half—not 92 percent—of the median income for a comparably sized family.
>
> Then Stockman counted as part of the income of program beneficiaries the value of health insurance coverage provided by Medicaid and benefits from living in subsidized housing—but he did *not* include in his median income figures for workers either the comparable fringe benefits for employer-paid health insurance or the tax subsidies for mortgage and medical payments that many middle-income families receive. This makes for a neat comparison of apples and oranges.
>
> When you do these comparisons properly, you find that the income and benefits of those participating in the federal programs were far below the living standards of average American families—even before the Reagan budget cuts took effect.[10]

Merit Goods

Some spending is justified primarily by an observation that the purposes of spending are especially worthy *in and of themselves.* Some economists have labeled preferences of this type as *merit goods,* though they have been unable to arrive at a consensus definition of the term. In my view, myth and tradition are largely responsible for instilling preferences to spend on merit goods. Call it the "Mom and apple pie" rationale for spending.

Perhaps the leading example is from budgeting for agriculture programs. The government extensively regulates farming and in some years has provided the majority of farmers' income. Although there have been notable failures of agricultural policy—for example, multimillion dollar payments to individual farms that reorganized to escape limits on income supports, and governmentally acquired surpluses that were so poorly stored they spoiled—support for agriculture spending has been robust. The political mobilization of agricultural interest groups and the intelligent use of the tactics described in the previous two chapters are surely part of the explanation. The symbolic merit good argument for the family farm is another.

> Few economic endeavors have any aura of romance and tradition. We don't get misty at the sight of a chain store framed against a prairie landscape or take comfort in knowing that each morning thousands of

10. Robert Greenstein, "Stockman is Still Cooking the Numbers," *Washington Post,* 19 June 1983, sec. B.

> lawyers head out into the predawn darkness to tend their lawsuits. Farming, though, occupies an honored place in our culture. Even big-city sophisticates who would sooner die than attend a Grange Hall dance find it reassuring that somewhere out there honest folk are working the earth much as it has been worked for centuries.[11]

Despite the fact that agriculture spending generally helps large farms more than it does small family farms, the social appeal of the family farm myth is clearly understood by advocates for agriculture, and they milk it for all it is worth.[12] As a respected observer of agricultural policy-making observed,

> A myth that explains much agricultural legislation is agrarianism or agricultural fundamentalism, or the agricultural creed, or commitment to the family farm, call it what you will. . . . Agricultural fundamentalism, in my judgement, was the prime mover behind the Food Security Act of 1985. The myth is embraced by many nonfarm people as well as by farmers, and, in my estimation, agriculture's legislative gains are not so much prizes won by political power as benefits conferred by an indulgent state. (Paarlberg 1987, 111–17)

Homeownership is another merit good. Like agriculture, homeownership is heavily subsidized by the federal government, and although the effects are very regressive, tax expenditure spending on homeownership is nearly impossible to cut. This is due in part to arguments that such cuts would threaten what all believe to be an exceptionally worthy goal. Consider a Mortgage Bankers of America ad placed in response to the Reagan administration's rather modest proposals to reduce tax subsidies for homeownership in 1986. The text led with the complaint that "the American Dream is Fading," and continued,

> Homeownership goes hand in hand with the promotion of family and other traditional values. It is linked to concepts of property rights, freedom of choice, and independence in one's lifestyle. Homeownership provides a way of building, preserving, and passing on wealth to future generations.[13]

---

11. Gregg Easterbrook, "Making Sense of Agriculture," *Atlantic Monthly,* July 1985, cited in *Congressional Record,* 26 June 1985, S 8883. See also Rapp 1987b.

12. On the roles of small and large farms, see Office of Technology Assessment 1986b.

13. *Washington Post,* 4 February 1986, sec. A. See also De Neufville and Barton 1987; Milgram 1979.

Macroeconomic Effects

Advocates of spending often try to show that spending will improve macroeconomic conditions. The general approach is to commission a study by economists who know how to manipulate assumptions and computations to come up with desired results. They show how spending creates jobs, how a program increases national income through a multiplier, or how cutting a program will be inflationary (because abandoned beneficiaries will have to pay more). During the latter 1980s, a favorite analysis was how spending would be trade enhancing—the most serious macroeconomic concerns of the era often determine the outcome that is emphasized in the analyses.

An example of a macroeconomic-effects argument is a widely disseminated analysis by a retired Stanford professor on the "Economic and Social Benefits of the REA Telephone Loan Program." Prepared to counteract proposals from the Reagan administration, the professor cited a cross-national study (mostly of developing countries) that calculated the growth in gross domestic product (GDP) that was attributable to increased use of telephones, and then estimated that "the GDP attributable to the REA Telephone Loan Programs would be about $850 million in 1980 and growing each year." He continued,

> This sum far exceeds any estimate of the cost of the program. Suppose that the cost to the Federal Government in interest support for the REA Telephone Insured Loans was 5.6%. . . . From these data, the cost to the federal government in interest support for the Telephone Loan Programs can be estimated at $130 million in 1979. The possible benefits in expanded gross domestic product from the Telephone Loan Programs are between six and seven times as large as the cost to the federal government in interest support.
>
> As impressive as this result is, the costs of the programs to the federal government were overstated in this calculation. . . . The REA Telephone Loan Programs have increased the taxable income of rural telephone companies by expanding the number of subscribers served, raising the quality and utilization of their services, and lowering their capital costs. Consequently, a substantial portion of the annual interest cost to the federal government is returned through higher income tax payments by the borrowers. Furthermore, the stimulus of the loans to economic activity results in additional tax revenues to the federal government, possibly making the REA Telephone Loan Programs net contributors to the federal treasury. (Parker 1981, 8–11)

This study provides a good illustration of the limitations of this form of argument—decision makers have learned from years of experience that nearly any desired result can be obtained when paid economists start cranking numbers. Controllers often responded to selective analyses by shifting toward a general equilibrium framework, in which the positive effects of a program are compared to the negative effects elsewhere, which had been conveniently ignored in the criticized analysis. "Yes, new highway construction may add jobs, but the tax increase to finance this construction will increase unemployment correspondingly," and so on. Yet despite this kind of challenge, macroeconomic arguments are still used frequently. According to a report by Burt Solomon,

> The dynamic that spurs studies is more often defensive. "You can't make an assertion around here and not have a number," a Senate committee aide said. "You have to have them because everybody has them, and you look unprepared if you don't." (1987, 1459; see also Stone 1993)

In addition, in a recession, the standards for showing positive macroeconomic effects decline. Many spending advocates argue: "This program deserves support for three reasons: jobs, jobs, and jobs." This justification is as simple as a meditative mantra, but despite its mystical nature, some decision makers find it a reliable way to cope with recession-induced stress.

Federal Responsibility

Primarily in Republican administrations, decision makers supported budget cuts for grant and benefit programs based on the rationale that dealing with some problems should not be the federal government's responsibility. One argument was programmatic: problems vary greatly across local jurisdictions, and the federal government is incapable of tailoring programmatic solutions to this diversity. Another argument was that the federal government is overburdened with problems of its own (minor ones like the national defense and macroeconomic policy) and should leave some problems to the state and local governments, consistent with the dual sovereignty planned by the Constitution.[14]

Spending advocates for these programs, especially from the state and local governments that receive most grants, responded with several counterarguments. One rationale they put forward is the view that only the federal government has the fiscal capacity to address certain problems. For example, when the poor are mobile, they move to generous states, but this disadvantages

14. For a recent discussion of these arguments, see Rivlin 1992.

generous states in the competition between states to keep taxes low. This pressures these states to reduce benefits. The federal government can compensate for this by offering targeted aid to low-capacity, high-effort governments.

In the recurrent debate over federal responsibility, spending advocates try to strip the devolution advocates of their "fiscal federalism" rationales and suggest that they were simply trying to save money by shifting costs. For example, in the mid-1980s, cities and counties claimed that "a vote to kill revenue sharing is a vote to raise local taxes." This was an especially good argument to make against an administration whose political power had grown out of the state and local tax revolts of the late 1970s. But many of the same state and local officials who resisted cuts in grants also criticized the federal government's unbalanced budget, crowing that they acted properly in balancing *their* budgets. Federal government officials, liberal and conservative alike, knew that state and local budgets were balanced only with the help of grants from the feds, which undermined the spending advocates' argument. Yet the political potency of the complaint that federal budget cuts had deleterious effects on state and local fiscal conditions probably was restored during the next recession, which could be blamed on federal mismanagement of the economy.

A typical controller tactic was to argue spending cuts provide better targeting. This threatened spending advocates in several ways. First, better targeting would cancel funding for the less-needy beneficiaries. Second, although it would temporarily *increase* funding for the more-needy beneficiaries, targeting could also cause the less-needy beneficiaries to stop promoting the program, and as the program's supporting coalition decreased in size, its political strength would decline. Both groups thus had incentives to argue back to controllers that programs were already well targeted. These debates often featured state-by-state printouts that showed the distributive effects of the actual policy, and the biases in these analyses often rivaled those found in the macroeconomic projections that were described above (Starobin 1987c). An illustration of the lengths advocates went to make this argument is shown in the following quote on revenue sharing, which was the prototype untargeted design.

> Revenue sharing is a targeted program . . . created not because the federal government had an excess of revenues to share, but because Congress recognized the need to use the larger and broader federal tax base to help mitigate fiscal disparities among state and local governments. (National League of Cities 1986)

Use of the word "targeted" apparently signified that they had found a (unspecified) denominator that showed that some beneficiaries got proportionately less than others! But some advocates recognized that this rhetoric would not retain force, and proposed to counter the Reagan administration attack by converting General Revenue Sharing into a program that would truly reduce fiscal disparities. The failure of the Congress to adopt this approach was explained by one of its sponsors.

> "If you asked everyone up here whether they like targeting, everyone would say yes," said Durenberger, an expert on federalism. "But when it comes down to specifics, each one thinks his state should be targeted."[15]

Leveraging

In corporate finance, *leveraging* is typically used to describe the ratio of debt to equity. Investors in a highly leveraged company can control a lot of assets with little investment, but they also bear the risk of substantial increases in debt-financing costs. The concept of leveraging has migrated to public policy debates, but its usage has been one-sided. It commonly signifies the idea that although the government spends only a little, society will benefit greatly. The mechanism for this wondrous result is that a program's costs will be largely covered by contributions from others.

To some extent, the leveraging argument has been used to make a virtue out of necessity. Program advocates compensated for spending cuts by seeking financial support from other sources—state and local governments, private developers, or charities. When they recognized the difficulty of recapturing the lost federal financing, they began to describe programs as leveraged so as to *retain* the remaining federal government financing. As a housing advocate told me, "We used to worry about the high local share, but now we call it 'leveraging,' and it's supposed to be good!" The argument was most attractive to conservatives who revere the private sector. Regarding the community services block grant, "Giving seed money to attract state, local and private money 'is a pretty good Republican policy,' says Senator Charles E. Grassley" (Kosterlitz 1986, 937).

An example of the leveraging tactic is provided by the reaction to the administration's 1985 proposed cuts in the Community Development Block Grant (CDBG) program. Among the ads run by the National Association of Housing and Redevelopment Officials was one titled "Why a 10-Percent Cut in CDBG Is More Than A 10-Percent Cut." The text included the projection that all the investments in planned CDBG projects would be lost without the seed money from the CDBG program. These arguments often penetrated the Con-

---

15. Howard Kurtz, "Targeting Federal Aid Raises the Question, Who's in Bull's-Eye?" *Washington Post,* 6 December 1983, sec. A.

gress. For example, during a debate on an amendment to terminate the Urban Development Action Grant (UDAG) program, nearly every opponent of the amendment made a statement much like Senator Riegle's.

> We have a leverage factor of 5 to 8 dollars in private investment for every single dollar of UDAG money. So for a very small percentage of Federal incentive we are able to trigger a very substantial private sector investment in projects put together by the private sector, carried out by the private sector, and managed by the private sector.[16]

Such conclusions were typically stated with a confidence that analysts of these programs rarely express (see, e.g., Eisinger 1988).

Spending Gaps

When long-term needs estimates are compared to proposed spending, the shortfall is a spending gap. The most obvious reason for identifying a gap is that the larger the estimated gap, the greater the apparent need for increased funding. An example is provided by a Senate aide who was an advocate of housing programs.

> We decided to look at the total universe of housing needs and draw up a plan for dealing with them. So we took the already assisted, those who met the 30 percent income limits, etc., and we came up with a number that defined the worst cases. Then we assumed that we'd eliminate the need in eight years, so we divided up the units so that FmHA would get thirty-three thousand units and HUD would take one hundred thousand. It really didn't make any logical sense, but it provided a rationale for what we wanted to do.

The controller response in such cases is to question both the size of the gap (it's smaller because there actually are fewer worst cases) and the period over which it must be closed (a longer period allows less spending each year).

Identifying a spending gap is sometimes an attempt to change perceptions of needs. One case was a bill—the Veterans' Health Care Guidelines Act, introduced by Senator Thomas Daschle—that would have required the secretary of veterans' affairs to report whether each budget "is sufficient to fund a level of care that fully meets the anticipated demand for such care" from *all* veterans. The bill was a response to VA's policy of rationing care if funding could not cover demand: veterans with service-connected disabilities were

---

16. *Congressional Record,* 17 October 1985, S 13468.

served first, and care could be denied to veterans suffering from non–service-connected disabilities, except for those who were indigent. (This design reflects different levels of earned rights.) Daschle and supporting veterans' groups were attempting to highlight the needs of those who might be rationed out of care by the system.[17]

The spending-gap tactic has a long lineage in defense policy debates, the most famous example being the (false) claim by Democrats in the late 1950s that there was a missile gap. In the 1980s, the spending-gap tactic was used at different levels of defense budgeting. At the highest level, spending advocates compared the percentage of gross national product (GNP) devoted to defense in the budget year to percentages from earlier years. Advocates were able to show that spending during the 1970s fell far below that of the 1960s. They labeled the 1970ss as "the decade of neglect" and argued that only continuous real growth in defense spending would close the spending gap. Even though the desirability of returning to the 1960s' level of defense spending was never fully explained, the frequent use of this argument suggests that it was viewed as effective.[18]

The spending gap tactic was also used routinely in the Five Year Defense Plan (FYDP), one of the central acts of the annual defense budget process. The FYDP estimated the necessary spending for responding to the "threats" against our country. The process of developing the FYDP followed the guidelines of a sequential rational-planning model, in which objectives were defined before alternatives were surveyed and programs selected. In other words, the threat estimates were generally defined without acknowledgment of a realistic aggregate-funding constraint. Many observers concluded that this method of preparing the FYDP pushed estimated spending requirements up, creating the opportunity for defense advocates to identify a spending gap. For years, spending advocates for defense opposed making the FYDP process more realistic, for fear that recognizing fiscal reality could stimulate decision makers to search for nonmilitary and nonbudgetary ways of responding to some threats (D. Morrison 1987b).

The Navy employed another spending-gap tactic to push for more spending. Early in the Reagan administration, it formally adopted the military strategy of trying to keep Soviet ships bottled up near their ports. To have a chance of succeeding, this forward-offensive strategy required the Navy to have many more ships than were in its inventory. The Navy identified six hundred ships as the minimum needed—the real number was actually a few ships more, but six hundred was a nice round number for rhetorical use. Though many in the Navy

---

17. *Congressional Record,* 19 April 1989, S 4429–30.

18. See *Budget of the U.S. Government, FY 1983* (1982); 3-16–3-18.

argued that they would never carry out the forward-offensive strategy because of the substantial risk of losing most of the ships to Soviet tactical nuclear weapons, the forward-offensive strategy was used to justify the desired buildup. The debate largely shifted to a consideration of when and how the target of the six-hundred-ship Navy would be reached (Tarpgaard 1982).

The infrastructure crisis is another example of the spending-gap tactic. The goals of this campaign were to increase federal spending on public works, and to adopt a capital budget for the federal government (which would reduce the visibility of this spending).[19] After the publication of the influential book *America in Ruins: Beyond the Public Works Pork Barrel* (Choate and Walter 1981), spending advocates made cost estimates for replacing deteriorated public works.[20] These estimates were often based on agency needs assessments (DeMaree 1982, 128). For example, the American Society of Civil Engineers claimed that "of the nation's 524,966 bridges, 223,200 are either 'structurally deficient' or 'functionally obsolete,'" but the engineering standards used to make these calculations were of dubious validity.[21] The flawed nature of these needs estimates were identified by a CBO report, which concluded that if inefficiencies in public works spending were eliminated, spending could *decline* and still replace the deteriorated infrastructure. But because of saturation by spending-gap arguments, media reports missed this point.[22]

The infrastructure crisis also illustrates one important aspect of the spending-gap tactic—the gap must not be too large. If the gap is extremely large, increasing spending might be viewed as devoting money to a hopeless cause. This potential problem was recognized by the National League of Cities, which concluded that one of its infrastructure surveys "shows that a steady but manageable investment over a number of years could and would enable communities to start work on the capital assets ranked as highest priorities" (Stanfield 1983, 860).

---

19. David A. Stockman, "Statement on Capital Budgeting and Public Infrastructure Policy," before the Subcommittee on Economic Development, Committee on Public Works and Transportation, U.S. House of Representatives, 3 May 1983.

20. The counties, cities, the Joint Economic Committee, the Government Finance Officers Association, and a national commission suggested by the public works committees all prepared such "needs estimates."

21. *Washington Post,* 9 December 1982, sec. A; testimony of George Peterson before the Subcommittee on Economic Development, Committee on Public Works and Transportation, House of Representatives, "Federal Capital Investment Budget Act of 1982," 15 September 1982, 55–60. See also Altshuler and Kaplan 1993.

22. *Public Works Infrastructure: Policy Considerations for the 1980s* (April 1983); Douglas B. Feaver, "Infrastructure Spending Called Billions Too Low," *Washington Post,* 27 April 1983, sec. A.

Disastrous Consequences

Advocates sometimes raise the prospect that the failure to spend money will have disastrous consequences. The rationale threatens decision makers with having to face the budgetary equivalent of "who lost China?"—the charge that not funding a program adequately led to deaths, unemployment, and so on. It has been used for safety programs, like that run by the Federal Aviation Administration. Portraying the system as "stretched to the limit," the FAA's advocates argued that cuts in spending (or slower than requested increases) would shortly produce planes falling from the sky. (Controllers could literally counter "Chicken Little!") Potentially disastrous consequences were also invoked in "too big to fail" bailouts like the rescue of Penn Central, Lockheed, Chrysler, and the Continental Illinois Bank. The government would have to subsidize these organizations to avoid, respectively, transportation bottlenecks, a hemorrhage of the defense industrial base, catastrophic unemployment, and financial meltdown.

For obvious reasons, warning of disastrous consequences was a common tactic in defense budgeting. An example is provided by the Reagan administration's argument in 1986 in favor of a *real* increase in defense spending (after the largest peacetime buildup in history):

> Failure to provide these necessary increases would risk:
>
> a return to the problems of the previous decade—a hollow Army, ships that can't sail, and aircraft that can't fly;
> discourage our allies from taking needed actions to strengthen their own military capabilities and inviting increased adventurism on the part of the Soviets and their allies; and
> weakening the administration's ability to negotiate a satisfactory arms reduction agreement.[23]

Of course, defense hawks and doves have long debated at what point of spending the rhetoric of disastrous consequences could be fairly applied. No one really knew the level of U.S. spending that would check "Soviet adventurism," so hawks tried to support their position by pointing to an (overblown) defense-spending gap with the Soviets as evidence that any U.S. reduction could fatally tip the balance. The doves, on the other hand, seemed to argue that the optimal level of defense spending would occur when the military was several orders of magnitude smaller. More U.S. defense spending was said to encourage wars because it showed our belligerence.

23. OMB, "Major Policy Initiatives," *FY1987 Budget* (1986), 12.

By the mid-1980s, defense policy analysts who were neither doves or hawks—the "owls"—weighed in with the limited argument that defense spending had reached the point of diminishing marginal effectiveness. (Few political decision makers gave a hoot for this kind of dispassionate analysis.) The hawks and doves remained polarized until the disastrous consequences argument lost much of its power when the big bad bear evolved into a less threatening creature. In response, advocates for defense spending faced a threat meltdown and searched for new goals for the military (fighting the drug war, providing humanitarian assistance) (D. Morrison 1990b, 1991b, 1992a). But the hawks' logic of disastrous consequences from not maintaining a large military retained some attraction. The Pentagon spewed out plans for becoming more involved in "regional contingencies," warning that not doing so would cause a massive loss of international influence.[24] Beneficiaries of defense spending played the game as well. My favorite example was the clumsy effort by General Dynamics to justify procurement of new cruise missiles. Their briefings to Pentagon officials suggested a variety of threat scenarios for use in the defense planning, with calculations of the number of missiles that could be deployed for attacks on Indonesian rebels and for helping Pakistan in a war with India! (D. Morrison 1991c). Kissinger's aphorism about defense planning being "weapons in search of a doctrine" applies here.

Occasionally, the rhetoric of disastrous consequences suggests disaster when no imminent disaster is projected. This is the familiar "slippery slope" argument, in which one small cut *inevitably* leads to evisceration of a program. For example, President Joseph F. Boyle of the American Medical Association was once quoted as saying that cuts in medical-education spending "could threaten the financial security of many institutions" (Demkovich 1985, 311). *Threaten* is the operative word here, used in the hope that decision makers will ignore questions about the specific effects of a small cut to worry about what might happen from a very hypothetical series of such cuts.

The Level Playing Field

Maurice Stans once described budgeting as "the uniform distribution of discontent." It is doubtful that most competitors in the budget process believe this, but they often employ the rhetoric of rough equity. This should be expected given the mixed-enterprise nature of our economy and the frequent subsidization of industry. But industry battles are not the only conflicts in which the ideal of the level playing field is cited. In 1991, Guy Gugliotta of the *Washington*

---

24. See, for example, Don Oberdorfer, "Strategy for Solo Superpower," *Washington Post,* 19 May 1991, sec. A. A similar 1992 Pentagon document suggested the United States would counter a Russian invasion of Lithuania—a country that the United States hesitated to recognize even as the Soviet Union was disintegrating.

Post searched through Congressional debates for mentions of the level playing field and found

> 30 computer-generated pages of paragraph-long samples from 67 members of Congress on 17 different subjects ranging from international trade to highways and campaign financing, to American agriculture and American industry, to women's rights, veterans rights and civil rights, to health care, national defense, the budget, pesticides, taxes, and space.[25]

Budgetary level-playing-field rationales usually justify spending by complaining that the subsidies provided to competitors are larger. An example was the debate over Medicare's reimbursement of the capital costs of hospitals. Subsidies to for-profit and not-for-profit hospitals came in different forms—for-profits received payments for their capital costs, and not-for-profits were exempted from taxes. During the period of high real interest rates of the 1980s, the not-for-profits felt at a disadvantage and lobbied for the receipt of comparable subsidies. When the administration decided not to make such payments, it undercut the

> "concept of equality of payments," Linda B. Miller[,] executive director of the Volunteer Trustees of Not-For-Profit Hospitals, told the House subcommittee on Feb. 14. For Congress to "deliberately perpetuate" the inequity that existing medicare law has created "would be ruinous," she said. (Demkovich 1983, 706)

Another example is how Amtrak justified its subsidy with the following:

> The issue of federal subsidies needs to be put into perspective. All modes are subsidized, air transportation being the beneficiary of a federally funded and operated air traffic control system receiving about $1.5 billion annually from general funds alone, and ground/highway transportation receiving massive subsidies for construction and maintenance of roadways, totaling $425 billion over the most recent 12-year period. Unlike all other transportation modes, Amtrak's annual appropriation must cover its operating and capital expenses as well as all related infrastructure costs.[26]

The level-playing-field argument is attractive because it conforms with the widely held public philosophy labeled "interest-group liberalism" by Lowi

25. "In Congress, a Cliche Is Worth a Thousand Speeches," 4 July 1991, sec. A.

26. W. Graham Claytor, Jr., "'Extreme Conclusions' about Amtrak," *Washington Post,* 22 June 1985, sec. A. The ground transportation subsidy estimate is absurdly high.

(1969). Lowi argued that our political culture assumes expansive intervention by the government in the economy and grants all organized interest groups the right to receive services from the government. Rather than critically examining the need for assisting each group, attention is focused on assuring an equitable distribution of subsidies among groups. This expectation of equal treatment creates pressure for spending increases.

Controllers can reverse the level-playing-field rationale by arguing it would only be fair to coordinate spending cuts for one program with reductions in the subsidies granted to competitors. Unfortunately for controllers, this tactic is often procedurally complicated by committee jurisdictions and the varied timing for different bills. In addition, though spending advocates may sometimes voice a desire for a field level to cricket standards, when conditions change, they may say they prefer a hilly golf course instead. For example, in 1991 the Pharmaceutical Manufacturers Association feared that discontent with the rapid increases in health care costs would force budget cuts. They ran a series of ads in Washington opinion-leader magazines that distinguished spending on drugs from other health care spending. These ads showed that the percentage of GNP spent on drugs remained steady from 1970 to 1990 (unlike total health spending, which more than doubled) and that the trade balance for drugs was more than $1 billion in the black.

The Structure of Budgetary Argumentation

Anton described the basics of budgetary argumentation as follows: "Agencies press for expansion using programmatic criteria while budget review officers attempt to negate expansion using financial criteria" (1967, 30). Spending advocates need to say something besides "we want the money!" because they recognize that the process emphasizes controlling costs. By convincing others that money will be well spent, they can shift attention from controlling costs to meeting other goals.

Controllers generally react to these arguments by complaining that "it still costs too much!" Yet they also know they often can't cut spending by just complaining about costs. Controllers also need to show that spending doesn't cause desired effects or that these effects are actually undesirable. This is not simply a strategic decision. Controllers often value efficiency and effectiveness as highly as economy. Among the most biting criticisms they could hear would be that they knew "the cost of everything, but the value of nothing."

So though controllers prefer to emphasize costs and spending advocates prefer to discuss programmatic effects, both sides often compare costs to effects. In fact, some of the arguments described above—investment and leveraging, in particular—especially help spending advocates because they allow favorable comparisons of effects to costs. For example, labeling spending as an investment transforms an effect into the metric used for controlling costs. It is then easier to argue that spending is acceptable because short-run costs will be fully offset by long-run benefits.

A Prospending Bias

What are some other notable characteristics of the process of budgetary argumentation? One is the bias in the stream of information received by budgetary decision makers. It is certainly easier to mobilize support for spending than for control of spending. Spending typically confers concentrated benefits and imposes dispersed costs, whereas control of spending typically confers dispersed benefits and imposes concentrated costs. People are especially motivated to organize to protect concentrated benefits, but face strong barriers should they wish to join with others to obtain dispersed benefits (Wilson 1973).

James L. Payne has observed that members of Congress (and other decision makers) receive not a stream, but a flood of positive information about the effects of spending (1990, 1991). To illustrate his conclusion, he compiled data that showed that prospending witnesses at appropriations hearings outnumbered antispending witnesses by a ratio of 145 to 1. This single measure is insufficient, because committees usually receive more negative information in other forums—for example, in unpublicized visits from opponents of spending. Yet though there is little valid data on the degree of balance in the information stream, its general bias seems undeniable. The boom box of support for spending often overpowers the tinny transistor radio of opposition.

Payne also argues that the repetitive broadcast of positive rationales for spending has created a "culture of spending." This culture features a "presumption of government efficacy," in which "the government is the appropriate instrumentality to solve any national problem" (1991, 28). Payne thinks this presumption is generally false, whereas I believe there are many problems that the government should and can solve. But though I do not share Payne's ideology, I agree that budgetary decision makers often seem to accept arguments that spending will work without sufficient skepticism about their validity. Too often, it seems, accurate information is outweighed by fluff. Remember Pike's observation about the claimed spinoffs from the space station?

> I was embarrassed for the company I was keeping. It was painful. It was deceptive.

Among many analyst-observers, these are all-too-common feelings. And a number of experienced informants told me of their perceptions that the deceptiveness of budgeting has increased over time. As one OMB analyst put it, previous budgets had "nothing purple in them, although a faint tint occasionally. Now, I can hardly believe what we put out."

Besides flooding decision makers with positive evaluations of spending, advocates may also try to rid the information stream of negative evaluations of spending. This tactic of *de*commissioning studies of spending is sometimes carried out in the open, as it was in the 1986 Urgent Supplemental Appropriations bill. A provision of this bill, which was sponsored by senators from Tennessee (TVA) and Washington (Bonneville Power Administration), stated that

> None of the funds appropriated under this joint resolution or any other provisions of law shall be used for the purposes of conducting any studies relating or leading to the possibility of changing from the currently required "at cost" to a "market rate" method for the pricing of hydroelectric power by the six Federal public power authorities, or other agencies or authorities of the Federal Government.[27]

The tactic of creating such thought crimes was also employed by advocates who prevented OMB studies of reducing REA subsidies, USDA studies of user fees for commodity inspection and marketing services, and executive-branch studies of selling naval petroleum reserves.[28]

Controllers are not free from blame in this regard. For example, some spending advocates charged the Reagan administration with using the thought-crime tactic in 1981, when OMB canceled funds for a number of studies of welfare spending, including the long-planned Survey on Income and Program Participation (SIPP), for fear that the results would be used to argue for greater welfare spending.[29] A more recent example was a bumbling attempt by USDA political appointees to recast findings of a major evaluation of the Women, Infants, and Children program. The draft study found positive effects from the program, and after it was judged technically acceptable by USDA career staff and an advisory panel, the political staff rewrote the executive summary to portray the program as ineffective. In this case, the rewrite was exposed by a GAO audit, and USDA apologized (GAO 1989c).

Comprehensible Arguments

Though decision makers hear more from spending advocates, they won't decide to approve spending unless the arguments of spending advocates are convincing. Why are some arguments for spending convincing and others not?

---

27. *Congressional Record,* 5 June 1986, S 6843–53.

28. A similar message was sent to GAO after it produced unfavorable audits of grazing and mining programs—the Congress cut its funding (Kuntz 1991b).

29. Stanfield 1981b; Ellen Goodman, "Killing the Bearer of Bad Tidings," *Washington Post,* 6 February 1982, sec. A.

We can begin to answer this question with some basic knowledge about political rhetoric. Many experts believe that arguments are most convincing when they are *interpretable* and *explainable.*

Ease of interpretation is important because of the dense character of the information environment. Political decision makers are continually bombarded with information and must find a way to cope with this "tower of babble." One way is to rely on advice from trusted experts, a process known as *cue taking* (Kingdon 1973). Another way is to tune out arguments that are too complex for decision makers to understand, given the time pressures they face and their cognitive limitations (Lau, Smith, and Fiske 1991). Successful spending rationales, then, are rapidly communicated by cue givers to cue takers or are simple enough for burdened decision makers to understand by themselves. They function as programmatic "aids to conceptualization" (again, apologies to Wildavsky). Such conceptual crutches are like Derthick and Quirk's description of the argument for deregulation of transportation

> The argument for reform had a simple, intuitive character and was sanctioned by a pattern of endorsements—providing cues that made it easy for Congressmen to be persuaded on the merits without investing much effort in making an assessment. (Derthick and Quirk 1985, 118)

Interpretable arguments allow decision makers to easily conceive of the nature of budgetary problems and the possibility of solutions.

Rationales for spending often must also be explainable to the public, because decision makers must often explain their actions to justify keeping their jobs (Kingdon 1973, 46–53). Members of the public, of course, devote little time and few brain cells to the consideration of a government's budget, but they often have strong opinions about how spending can potentially affect them. The challenge for spending advocates is to find arguments about spending that can be readily repeated by politicians to this challenging audience, in order that politicians will gain credit or avoid blame for their actions (Arnold 1990).

Metaphors are often the most efficient form for this task, particularly because they can stimulate a simple emotional reaction that short-circuits a more critical analysis (Lakoff and Johnson 1980). I saw one of my favorite prospending metaphors (as a professor and a parent) on a bumper sticker: "Education Cuts Never Heal." The slogan triggers emotions by suggesting that budget cuts are analogous to physical injury and disability. It also implies that Band-Aids are no cure: cuts reduce quality and cause students to forever lag behind the students with an uninterrupted first-rate education.

The power of metaphors to force a snap judgment on the effects of spending can be found in many programs. For example, several informants explained the demise of the Comprehensive Employment and Training Act

Public Service Employment program as a result of "leaning on their shovels" stories. Another case was the Reagan administration's proposal to cut nutrition spending that was torpedoed by the controversy over ketchup as a vegetable, though the "ketchup regulations" were generally misperceived and had little to do with the proposed spending cuts.[30]

Tailoring Rationales

Developing the right message about the effects of spending is much harder than developing the right form.[31] The main difficulties are that the goals of individual decision makers change over time, and at any time, groups of decision makers differ over goals. To be most successful, spending advocates and controllers must change their arguments to match the goals of targeted decision makers at specific times.

One approach is to send the message that spending addresses important conditions that have moved high on the problem agenda. For example, the disastrous-consequences argument worked well for defense spending after the Iran hostage debacle of 1979–81. The chain of logic was simple: the "decade of neglect" produced an insufficiently trained military that took too few of its unreliable helicopters in the failed attempt to rescue the hostages. Because we had depreciated our armed forces, the argument went, not only could we not deter the Soviets from invading Afghanistan, we couldn't even carry out a "simple" exercise against a third-rate military power! This argument was very influential in support of the defense buildup.

Another timing approach is to emphasize the potential of a novel solution: we've had this problem forever, but now we finally *know* how to solve it, so let's spend some money! A tortured argument of this type was made during the oat bran craze in 1988–89. When medical journals reported that gorging oat bran was an especially effective method of lowering cholesterol levels, many people started eating daily rations of (fat-laden) oat bran muffins. Naturally, members of Congress then served up the argument that increased federal spending for oat production would reduce market prices, promote consumption, and improve the public health. This case illustrates the risk of a novel solution. It wasn't long until people learned that oat bran was not a magic bullet against cholesterol: novelty wears off. Like Anthony Downs's "issue-attention cycle," in which attending to an issue become less attractive as the downside of dealing with it becomes more apparent, there is a solution-acceptance cycle (1972). Analysis typically shows that solutions don't work as well as originally

30. For an extensive catalog of political metaphors, see Safire 1978.

31. This section relies heavily on Kingdon's discussion of "coupling" (1984, 181–93).

thought. For example, the investment argument is convincing for only a limited time absent some documentation. Conservative congressman Robert Walker exposed this drawback when he complained in a debate over funding the Economic Development Administration that

> we are told by all kinds of people, "It pays its own way." How often have we heard that on the floor with regard to programs? Every program that we have asked to be cut in this House over the last couple of years, we have had at least one person come to the floor and say, "Do not worry about this program, it pays its own way." Good heavens, my friends, we have got 200 billion dollars' worth of deficit. These programs cannot all be paying their own way or we would not have deficits.[32]

Spending advocates can avoid this risk by shifting rationales. The following example replaces a disgraced macroeconomic-effect argument with a spending-gap argument.

> "Are public works jobs the most cost effective? Probably not. But we have a tremendous need for infrastructure repair," said Joint Economic Committee Chairman Henry S. Reuss, D. Wis., who worked on the preliminary House jobs proposals. (Donnelly 1982, 2871)

Although it is important to have temporally influential arguments, spending advocates also find that they need justifications for spending that provide stable support over time. Spending is more likely to be acceptable when it conforms with culturally based concepts about the legitimate roles of the government and about the classes and groups most deserving of governmental support. Spinoff arguments, for example, agree with our embrace of growth-oriented economic policy. Level-playing-field arguments bear a slight but sufficient resemblance to our preference for democracy.

While some arguments may be persuasive at any point in time, they still may not apply to particular programs: Medicaid spending on long-term care for eighty-five year olds is clearly not an investment, whatever its other merits. In other words, the persuasiveness of rationales is partially contingent on the types of programs to which they are applied. Advocates who do not limit their arguments to the most plausible will look foolish. Consider the following from a UPI story of 31 July 1985 (copied in a policy report of the Cato Institute).

> President Reagan's tax reform plan, Congress was told Wednesday, could mean the end of the American Christmas tree. . . .

32. *Congressional Record,* 17 July 1985, H 5787.

> It could, [a National Christmas Tree Association spokesman] said, return the United States to the days of having to look outside its own borders for Christmas trees. . . .
>
> The plan [Keith] Jacob charged, would hurt an industry that "is entirely a family-oriented enterprise." "Also victims," he noted, "would be numerous youths. . . ."
>
> "Another beneficiary of the proposals of the Treasury Department is the Oriental manufacturer of plastic trees which utilize non-renewable petroleum resources." (Cato Institute 1985, 16)

Staying quiet would probably have been the best tactic for this group.

That being said, it is important to put forward a plausible rationale for its full worth. For example, since the fear of creating uncontrollable programs has made it difficult to create entitlements, the truly needy and earned-right arguments must be made forcefully to create the perception that beneficiaries really deserve their benefits. An example was the failure of the Senate to adopt a proposal to fund a "demonstration program" to compensate victims of toxic wastes through the Superfund tax. The sponsor of the proposal, Senator George Mitchell, sought to use the "camel's nose" tactic,

> arguing in vain that the provision was a "cautious, limited effort" to determine the need for victims' assistance. "This is not an entitlement program. This is not a national health insurance program," he said.[33]

By failing to communicate that people *should be* entitled because they had been victimized, Mitchell gave away a powerful argument for its adoption.

Because budget decision makers are segmented into different groups by their backgrounds, ideologies, and goals, rationales should also be tailored to the intended recipients. Robert Bell has found that arguments about housing spending that were based on public-finance theory were received in different ways by the three institutions that made policy on housing—OMB was highly receptive, HUD was receptive only when its political leadership had been trained in economics, and the Congress rarely was (Bell 1985). Similarly, investment arguments for social programs can convince moderate conservatives, but not strong conservatives who would rather end state intervention in the private sector than intervene more efficiently.

The common distinction between "rifle" and "shotgun" lobbying is useful for understanding how spending advocates deal with the challenge of segmentation. The shotgun approach is to distribute a list of supportive rationales, and

33. Cass Peterson, "Toxic Waste Compensation Plan Rejected," *Washington Post,* 25 September 1985, sec. A.

to let targets pick and use the rationales that are most attractive. This approach can be most effective when the arguments are meant to be supportive rather than directly persuasive. This was the approach of the Reagan administration's *Major Themes* volume, primarily to promote the control of spending. An aide to Stockman explained,

> From our Hill background, we knew it was not enough to have one to three people on your side. Rather, you need a lot of people. On many issues, there are a lot of legislative assistants and members who can be swayed. They want a set of ironclad arguments to defend themselves when they do the right thing. *Major Themes* was produced not to help them make up their minds, but rather so they could feel it was all right to cut budgets as well as to fund particular projects.

The "rifle" approach tailors arguments very specifically to respond to the idiosyncratic beliefs of one or several decision makers. Consider the case of a high-level OMB officer who told me,

> On black lung, our examiner would make a cogent case about abuse—he had anecdotes and also good analysis, good enough to conclude that this program was not going in the right direction. But we never figured out how to get those kinds of things to the Hill. More and more, I realized that it wasn't the facts that persuaded the Hill, it was the emotions.

The same person confessed,

> We'd ask "What percentage of new lines are going up in urban areas?" and the answer was "a majority." But I remembered about REA, because I grew up on a farm and we didn't have electricity until I was twelve. The warm glow I have carries into the Congress and negates the good analysis that "proves" the program should be cut.

This is one reason why lobbyists who know decision makers intimately are so valuable to advocacy groups.

Though they are often outshouted, controllers are not indefensible in budgetary policy argumentation. Their opening is created by the mere plausibility of the rationales put forward by spending advocates: since decision makers often have low validity standards, spending advocates rarely need to put forward ironclad rationales. This leaves rationales subject to counterattacks from controllers. Controllers can't attack all rationales—they are too busy counting the change—but selective attacks can be effective.

Albert O. Hirschman discusses this topic brilliantly in a recent book called *The Rhetoric of Reaction,* which covers three centuries of ideological debates over social reforms. He categorized conservative reactions to proposed reforms into three generic arguments:

> According to the *perversity* thesis, any purposive action to improve some feature of the political, social, or economic order only serves to exacerbate the condition one wishes to remedy. The *futility* thesis holds that attempts at social transformation will be unavailing, that they will simply fail to "make a dent." Finally the *jeopardy* thesis argues that the cost of the proposed change or reform is too high as it endangers some previous, precious accomplishment. (1991, 7)

I find this framework to be enlightening for budgeting as well. For example, opponents to building the B-2 bomber seized on the futility argument by highlighting studies that questioned whether the bomber would ever be stealthy. This attacked the linchpin of the program—its crucial rationale. But controllers create a risk by claiming that a spending proposal is futile—spending advocates can then argue that spending more won't be futile.

A broader attack on the B-2 was made by Congressman Ed Markey, who used the perversity, futility, and jeopardy arguments, among others.

> B-2, or not B-2: That is the question.
> Whether 'tis nobler in the mind to suffer the slings and arrows of outrageous expense.
> Or to take arms against a sea of deficits,
> And by opposing end them. To cut; to spend;
> No more; and by a cut to say we end the heartache and a thousand cost overruns
> That B-2 is heir to. 'Tis a consummation
> Devoutly to be wished. To cut; to spend;
> To spend? Perchance stretch-out! Ay, there's the rub;
> For in those stretch-outs what new overruns may come,
> When we have shuffled off deciding,
> Must give us pause. There's the respect
> That makes calamity of delay.
> For would Stealth bear the whips and scorns of time,
> The lack of mission, the untried technology,
> The great expense, the inevitable delays,
> The excessive secrecy, and the cuts
> That must be made for Gramm-Rudman target's sake.
> When we ourselves might today Stealth's termination make
> With a bare majority. Who would new tax burdens bear,
> To pay its 70 billion dollar pricetag,

When the dread of a turkey worse than B-1,
A flying Bat-winger bomber whose cost per pound,
Is that of gold, puzzles the mind
And makes us rather keep those bombers that we now have
Than to fly to others that we know not of?
Thus conscience should make cautious legislators of us all;
And thus the hue of B-2 boosterism
Must be replaced with the sober cast of thought,
And this enterprise of great pith and moment,
Be halted now before it further proceeds.
A handsome bomber yes, but better
Not to be.[34]

Perhaps this effort at ridicule was a bit too cute. For another example, consider the tactics of the opposition to a committee appropriation of $6 million to NASA for its SETI program, which stood for the Search for Extraterrestrial Intelligence. Rep. Silvio Conte came to the floor, and said that

> of course there are flying saucers and advanced civilizations in outer space. But we don't need to spend $6 million this year to find evidence of these rascally creatures. We only need 75 cents to buy a tabloid at the local supermarket.

He then exhibited tabloids with the following headlines:

"Blimp Scared UFOs Away From Stadium"
"Noah's Ark Was Built By Space Aliens"
"Webbed Creatures Vanishing From Earth By Leaps And Bounds—
Space Aliens Stealing Our Frogs"
"UFO Flies Out Of The Ocean!"
"Magic Ray From This UFO Cures 22 People!"

He closed with the following:

> This amendment gives us a chance to prove that there is still intelligent life on Earth. Let us save our hard-earned money and let the space aliens spend their currency to find us.
>
> If we continue to fund this dog—a Golden Fleece award winner in 1978—then we should seriously consider funding of an even more ambitious program—SCI: Search for Congressional Intelligence.[35]

34. *Congressional Record,* 26 July 1989, H 4284.
35. *Congressional Record,* 28 June 1990, H 4355–58.

Believe it or not, this program survived Conte's inspired ridicule, but other programs with barely plausible rationales may be susceptible to similarly inventive attacks.

Summary

The desire for a definitive budgetary standard has focused attention on the costs of spending. The flip side of this has been less critical scrutiny of arguments about the effects of spending. Though controllers have certainly tried to counter the misimpressions created by the rhetorical tactics of spending advocates, they have often failed. Even though accounting controls and budgetary decision procedures have been strengthened, spending advocates have often protected programs with convincing arguments about the effects of spending.

Chapter 8

Budget Structures and Budget Reform

During the winter of 1990, the Jim Beam Distillery Company highlighted the seven-year aging of its sour mash bourbon by advertising it was "Made When the Deficit Was Still Payable." The black humor worked because few believed that the huge deficits initiated in the second year of the Reagan administration would be largely and permanently reduced. Nor was there much public confidence that most individual spending programs and tax preferences would be made more effective and economical. Many people had concluded that the budget process was an abysmal failure, but disappointing policy outcomes were not the only reason. Also indicted were the most visible features of the budget process: its complexity, innumerable delays, and high degree of conflict.

Many participants in the budget process have responded to such criticisms with the aphorism: "the process is not the problem, the problem is the problem." Their admirable intent was to focus attention on the difficult policy tradeoffs that must be made if the deficit is to be reduced. But most didn't act as if they believed what they were saying. Often, soon after they stated "the process is not the problem," they immediately suggested specific improvements to the *process.* They recognized that process and problems are interrelated, that reforms to the process could enable controllers to deal more successfully with challenges from spending advocates.

In contrast to this general preference for reform of the budget process, some critics argued that a "panic of responsibility" had overemphasized the economic and political costs of large deficits (White and Wildavsky 1989, 426). Because they suggested that these costs were small, they claimed there was little need to reform the budgetary process. The delays and conflict were troubling, but also necessary attributes of democratic decision making (White and Wildavsky 1989).

This perspective deserves some consideration, for politicians clearly would be guilty of gross displacement of goals if they shifted all attention from serious social problems in order to develop the *perfect* budget process and produce the *optimal* budget outcome. On the other hand, many observers, including myself, have concluded that the probable results of continuing to run huge deficits are highly undesirable. Huge deficits will likely so reduce national savings and private investment that economic growth will be markedly slowed; we might even become notably poorer. Allowing failing programs and tax policies to continue will limit our flexibility to allocate budgetary resources to new problems. Finally, recurrent budgetary failures will increase public discontent with government above its already high level.

Macroinstitutional Reforms

Assuming this latter perspective is widely shared, how then should we reform the budget process? Most political scientists would argue that since institutional characteristics of the Congress and the presidency are to blame for budgetary problems, reformers could try to change these characteristics. These characteristics are normally explained by referring to congressional incapacity, presidential unwillingness or inability to lead, and divided government.

Congressional Incapacity

The argument of congressional incapacity is that the Congress usually is structurally unable to carry out a function—budgeting—that seriously challenges the more hierarchical executive branch (Kamlet and Mowery 1985). It starts with the observation that members are strongly motivated to be reelected and recognize they must place great weight on the short-term desires of the electorate and interest groups to attain this goal. The member's dilemma is that the electorate and interest groups tend to punish politicians who are perceived to have imposed costs on them, but responsible budgeting *requires* the imposition of costs. Members who want to be reelected must therefore avoid *looking* responsible for imposing costs. They can do this only if a skillful leadership designs deficit-reduction packages and schedules votes in ways that reduce the ability of constituents to determine blame (Arnold 1990).

The argument suggests that one shouldn't expect this to happen frequently. The Congress is a decentralized organization that decides collegially (Hedlund 1984). This usually means that deficit-reduction proposals must be voted on in so many combinations and on so many occasions that members of Congress are almost always placed at risk at electoral retribution. But it is true that on occasion, Congress *has* simplified its structure and procedures and given more power to leaders. These reforms were usually adopted in response to challenges to its institutional reputation. For example, President Nixon's impoundments provided the impetus for passage of the Congressional Budget Act.

Since the scandals of 1991 and 1992 produced what is probably the historic low in the reputation of the Congress (and that's saying something!), it is not impossible that significant congressional reforms will be adopted. But the history of congressional reform is littered with failures, and most centralizing reforms were weakened after a few years. Electoral incentives usually create strong pressures to decentralize. Members will probably not let party leaders keep internal resources, making it difficult for leaders to convince party members to risk electoral retribution and vote for responsible deficit-reduction packages. Members also typically refuse to grant sufficient gatekeeping or other powers to committees, reducing the chance that they will provide leadership. As described above, the committee in the House that could best fulfill this role—the House Budget Committee—is often said to be too accommodating toward spending advocates because its membership is rotated from and to committees dominated by spending advocates.

Presidential Leadership

A traditional institutional solution for congressional incapacity is a strong president. Many hope the president would lead by proposing a responsible budget policy and then use all of the powers of the presidency to bring the Congress into line. But recent experience shows that the desire to exercise such leadership is not guaranteed. Its lack was conspicuous under President Reagan, who even though he was the most charismatic and rhetorically conservative executive in decades, paid only lip service to the deficit, giving a peculiar reading of the presidential role Clinton Rossiter identified as the "Manager of Prosperity" (1956, 25–27). His successor apparently could have cared less about budgetary leadership, disavowing the only deficit-reduction agreement of his administration just days after its completion.

As is the case with the Congress, the electoral incentives facing a president reduce the likelihood of budgetary responsibility. A presidentially supported deficit-reduction plan necessarily imposes costs on interest groups, who can react by withdrawing support from the incumbent president and the president's party in the next election cycle. More importantly, deficit reductions impose costs on voters. Many cost bearers are likely to remember costs, and some will not absolve the president nor the president's party for imposing these costs. Deficit reductions may also reduce economic growth for a period of time, and as President Bush learned, rule number one for the incumbent presidential party is "don't have a recession before the election." Therefore, if a president is to lead on the budget at all, it may be more likely shortly after the election than before the hoped-for reelection.

But the electoral dynamic also reduces the possibility that a president will lead shortly after being elected. Presidential leadership often relies upon having developed an electoral mandate, but it is difficult to develop a mandate for deficit reduction. As President Clinton's campaign illustrated, a candidate for the presidency is expected to promise benefits rather than burdens, even if most expert opinion and a good deal of public opinion suggest burdens are in order. Presidents who wish to budget responsibly thus must change the message they send to the public soon after they take office (which President Bush never did after his "read my lips" bluster). This shift must occur when a president is dealing with another significant barrier to leadership: the president is at the bottom of the learning curve in how to carry out presidential responsibilities. But even if the president quickly moves up this curve, the president still must convince a Congress that has its own reasons to balk at deficit reduction.

Divided Government and Responsiveness to the Public

From 1981 to 1992, huge deficits were often blamed on divided government. The implication was the return of unified government would lead to significant deficit reduction. In 1993, the control of government was newly unified. In addition, the Clinton administration was inclined to lead, and a Congress chastened by scandal seemed to be more likely to follow than it had in the past. Yet the unified government of 1993 struggled to impose a deficit reduction that was *smaller* than the amount imposed by the divided government of 1990. Why?

The perceived flaw of divided government is that responsible budget compromises are harder to reach because opposing parties are naturally reluctant to abandon strongly held policy preferences (for defense spending, for cost-of-living adjustments, against tax increases, and so on). Their easiest method of compromise is the logroll that accepts all of the deficit *increases* proposed by both sides. These irresponsible bargains are often camouflaged by gimmickry.

> Van Dorn Ooms, the House Budget Committee's chief economist, cites what he calls the Gresham's Law of Budgeting: Bad numbers tend to drive out good. . . . "It's a competitive situation" between the White House and Congress, he said, "and if someone preempts the process by using bad numbers that make the world look rosier, that puts tremendous pressure on everyone else to follow suit." (Rauch 1986c, 2289)

With the aid of gimmickry, the free lunch becomes the daily special, as politicians tell the public that taxes can be low and that spending can be high—simultaneously.

The responsible alternative is to circle the wagons in a budget summit, a process in which parties jointly assume responsibility for initiating and adopting deficit reductions (Weaver 1986). The 1981–92 period showed, however, that many ruts impede an orderly circling of the wagons. Notably, each party is tempted to exploit opportunities to blame the other for advocating the imposition of costs on constituents. In addition, the procedural improvisations that were intended to cope with divided government often created new problems that rivaled the old (Schick 1990). For example, sequestration under Gramm-Rudman-Hollings was intended to force bargaining between the president and the Congress. It did not do this because its self-binding means of discipline was not credible. And while sequestration may have checked the growth of discretionary spending, it also *lessened* the pressure to control the costs of mandatory programs; consequently these programs continued to grow out of control.

Divided government deserves a better defense than it was given by most of its critics.[1] In particular, more skepticism should be directed at the first assumption of the unified-government argument: that the public strongly desires deficit reduction. At one time, this was a safer assumption to make. In this earlier, simpler world, the informal but widely supported *fiscal constitution* was a norm that required a balanced budget (or no more than a very small deficit). Following the popularization of Keynesian economics in the 1960s, support for that expectation weakened. Deficits became more acceptable if they reduced unemployment or stabilized the economy in other ways, financed investments, or even redistributed income. Supply-side advertising for the free lunch further weakened the fiscal-constitution constraint (Savage 1988).

Acceptance of the legitimacy of deficits was also spurred by the absence of immediate penalties for running deficits. The courts could not prevent deficits because, unlike in most state and local governments, there was no constitutional prohibition against deficits. Nor did creditors cut off the supply of credit—as they do for state and local governments that continually run deficits—because the size and wealth of the United States made this course unnecessary. Initial warnings about the dangers of large deficits also proved false—neither rampant inflation nor deep depression resulted.

Now, the consensus among economists is that deficits are dangerous because they reduce long-run economic growth. Government deficits reduce national savings, and a reduced national savings rate makes less capital available for investment. Less investment reduces productivity growth and thereby reduces economic growth. But the plain fact is that for most of the past two decades, this argument did not worry the public that much. And although public concern about the deficit has certainly increased in recent years, there are several reasons to question whether public concern about the deficit will grow much more. First, the argument about the relationships between savings, investment, and growth is relatively complicated. It may be that the people who are most receptive to this argument have already been reached, and that the

1. For an empirical examination of the supposed flaws of divided government, see Mayhew 1991.

remaining citizens will be harder to convince. These citizens may find more attractive the simpler arguments from spending advocates about how specific deficit reductions create immediate harm.

Second, many people apparently prefer to avoid definite short-run costs *even if* this probably prevents the enjoyment of long-run benefits. In addition, the forecast of diminished *growth* from high deficits still leaves succeeding generations with a *better* standard of living than their predecessors. Though this standard is far below what future generations *could* enjoy, the present generation may prefer not to sacrifice so that future generations will be *much* better off. Finally, even if there is some desire to sacrifice, there is no urgency for action. Elected politicians can tell controllers to wait one more year—until after the election—because the reduction in long-run economic growth from the year's inaction will be small. But to win, the electoral victors probably will promise to protect the interests of many spending advocates, which then postpones action for another year if these promises are honored. This is an interesting dynamic in a country with a two-year electoral cycle.

In sum, a unified government should not be the magic bullet for deficit reduction. Quite the opposite if the public typically attaches blame for the short-run costs of deficit reduction and does not fully appreciate the long-run benefits. When the public wants to live well *now,* a single party in control of government that budgets responsibly is at *greater* risk than the parties to a divided government who circle the wagons. In the former case, the citizens will know who to blame. In the latter case, citizens may be confused, especially if the divided parties agree to disagree after they act.

Blaming the controlling party is especially easy because the public will already believe that this party is predisposed to increase taxes (Democrats) or cut spending (Republicans). Pragmatic deficit reduction plans require both—eliminating a deficit by only increasing taxes or by only cutting spending is unrealistic. But the controlling party risks retribution even by advocating a balanced plan because it exposes itself to a convincing "we told you so" charge from its opponents. This risk is ironic, because all the plans that have been developed by cooperating divided parties have balanced spending cuts with tax increases.

Of course, should the public learn to value the long-run benefits of deficit reduction over the short-run costs, there would be more reason to hope that unified government will produce deficit reductions. There are some indications that the public is moving in this direction. The recession of 1991 caused many people to think about more than the temporary reduction in national income, and ask why economic growth over the past two decades had been so slow relative to growth in the past. The logic that reducing the deficit could increase investment, productivity, and economic growth was picked up first by Senator Tsongas and then by Ross Perot in the 1992 presidential campaign. Both candidates received surprising support. They are now trying to organize the nascent deficit-reduction movement that came out of these campaigns into an influential lobby and electoral force. (Americans for Root Canals?) If they do—against the odds—then perhaps unified government will perform as its advocates have hoped.

Budget Structure Reforms

Without denigrating the importance of thinking about these macroinstitutional reforms, the perspective of this book suggests that advocates of budget process reform should also recall Senator Everett Dirksen's maxim: "A billion here, a billion there, pretty soon it adds up to real money." Dirksen was suggesting that members of Congress should scrutinize requests for small expenditures even though they are of relatively inconsequential size. By paying attention to the trees as well as the forest, he implied, sick trees could be thinned out and the forest's health would improve.

Thinking only about macroinstitutional reforms is equivalent to looking only at the forest and ignoring the trees. The trees are important. For example, a president who desires to reduce the deficit will be frustrated if accurate cost estimates are unavailable, if members of Congress accept tortured rationales for spending, and if programs are procedurally protected from frequent budget scrutiny.

More generally, budgeting is not just a macroinstitutional conflict; it is also a competition between coalitions over individual programs. This means that reform of the budget process necessarily involves changing the structure of the competition between spending advocates and controllers over individual programs. In fact, this has been an unheralded method of reform. Chapters 4 through 7 showed how many controller proposals have been adopted over past decades: in legislation from the Congressional Budget Act through the Budget Enforcement Act, and in administrative decisions on the recommendation of experts from the President's Commission on Budget Concepts to the current comptroller general.

One lesson from these studies is that controllers often have to wait a long time for their victories. Consider the control of the many accounting and financing tactics associated with credit programs—the asset sales and loan prepayments, the use of the FFB as an off-budget spigot, the substitution of guaranteed loans for direct loans, and the creation of government-sponsored enterprises. Since at least the mid-1960s, controllers had sought accounting rules that would report the costs of credit on a basis comparable to other forms of spending. A first barrier was overcome when the President's Commission on Budget Concepts recommended that the subsidies delivered by credit programs be calculated separately from their financing. Yet implementing this principle became possible only after controllers resolved some major conceptual and measurement problems, and this took a great deal of work over a long time. As the technicians worked on these problems, politician controllers like Representative Willis Gradison of Ohio proposed various credit reforms over and over. They often failed—the Appropriations Committee would hear nothing of the idea for years—but they sometimes won when conditions were favorable. Then, in 1985, as recounted in chapter 4, OMB director Stockman took advantage of an opportunity to control FFB financing. In the latter 1980s, the Congress was embarrassed enough by its orgy of loan-asset sales and prepayments to decide not to count these as budgetary savings. And in 1990, concern about the tendency to shift costs into the future through loan guarantees kept credit reform in the Budget Enforcement Act. In sum, controllers eventually *did* use credit reform to close the barn door, *but* many horses had escaped over the previous twenty-five years.

Though controllers have often succeeded after long struggles, they have also lost more than a few. My agenda for structural budget reform was developed after considering these losses. It has four major recommendations.

Recognize the Legitimacy of Multiple Goals for Budgeting

For many years, federal budgeting emphasized controlling the budget-year deficit. There were two rationales for this emphasis. First, by minimizing the budget-year deficit, the government would have to borrow less over the short run. Second, controlling the budget-year deficit could allow the government to stabilize the economy through fiscal policy. But as the government ran large deficits, it became apparent that there was little financial need for the federal government to control short-run borrowing. Lenders were willing to lend huge amounts, given the government's likely ability to repay. In addition, economic theory and negative evaluations of antirecession jobs programs suggested that fiscal policy was not an effective stabilization tool.

A paradox of budgeting during the 1980s was that though the rationales for emphasizing the budget-year deficit weakened, decision makers continued to focus on the budget-year deficit. Partially countering this focus were the multiple-year forecasts of budgetary policy that budget controllers started to prepare. But the fixation on the budget year was still strong—what better example is there than the harsh sequestration penalties for not meeting the annual deficit targets set by Gramm-Rudman-Hollings?

This fixation on cash flow was generally counterproductive. It led to inefficient, last-minute, cut-what-can-be-cut reductions. It also encouraged spending advocates to use obligation and financing tactics. This produced greater uncontrollability, and the economic costs—termination penalties in leases, the additional borrowing costs from agency debt-type borrowing, subsidies to guaranteed loan originators, and so on—were substantial.

A reasonable conclusion is that attention should be shifted from annual cash flow to the long-term effects of the government's financial transactions. Adoption of accrual accounting is necessary for this objective, but it is not the complete answer. One risk is that a focus on accruals would substitute hyperopia for myopia. It would be better to recognize the legitimacy of multiple goals for budgeting, including the goals of controlling the ability of agencies to obligate funds, of allocating limited funds to higher uses, and of promoting national saving and investment over the long-run. As the President's Commission on Budget Concepts concluded: "It is not possible for one number to portray the scope, character, and economic effects of the Government's financial plan." While I earlier argued that the commission was optimistic when it suggested that the desire for one number could be withstood, maybe the experience of the past twenty-five years has informed more of us that multiple goals for budgeting and multiple measures of outcomes are desirable.

Support Development of Generally Accepted Accounting Principles for the Federal Government

Multiple measures that support multiple legitimate goals will not be easy to develop. One indicator is the variance among proposals that have been made by the accountants and economists who are confident that they have designed the best accounting system for the federal government.[2] Knowledge about the development of private sector "Generally Accepted Accounting Principles" (GAAP) shows that this confidence is misplaced. *Generally accepted* means that GAAP principles and practices are defined socially. They are proposed by standard-setting organizations that are staffed by experts and predisposed toward control.[3] But then standards are revised through a long process of comment and debate, and tough standards are sometimes watered down to accommodate influential groups. (The accounting treatment of pensions is instructive.) The process is imperfect, but it serves the basic needs of most users of accounting information.

For the first time, a somewhat similar process has been established in the federal government. The Federal Accounting Standards Advisory Board (FASAB) was created in 1990 by a joint agreement between OMB, Treasury, and GAO. To date, board members have had civil discussions about accounting issues and made some progress in establishing new standards. While the board

2. For example, see GAO 1985b; U.S. Department of Treasury, *Consolidated Financial Statement of the U.S. Government* (annual); Kotlikoff 1992; and Eisner 1986.

3. The Financial Accounting Standards Board sets standards for the private sector, and the Government Accounting Standards Board sets standards for state and local governments.

will be addressing some very difficult conceptual issues in a very political environment, it could begin an educational process that would show the drawbacks of current accounting practices and the advantages and disadvantages of alternatives to these practices (Bramlett 1991; Bramlett and Rexford 1992). The FASAB's decisions will more likely support responsible budgeting if the media pays attention to its decisions and public activists support tough standards.

The procedural equivalent of accounting standards—scorekeeping rules—have already been improved through a similar negotiation between budget agencies. These rules could be published routinely. While there is a risk that publication could provide a manual to spending advocates on how to get around the rules, publication would also make inconsistencies in scorekeeping decisions more obvious.

Increase Understanding of the Effects of Spending

As problematic as are current federal accounting practices, typical beliefs about the effects of spending are often much more inaccurate. Decision makers often seem to blindly accept rationales simply because they are familiar or persuasively argued.

How can decision makers be encouraged to use analyses more often and to use them properly? One strategy would be to increase the supply of analyses of the efficacy of spending. The assumption of this approach is that if decision makers were to receive more disinterested analyses, there would be less of a prospending bias in the stream of information that flows to them. A balanced stream would increase skepticism about claimed effects and encourage more selective approvals of spending proposals.

To carry out this strategy, agencies could be required to create or improve performance and program budgeting systems, more evaluations could be commissioned, and academic and other experts could be invited to participate on commissions that would resolve controversies about the efficacy of spending. An extension of the strategy would have controllers frequently market short, convincing arguments against failing programs.

Of course, the supply approach has already been tried—high-quality analyses of the effects of spending are often readily available. This suggests that the reforms should also be considered for the demand side, to counter the often strong incentives for decision makers to ignore or misuse analyses. Many experts on policy analysis describe some tricks of the trade that analysts can use to encourage decision makers to pay attention or limit their misinterpretations or distortions.[4]

4. For examples of these techniques, see Meltsner 1976; and Weimer and Vining 1992.

Clearly, less progress has been made improving the quality of beliefs about the efficacy of spending than there has been in reforming budgetary accounting or decision procedures. Perhaps this can be explained by referring again to the long-standing public philosophy of interest group liberalism. Since every interest group "deserves" something from government, they can get by with weak program rationales. This perspective has clashed with the newcomer tax revolt, and the result is a muddle: taxes can't be raised, but programs can't be terminated. To reduce the deficit, one or both of the perspectives have to give way. In place of the tax revolt, citizens would acknowledge their responsibility to pay taxes for the services they demand if they continue to hold to interest-group liberalism. In the place of interest-group liberalism, we would need a more explicit, coherent, and limited philosophy of the legitimate role of the government. With this philosophy, we would refuse to spend money on programs that had fully met their original goals, on programs that hadn't worked in the past, or on programs that weren't considered central responsibilities of the federal government. Doing so would allow us to grant more funds to underfunded programs that could work or to experimental programs.

Selectively Change the Structure of Budgeting for Individual Programs

Remaining for discussion are reforms of budgetary decision procedures and policy designs, and first on the agenda must be reforms of mandatory programs. The most recent proposals take two approaches. One focuses on reforming national health care, as the federal programs that finance health care are the main sources of growth in mandatory spending. This approach is beyond the scope of this book. The second approach would extend the sequestration procedure to mandatories, in the hope that the threat of sequestration would produce reconciliation bills that significantly reduced mandatory spending. Some proposals for expanded sequestration would also impose a tax surcharge if deficit reduction targets are not met.

It is not immediately apparent that sequestration would work with mandatory spending. For discretionary programs, sequestration reduces appropriations for each account, and administrators use existing discretion to make do with less. But most administrators of mandatory spending have little or no discretion to change benefit levels or select among eligible beneficiaries, and members of Congress will not likely grant such discretion if sequestration were used for mandatory spending. Instead, the Congress would probably write detailed and different sequestration procedures for each mandatory program (there is no such thing as a typical entitlement). But the logic of this procedure is perplexing: reductions in mandatory spending would be written into law, but would take effect only if the Congress *failed* to pass a reconciliation bill that reduced mandatory spending by a similar amount.

Why would members of Congress and the president act this way? In 1985, sequestration was projected to produce cuts without politicians being blamed for pulling the trigger—although they had aimed and loaded the gun. Of course, it didn't. In both 1987 and 1990, politicians spiked the gun by shifting the deficit targets. It seems unlikely that an "automatic" sequestration of mandatories (not to mention an "automatic" tax surcharge) would protect decision makers from blame when the earlier sequestration process failed.

Because mandatory spending takes such different forms, control of mandatory spending requires that the programs be reviewed one at a time, and that some of the structural characteristics that currently protect them be changed. To return to the forest and trees metaphor, sequestration of mandatories gives the appearance of a clear-cut, but only selective pruning will improve the forest. The most effective types of pruning will make indexing provisions less generous, reverse revenue dedications, and shrink classes of beneficiaries. Some mandatory programs could be made entirely discretionary. Reconciliation is the appropriate procedure for this program-by-program reduction of mandatory spending, but only if leaders force committees to comply with instructions. A procedural alternative would be the sunset procedure that was discussed extensively during the late 1970s but never enacted. Under this procedure, no programs would be permanently authorized—all programs would be routinely considered for reauthorization on a rolling schedule. Sunset would shift the burden of justifying mandatory provisions to spending advocates.

Changes in the policy design of mandatories could be complemented by changes in arenas and decision frequency. Most desirable, in my opinion, is a procedure that would force comparisons between tax expenditures and regular spending programs by functional areas. Unfortunately, the jurisdictional problem is daunting, as the tax-writing committees have a long history of protecting their powers. Because these committees can reduce some tax spending, they can finance expansions of other programs under the pay-as-you-go procedures. Other committees should be given the same opportunity.

Summary

My reform agenda might be characterized as, "The country is going broke overestimating the rationality of the budgetary process." This, of course, is a play on one of H. L. Mencken's most famous witticisms: "No one ever went broke underestimating the intelligence of the American voter." But my reform agenda actually requires that Mencken was wrong, that those who dislike current budget outcomes and the current process will become active. Absent such mobilization, macroinstitutions will be allowed to temporize. Absent such mobilization, spending advocates will ensure that proposed accounting reforms will be weakened, that unquestioned rationales will support unnecessary programs, and that mandatory spending will keep growing.

I recognize that such political mobilization is unlikely. Future generations would be the main beneficiaries of reform of the budget process, and they obviously cannot be mobilized; only their altruistic predecessors can be. It seems even less likely that a structural reform agenda will move many souls—I don't anticipate tens of thousands marching down the Mall shouting, "Relentlessly apply the full funding principle!" While this suggests that budget deficits will remain with us, it does have the benefit—from my perspective—that this book's ideas about structural budget tactics will retain some validity.

Appendix: Methodological Issues

Researchers who use qualitative methods to understand a complex process risk losing perspective. They can overemphasize interesting cases and neglect the boring but still important cases. The best way to guard against this problem is to exercise diligence and care when interviewing, participating, and thinking. The first part of this Appendix describes how I carried out these activities.

My qualitative methods, even if used perfectly, did not enable me to prove beyond a doubt that structural strategies were the best choices for the advocates that used them, or even that these strategies had a positive effect. Therefore, this study is properly understood as interpretive and suggestive. I am quite willing to admit to the possibility that I overemphasized the importance of budget-structure strategies—perhaps working in a budget office makes one the functional equivalent of the police officer who learns to believe that violent, irresponsible, bizarre, or perverse behaviors are the norm. The second part of the Appendix discusses this issue of emphasis.

The Methodological Approach Used for This Research

The base method for this study was participant observation. I was employed by the Congressional Budget Office from April 1981 through July 1990 as an analyst in its Budget Process Unit. This unit was part of the Budget Analysis Division, the division responsible for preparing budget estimates, scorekeeping of congressional budget actions, and analysis of reforms of the process. In this environment, the accuracy of academic criticisms of the theory of budgetary incrementalism became quickly apparent. However, in contrast to those participant observers that enter the field with a research focus, my emphasis during my first years at CBO was more on participation than on theory-oriented observation. Then, in 1984, I wrote a report on the budgetary status of the Federal Reserve (Meyers 1985). Besides learning about the Federal Reserve's strange budgetary history, I benefited intellectually, if not emotionally, from its staff's efforts to influence the content of the report. I began rummaging through my files and my memory of experiences at CBO for interesting cases, new leads, and possible counterexamples to emerging ideas. This research method was heavily influenced by Glaser and Strauss's *The Discovery of Grounded*

Theory (1967).[1] They argue for a qualitative research method in which one constantly compares different cases in order to develop useful concepts and theories. Case selection is determined more by prospective theoretical utility than by the concern that the sample of cases accurately reflect the characteristics of the universe. The grounded-theory approach is enabled by the use of different qualitative research approaches—direct observation, interviewing, analysis of printed sources—in appropriate situations. Although this methodology did prove to be very useful, I did not follow the strict coding procedures advocated by some of its proponents (Lane 1990).

I began by conducting thirty-four interviews during a leave of absence from CBO in October and November 1985. Most of the informants were old hands in budgeting—OMB examiners, CBO analysts, congressional staffers, agency budget and program directors, lobbyists. Many had experience in several of these roles. I selected the interviewees on the basis of these employment characteristics, on whether potential interviewees had reputations for being wise owls, and with a concern for balance across program areas. I make no claim, though, to the representativeness of this initial group of informants.

I always told the interviewees of my background at CBO, which had advantages and disadvantages. It conveyed the message that I knew something about budgeting and perhaps wouldn't be too ivory tower in approach (a real minus to most Washington elites). As most interviewees probably saw CBO as a relatively objective institution with which they would like to keep good relations, I believe that my access to these people was enhanced by my employment status. On several occasions, however, I felt that interviewees were not being very forthcoming to me because they viewed CBO as a potential threat. (I have also left out of this book a number of cases that would serve to document my theory, but which I must keep to myself so as to not violate professional and personal confidences.) In addition, my controller status while at CBO, and my continuing support for deficit reduction after leaving, made it inappropriate to question some participants about the relative importance of incremental and budget-structure strategies.

In my opinion, these problems were more than offset by the extremely open responses that I obtained from most of the informants. I would commonly phrase questions about sensitive topics in a way that indicated that I knew a fair amount about budgeting—in effect, that I was in on some of their secrets (Dexter 1970; Smigel 1969, 17–35). I believe that this encouraged informants to be forthcoming, especially because a number of informants provided me with memos and other documents that are quoted in the text; several provided

1. See also McCall and Simmons 1969; Taylor and Bogdan 1984; Fenno 1978, 249–95; Fenno 1986, 3–15; and C. Mills 1959.

or showed me documents that contributed to my understanding but that may not be cited.

This experience confirmed a reputed major strength of participant observation, in that it allows the researcher to understand special language, which is rife in budgeting. It may even be a necessary method when the process that is being studied involves subterfuge, broken rules, and participants covering their tracks, as I argue budgeting does. Taylor and Bogdan comment,

> In contrast to participant observers, interviewers lack the first-hand knowledge of how people act in their day-to-day lives. This can make it difficult to sort out the difference between purposeful distortions and gross exaggerations, on the one hand, and genuine perspectives (which are necessarily "subjective" and "biased"), on the other. (1984, 99)

After my leave from CBO, I analyzed budget documents and secondary sources, and carried out uncounted mini-interviews over the phone and in person. I often used a nondirective interviewing style to try to minimize informant reactivity.

Although I took care to avoid the typical pitfalls of qualitative research, I found it impossible to overcome one completely. A danger of participant observation is that one's personal involvement will seriously distort perceptions of the subject of the study (Becker 1958). It was often difficult to shed the participant's worldview—that of a budget officer—for the observer's: I came to view some advocates more as perpetrators than as participants. This probably caused me to overemphasize the importance of accounting gimmicks early in my rcsearch, because I was part of an organization that was actively trying to stop them. Moving from CBO to academia gave me a better perspective on this issue. Although this book was completed later than I had planned, the time to reflect on what I had seen and the passage of the Budget Enforcement Act of 1990, led me to rate the success of controllers in reaching their goals much higher than I had originally.

An Overemphasis on Budget-Structure Strategies?

As stated above, qualitatitive methods prevented me from testing the comparative worth of incremental and budget-structure strategies. Since case selection with grounded-theory methods is determined more by prospective theoretical utility than by the concern that the sample of cases accurately reflect the characteristics of the universe, my sampling rule was to actively search for nonincremental cases (Glaser and Strauss 1967, chap. 3).[2] I thought incrementalism was an impoverished theory, and my purpose was to develop something different. In any event, my mind boggled at the thought of trying to develop a representative sampling frame—of outcomes, strategies, or resources—and then researching the appropriate cases. Nor did I want to lose the degree of concept density that I achieved with the grounded-theory method.

My methods could have produced a bias toward observing structural strategies when actually they were quite rare. On the other hand, in contrast to most previous studies of budgeting, the range of cases covered here is quite wide. These studies solved the problem of potentially overwhelming complexity by studying only a subset of the budget. Note, however, that the simple appropriations accounts included in the Fenno sample now constitute only less than 10 percent of the government's outlays. And it is surprisingly easy to find numerous examples of structural tactics when looking into the history of the Fenno sample accounts, or when struggling through their P and F statements. Included in the sample are a number of accounts that were featured in this book, including the Rural Electrification Administration, the Bureau of Land Management, NASA, the Bureau of Reclamation, the Corps of Engineers, the Patent Office, the Bonneville Power Administration, and the Bureau of Public Debt.

Another reason to accept the popularity of structural strategies is that it is relatively easy to find reports of their use elsewhere and at other times. For example, leasing, dedicated funds, public authorities, and accounting gimmicks are quite popular in state government budgeting.[3] One can also find examples of structural strategies from the era that incrementalism is thought to describe so well—the 1950s and 1960s. One useful source is a staff paper by Naomi Sweeney for the President's Commission on Budget Concepts, which describes a number of the tactics discussed in this book (1967). Another is one of Wildavsky's targets, Smithies's *The Budgetary Process in the United States.* For example, this study included the following statements on agricultural budgeting.

> Preferred budgetary positions, however, have been created not for the agricultural program as a whole but for important segments of it . . . these are open to criticism on the grounds that they obstruct the formulation of a well-balanced agricultural program within the limits imposed by the whole agricultural budget. . . .

---

2. For examples of other samples designed to ensure variance in what was being observed, see Fenno 1978, 253; and Kingdon 1984, 219–20.

3. See, for example, *Connecticut's Off-Budget Funds: Out of Sight Out of Mind* (Hartford: Connecticut Public Expenditure Council, June 1984); Anthony 1985; Hale and Douglass 1977; Cothran 1986; Kirkland 1983.

> There can be little question that but for the permanent appropriation either the total agricultural budget would be smaller or other agricultural programs would receive a larger share of it . . . since these payments parade under the banner of conservation, they undoubtedly receive more favorable budgetary treatment than they would if they were proposed as subsidies. . . .
>
> When general research cuts are made by the President or the committees, they appear to result more from considerations of budgetary expediency, including the impossibility of cutting the sheltered programs, rather than from deliberate general consideration of the requirement of research (Smithies 1955, 362–69).[4]

Or return to a famous letter President Thomas Jefferson wrote his secretary of the Treasury in 1802, explaining what might be called Hamilton's "structural strategy."

> In order that he might have the entire government of his machine, he determined so to complicate it as that neither the President nor Congress should be able to understand it, or to control him. He succeeded in doing this, not only beyond their reach, but so that he at length could not unravel it himself. He gave to the debt, in the first instance, in funding it, the most artificial and mysterious form he could devise. He then mounded up his appropriations of a number of scraps and remnants, many of which were nothing at all, applied them to different objects in reversion and remainder, until the whole system was involved in impenetrable fog. (1904–5, 9:358–59)

Apparently the fog bank described in chapter 2 has been around for a while.

Of course, only quantitative tests can provide definitive evidence about the extent of use and effectiveness of budget-structure strategies. To carry out these tests, controls would have to be developed for levels of political resources and context, and budgetary outcomes would have to be measured accurately. If the arguments in chapters 1, 2, and 4 are accepted, this is a research opportunity only for those with fat wallets! Reported budget outcomes must be adjusted to take account of the fact that programs can receive funding or have new constraints imposed at different times during the year (e.g., from supplemental bills or from authorization limits), be financed from both on-budget and off-budget sources, and that some funding is available for multiyear periods. Recasting historical data for such tests will be difficult

4. The chapter after the agriculture chapter is a description of the budgetary advantages enjoyed by revolving funds, government corporations, and guarantee programs.

because changes in government accounting practices make it extremely difficult to understand and modify lines in older budget statements.

Perhaps the ideas in this book at some time will be judged worthy enough to merit such testing. Absent such tests, the plausibility of the structural strategy approach will be assessed by practitioners. Among the best tests will be whether current or former participants in budgeting processes find my observations to be consistent with their experiences, and whether future participants feel that they were forewarned.[5]

5. On this method of assessing validity, see Fenno 1978.

Afterword to the Paperback Edition

This book intentionally ignored the formal institutions of American government to focus on the procedural and informational structures of budgeting. Yet any observer of budgeting from 1993 through early 1996 should have been struck by the impacts on budgetary outcomes of partisan competition and of the Madisonian "sharing" of powers. The deficit was substantially reduced over this period, but 1995 and 1996 also produced a historically significant stalemate—a dozen continuing resolutions, a three-week shutdown of many agencies and programs, and placement of the United States on a credit watch because failure to raise the debt ceiling might cause a default on debt payments. How did this happen, and what role was played by budget structures?

Shortly after the final draft of this book was completed in 1993, the Democratically controlled Congress passed legislation that would reduce the deficit by more than $400 billion over five years. A unified government had performed as the advocates of partisan responsibility had hoped; no Republicans voted for the plan, understandable behavior given the plan's reliance on tax increases for the rich and spending reductions for defense.

Though the public had often declared its support for deficit reductions, the Democrats received no electoral credit in 1994 for their 1993 actions. Instead, the Republicans gained full control of the Congress for the first time in forty years. The Democrats then resolved that the Republicans would bear the onus of budgetary responsibility; President Clinton's fiscal year 1996 budget implicitly dared the Republicans with "you go first."

The House Republicans accepted, attacking the established order of policies using their "Contract with America," a campaign pledge to consider ten sets of proposals that had tested well in focus groups and polls. More a broadside than a defensible contract, it promised lower taxes *and* lower spending *and* balance. Republicans often distracted attention from the mathematical inconsistency by supporting a balanced budget constitutional amendment. Enacted by a large majority of the House, the amendment failed by the slimmest of margins in the Senate.

The surprising legacy was a strengthening of the Republican commitment for balance; though Republicans had argued that only the amendment would provide the necessary "discipline," even absent this cover they proposed a massive plan and claimed it would balance the federal budget in seven years. The next surprise was that they pushed significant components of this plan through the House, the Senate, or both bodies. In the end, however, presidential vetoes and public opposition prevented most of the plan from being enacted into law.

From 1993 through early 1996, the positions and actions of the parties (and from 1995 through early 1996, the branches) were so opposed that the budgetary process was like a war. Extending that analogy, the Republicans of 1995 resembled the armies that invaded Russia but failed to conquer it. They had creative leaders, were well-organized, and used better technology than their opponents. Yet though most Republicans (including the freshmen shock troops) were experienced politicians, much of that experience came on easier terrain; the novelty of the 1995 context led them to make fatal strategic blunders. One was assuming that President Clinton's typical preference of compromise over conflict would cause him to not wield his veto—the equivalent of expecting a "short and mild" winter in Russia (*any* winter in Russia is comparatively long and deep). The other strategic blunder was equivalent to slighting the mass and bravery of the Russian people; put simply, balancing the budget is always difficult because of widespread, effective political opposition to the policy changes necessary for balancing.

Yet almost all Republicans wanted to balance only by reducing spending; many new members were even more ambitious, proposing tax reductions that would be offset by deeper spending cuts. They recognized their actions would antagonize some organized interests, but they claimed to prefer changing budgetary policies over long Washington careers. Some of the more experienced Republicans were less sanguine about the difficulties they faced—House Majority Leader Richard Armey, a strong advocate of deep cuts, responded to the Democrats' call for specifics during the balanced budget debate by admitting

> The fact of the matter is once members of Congress know exactly, chapter and verse, the pain that the government must live with in order to get to a balanced budget, their knees will buckle.[1]

Armey knew that specificity would force citizens to confront their ambivalence about balanced budgets, which they supported in general but

1. Andrew Taylor, "Amendment Remains a Gamble Despite Its Popularity," *Congressional Quarterly Weekly Report,* 14 January 1995, 141.

often opposed in practice when asked to choose means for balancing. And early specificity would help organized interests mobilize and use structural protections to counter proposed reductions. But budget legislation, unlike constitutional amendments, must be specific, so the Republicans soon confronted this problem.

Killing or eviscerating domestic discretionary programs led their agenda. The fiscal year 1996 appropriations bills made historically significant reductions, and both the Republicans and President Clinton extended real cuts in these programs into the twenty-first century by extending and lowering the appropriations caps created in 1990. One reason was that many appropriated programs had long been protected by Democratic majorities despite doubts about effectiveness (for example, employment training); the new regime naturally placed such programs at risk, despite frequent Democratic attempts to justify them as "investments." Other programs were cut because they regulated the Republicans' political base (for example, the Environmental Protection Agency). The Republicans also showed more self-restraint on distributive earmarks, and eventually enacted a close-substitute to the line-item veto that gave the President "enhanced rescission" authority (though its constitutionality was questionable).

The procedural ease of discretionary limits undoubtedly made them attractive as well, though to some degree that ease served as a crutch. On numerous occasions when controllers had to give up on proposals to limit mandatory spending, they made up the differences by increasing projected discretionary savings, typically by making the spending caps lower in the far outyears. That control tactic implicitly assumed that large operating efficiencies could be continually found, and that political and policy contexts would continue to support downsizing of the federal government; good grounds exist for doubting both assumptions.

The Republicans also went after mandatory spending, but were less successful in adopting cuts that President Clinton could support. They particularly focused on means-tested entitlements like Aid to Families with Dependent Children, Supplemental Security Income and disability insurance, foster care, nutrition programs, and Medicaid. The policy redesigns limited eligibility, revoked entitlement status, and blocked and capped grants to states. Generally described as "welfare reform," the supporting rationales included that state administration would be more efficient than federal administration and that monetary disincentives for beneficiaries would substantially reduce their dependencies. Most influential was the argument that programs should not be federal responsibilities; a related rationale, though supporters rarely said it publicly, was that devolving responsibilities to the states would force them to bid benefit levels and tax rates down—the so-called race to the bottom.

One reason why most of these proposed savings were not enacted, at least by early 1996, was that the plan was so unbalanced. The Republicans' greatest political vulnerability has long been the perception that they pick on the poor, and President Clinton used that vulnerability to embarrass the Republicans about the depth of their proposed cuts. The Republicans made that easier by protecting taxes and defense from cuts; they couldn't claim that sacrifices would be widely shared. The Democratic tax changes of 1993 had made effective tax rates for the rich relatively high by historical comparison, probably precluding even higher rates on them, but the Republicans ruled out discussion of other tax options such as a broad-based increase in rates, an environmental/energy responsibility tax, or eliminating tax preferences. President Clinton paid only lip service to the latter two options.

The Republicans also opposed further downsizing of the military, despite its size in comparison to other countries (the United States held about half of the world's military resources), discontent with peacekeeping and humanitarian assistance, and the public's shift toward isolationism. The Republicans argued that the force structure had already been cut enough if the United States wanted to be dominant, that favorable strategic conditions would not continue indefinitely, and that the physical depreciation of military hardware required new investments just to maintain current levels of military force.

Republicans did propose cuts in non-means-tested entitlements, but here they also had only limited success. Proposed reductions for federal retirement programs—employees would contribute more from pay, and benefits would be calculated from a less generous base—were pulled back for lack of support among moderate Republicans. The politics of blame-generation for Social Security kept it "off-the-table," as is generally the case, though Social Security and many other entitlements were at risk from technical reductions to cost-of-living adjustments (COLAs). A consensus developed that the Consumer Price Index overstated actual inflation, and one seriously considered option was to direct the Bureau of Labor Statistics (BLS) to fix that bias, thereby decaffeinating the COLAs; fear of blame-bearing for "cutting Social Security" watered down projected savings into an assumption that the BLS eventually would make the change.

Health presented the largest opportunity for deficit reductions, and the Republicans focused on Medicare, justifying proposed cuts as the only way to save a system that was rushing toward insolvency. Yet cuts in medical services and reimbursements are never easy to adopt, and the Democrats were ready to counterattack after their treatment by the Republicans in the comprehensive health reform debacle of 1993 and

1994. They did so with a skillful public relations campaign that the Republicans appropriately nicknamed "Mediscare"; the Democrats positioned themselves as fiscally responsible protectors of essential programs by proposing substantially smaller cuts.

Finally, a strange-bedfellows coalition of conservative deficit hawks and Secretary of Labor Robert Reich, the most articulate liberal spokesman in the government, argued that deficits should be reduced by ending "corporate welfare." Though this approach resonated with the public, those subsidies were heavily defended with campaign contributions and rationales for their necessity (for example, to enable a level playing field for international trade); both parties drew back from most initial plans to reduce these subsidies. Agricultural subsidies provide somewhat of a contrast. The 1996 farm bill created a new spending design for major commodities, delinking most payments from production levels and phasing down these payments over seven years; the intent of some sponsors was to create an opportunity at the end of this period to shift entirely to market incentives. But the short-term price of the plan was an increase in near-term subsidies, which without the new law would have fallen because of tight commodity markets.

What role was played by budget structures from 1993 to 1996? To begin with tactics, and in reverse of the order used in this book, the summary above reflects the high quantity of arguments about the policy effects of spending. This is often not the case when large deficit reductions are considered, as debates about options degenerate into arguments about exactly how much might be saved rather than how cuts change programmatic results. There certainly were disagreements of the former type, but partisan conflict brought effects rationales to the center of the debates; many were oriented to the single dimension of big government versus small government.

Given the widespread support for deficit reduction, few advocates successfully used the tactics of budgetary policy design to expand spending. Almost all policy design proposals were pushed by controllers wanting to retrench entitlements, both by reducing automatic growth and by granting spending discretion to those facing incentives to reduce; controllers picked on discretionary spending because this policy design exposed programs to reductions. In the House, they also developed a new procedure called the "lockbox," which prevented cuts to appropriations bills from being saved and credited to later appropriations bills that would exceed targets.

Nor did many advocates modify budgetary decision tactics; the procedural controls established by the Budget Enforcement Act remained largely intact. Strong expectations of deficit neutrality protected the pay-as-you-go rules, which limited opportunities to adopt new entitlements and tax expenditures. Pay-as-you-go was modified, however, by removal of the "firewall" between mandatory and discretionary arenas—tax cuts could be financed by savings in discretionary appropriations. Fiscal stress also heightened within-arena conflicts, particularly within appropriations subcommittees. Since this was the case in all arenas, trying to escape an arena provided little if any tactical advantage. An important exception was the large appropriations increases for crime reduction programs, which were walled-off into a "trust fund" and "financed" with savings from reducing the number of personnel in federal agencies.

Spending advocates did continue to game scorekeeping practices. For example, the Republicans dropped their controller stance when they proposed tax cuts, which they tried to protect by backloading costs beyond the seven year target date for a balanced (temporarily) budget (at least the window was now seven years long rather than five). Spending advocates also continued using accounting tactics, though many of the egregious gimmicks of the past—declaring off-budget status, for example—were out of bounds. For some of the disputes about accounting rules, the complexity of the transactions and the proposed ways of counting them hinder making the players and their tactics clear, particularly in the limited space available here, but a few examples are worth a mention. One is student loans, and particularly how to calculate the costs under two loan delivery alternatives: guaranteed and direct. Prior to adoption of credit reform, new guaranteed loans looked relatively cheap, even with payment of a generous subsidy to originators, because the costs of default were not recorded until years after origination. After credit reform, direct loans looked relatively cheap because the full costs of guaranteed loans were now approximated in the budget year, and because administrative costs were excluded from cost calculations (administering direct loans is more costly than guaranteed loans). With the Republicans favoring guaranteed loans and the Democrats favoring direct loans, they fought over how scorekeepers should be directed to count these administrative costs.

Another area for accounting tactics involved asset sales, as the rules were relaxed to allow crediting as deficit reductions of the proceeds from the sales of physical assets. The administration and Members of Congress manipulated the details of several proposals—varying which physical assets would be sold, how they would be sold, and when they would be sold—in order to plug holes in budget plans. Yet another area of complex accounting described in chapter 4 was that of budget authority for subsidized housing, in which I mentioned that Housing and Urban Development might logically count assistance as lasting only 1 year; this comment was meant sarcastically but it came true in practice. A final example of accounting tactics was a simple replay—defense spending advocates forced abandonment of the full-funding rule by financing major Navy ships for only the first year of construction.

So some accounting tactics prevented some deficit reductions from 1993 through 1996, as did other actions of spending advocates, particularly arguments about the effects of spending cuts. But in general, controllers improved their position in the control and advocacy dynamic. High fiscal stress and decades of controller tactics had significantly reduced the probability that budgetary controls could be avoided; spending advocates often abandoned the search for tactical opportunities, deciding the risk of antagonizing controllers was too great. This suggests that the structure of the budget process probably played little if any role in the difficulties experienced by the Congress and the president, leaving the broader factors of institutional conflict, partisan competition, and public ambivalence as the main explanations for the failure to balance the budget.

But it is probably unwise to make such a clear distinction between budget structures and the political system in which they reside. Consider the expectations for budgeting described in chapter 3—definitive information, a routine schedule, and the demonstration of central control. Interbranch conflict contributed to the perception that the process lacked definitive information, a problem best shown by a very partisan dispute over whether the "real numbers" were produced by OMB or by CBO. Partisan ideologies also reduced the quality, if not the quantity, of arguments about the effects of spending. The expectation of the routine schedule was replaced with a competitive obsession to balance at the end of seven years, and this attempt at "septennial budgeting" understandably broke down—it's demanding enough to try to understand the long-run implications of current actions; it's far more difficult to make some difficult decisions that could wait until the long-run arrives. And demonstrating central control within the process, as usual, was prevented by the structure of the branches and the internal organization of the Congress.

The conclusion of this book set out several recommendations for changing the budget process in order to adopt sensible deficit reductions. Despite the pessimistic points made in this afterword, it's easy to see some progress. That deficits should be reduced is now the consensus, and the needed debate on the appropriate size and responsibilities of the federal government is at least ongoing, though the quality of the debate could clearly be improved. The 1993 Government Performance and Results Act has agencies trying to integrate performance measurement and budgeting in a more feasible way than was tried in previous attempts like PPBS. It will still be a daunting task, but the more important challenge is how this bureaucratic process can be intergrated with the public debate about the effects of spending.

The main progress on the accounting front is that the Federal Accounting Standards Advisory Board has developed standards that will guide improvements in budgetary accounting practices. On the other hand, it has not resolved the most important controversies, especially over how to count the likely costs of long-lived commitments.

A final indicator of progress is that the recurrent focus on controlling the budget-year deficit has been replaced with an understanding that reductions must be made gradually over a multiyear "glide path." Yet this debate has been misguided in its concentration on the goal of reaching a balance of revenues and outlays by the end year of the glide path. In the first place, this implies that maintaining an adequate cash-flow from tax revenues is the main function of budgeting; that makes little if any sense for the federal government. Second, reaching that goal, especially with the policies currently under consideration, does almost nothing to avoid the guaranteed fiscal danger of the future. That danger is caused by the interaction of the aging of the population and the design of Social Security and health care programs. Averting this danger will be aided by improvements in the structure of budgeting for entitlements—accurate accounting practices, flexible program designs and decision procedures, and valid justifications for this spending—but political leadership and public learning will be more important.

References

Alonso, William, and Paul Starr, eds. 1987. *The Politics of Numbers.* New York: Russell Sage.

Altshuler, Alan, and Marshall Kaplan. 1993. "Whatever Happened to the Infrastructure Crisis?" *Governing,* July, 59–67.

Anthony, Robert N. 1985. "Games Government Accountants Play." *Harvard Business Review* (September-October): 161–70.

Anton, Thomas J. 1966. *The Politics of State Expenditure in Illinois.* Urbana, Ill.: University of Illinois Press.

———. 1967. "Roles and Symbols in the Determination of State Expenditures." *Midwest Journal of Political Science* 11 (February): 27–43.

Anton, Thomas J., Jerry P. Cawley, and Kevin L. Kramer. 1980. "Making Outlays Sense." In *Moving Money.* 103–24. Cambridge, Mass.: Oelgeschlager, Gunn, and Hain.

Armbrust, Earl A., William A. Isaacson, and R. Mark Musell. 1983. *The Federal Buildings Program: Authorization and Budgetary Alternatives.* Washington, D.C.: Congressional Budget Office. June.

Arnold, R. Douglas. 1990. *The Logic of Congressional Action.* New Haven: Yale University Press.

Auten, Gerald, Barry Bozeman, and Robert Cline. 1984. "A Sequential Model of Congressional Appropriations." *American Journal of Political Science* 28:503–23.

Axelrod, Donald. 1988. *Budgeting for Modern Government.* New York: St. Martin's.

Axelrod, Robert. 1984. *The Evolution of Cooperation.* New York: Basic Books.

Bailey, John J., and Robert J. O'Connor. 1975. "Operationalizing Incrementalism: Measuring the Muddles." *Public Administration Review* 35:60–66.

Bardach, Eugene. 1972. *The Skill Factor in Politics.* Berkeley and Los Angeles: University of California Press.

Barnes, James A. 1990. "$100K-Zzzzz." *National Journal,* 4 August, 1915.

Bassein, Richard, and Paul R. Schulman. 1985. "Modelling the Growth (and Decline) of Federal Agencies and Programs." Working Paper 85–1, Institute of Governmental Studies, University of California, Berkeley.

Becker, Howard S. 1958. "Problems of Inference and Proof in Participant Observation." *American Sociological Review* 23:652–60.

Behn, Robert D. 1985. "Cutback Budgeting." *Journal of Policy Analysis and Management* 4 (Winter): 155–77.

Bell, Robert. 1985. "Professional Values and Organizational Decision Making." *Administration and Society* 17 (May): 21–60.

Benenson, Bob. 1993. "House OKs Agriculture Spending with Most Grants Unscathed." *Congressional Quarterly Weekly Report,* 3 July, 1723–25.

Berry, William D. 1986. "Testing Budgetary Theories with Budgetary Data: Addressing the Risks." *American Journal of Political Science* 30:597–627.

———. 1990. "The Confusing Case of Budgetary Incrementalism: Too Many Meanings for a Single Concept." *Journal of Politics* 52 (February):167–96.

Berry, William D., and David Lowery. 1989. "Convergence and Divergence in Empirical Analyses of Fiscal Politics." *American Politics Quarterly* 17:447–76.

Bickers, Kenneth. 1991. "The Programmatic Expansion of the U.S. Government." *Western Political Quarterly* 44:891–914.

Birnbaum, Jeffrey H., and Alan S. Murray. 1987. *Showdown at Gucci Gulch.* New York: Random House.

Blais, Andre, and Stephane Dion, eds. 1991. *The Budget-Maximizing Bureaucrat: Appraisals and Evidence.* Pittsburgh: University of Pittsburgh Press.

Blose, Laurence E., and John D. Martin. 1989. "Federal Government Leasing: Costs, Incentives, and Effects." *Public Budgeting and Finance* 9 (Summer): 66–75.

Blum, James L. 1987. Remarks before the American Association for Budget and Program Analysis. 9 April.

Boseman, William C., and Christine Matthews Rose. 1988. *Equity, Excellence, and the Distribution of Federal Research and Development Funds.* Congressional Research Service. 25 April.

Bosworth, Barry, Andrew Carron, and Elisabeth Rhyne. 1988. *The Economics of Federal Credit Programs.* Washington, D.C.: Brookings.

Bozeman, Barry. 1977. "Acquisitiveness in Public Agencies: The Influence of Past Budgetary Success and Personnel Structure." *American Politics Quarterly* 5:517–29.

———. 1987. *All Organizations Are Public.* San Francisco: Jossey-Bass.

Bozeman, Barry, and Jeffrey D. Straussman. 1982. "Shrinking Budgets and the Shrinkage of Budget Theory." *Public Administration Review* 42:509–15.

———. 1990. *Public Management Strategies.* San Francisco: Jossey-Bass.

Bramlett, Robert W. 1991. "The Federal Accounting Standards Advisory Board: An Introduction for Non-Accountants." *Public Budgeting and Finance* 11 (Winter): 11–19.

Bramlett, Robert W., and Frank Rexford. 1992. "The Federal Accounting Standards Advisory Board: A View of Its Role One Year Later." *Public Budgeting and Finance* 12 (Winter): 87–101.

Burkhead, Jesse. 1956. *Government Budgeting.* New York: John Wiley.

Caiden, Naomi. 1982. "The Myth of the Annual Budget." *Public Administration Review* 42:516–23.

———. 1984. "The New Rules of the Budget Game." *Public Administration Review* 44:109–18.

———. 1990. "Public Budgeting in the United States: The State of the Discipline." In

Naomi Lynn and Aaron Wildavsky, *Public Administration: The State of the Discipline,* 228–55. Chatham, N.J.: Chatham House.

Caldeira, Greg A., and Andrew T. Cowart. 1980. "Budgets, Institutions, and Change: Criminal Justice Policy in America." *American Journal of Political Science* 24:413–38.

Calmes, Jackie. 1989. "Leon Panetta: Wearing Two Hats." *Congressional Quarterly Weekly Report,* 28 October, 2853.

Camia, Catalina. 1993. "With Grazing Fee Hike Certain, Question Becomes How Much." *Congressional Quarterly Weekly Report,* 7 August, 2150–51.

Caro, Robert. 1982. *The Path to Power.* New York: Random House.

Cato Institute. 1985. *Cato Policy Report,* September, 16.

Center for Defense Information. 1982. "OMB and the Pentagon: Adversaries or Collaborators?" *Defense Monitor,* 2 November 1982.

Children's Defense Fund. 1986. *Children's Defense Fund Reports,* February–March, insert.

Chite, Ralph. 1989. "FmHa Losses and the Federal Budget." Congressional Research Service. 18 January.

Choate, Pat, and Susan Walter. 1981. *America in Ruins: Beyond the Public Works Pork Barrel.* Washington, D.C.: Council of State Planning Agencies.

Civiak, Robert L. 1985. "Cost Accounting, Pricing, and Cost Recovery in DOE's Uranium Enrichment Program." Congressional Research Service. 9 October.

Clark, Timothy B. 1983. "Congress Avoiding Political Abyss by Approving Social Security Changes." *National Journal,* 19 March, 611.

Clark, Vance L. 1987. Letter to Senator William Proxmire. 1 June.

Cloud, David S. 1989a. "Committee Tries to Force-Feed Aerospace Plane Funding." *Congressional Quarterly Weekly Report,* 5 August, 2029.

———. 1989b. "Lawmakers to Weigh Farm Bill amid Budget, Trade Fears." *Congressional Quarterly Weekly Report,* 18 February, 318–19.

Cogan, John F. 1988. "The Evolution of Congressional Budget Decisionmaking and the Emergence of Federal Deficits." Working Paper in Economics E-88–33, Hoover Institution.

Cohen, Michael D., James G. March, and Johan P. Olsen. 1972. "A Garbage Can Theory of Organizational Choice." *Administrative Science Quarterly* 17 (March): 1–25.

Congressional Budget Office (CBO). 1977. *Advance Budgeting: A Report to the Congress.* March.

———. 1983. *Public Works Infrastructure: Policy Considerations for the 1980s.* April.

———. 1987a. *An Analysis of the President's Budgetary Proposals for FY 1988.*

———. 1987b. *Trends in Public Investment.* December.

———. 1988. *The Status of the Airport and Airway Trust Fund.* December.

———. 1989. *The Economic and Budget Outlook: Fiscal Years 1990–1994.* January.

———. 1990a. *The Economic and Budget Outlook, Fiscal Years 1991–1995.* January.

———. 1990b. *The Federal Deficit: Does It Measure the Government's Effect on National Saving?* March.

———. 1991. *Controlling the Risks of Government-Sponsored Enterprises.*
Congressional Research Service. 1981. *Indexation of Federal Programs.* Printed by the Senate Budget Committee. May.
Conlan, Timothy J., Margaret T. Wrightson, and David R. Beam. 1990. *Taxing Choices: The Politics of Tax Reform.* Washington, D.C.: Congressional Quarterly Press.
Cooper, Ann. 1986. "Trade Aid May Be Salvaged." *National Journal,* 11 January, 88.
Cooper, Joseph, and William F. West. 1988. "Presidential Power and Republican Government: The Theory and Practice of OMB Review of Agency Rules." *Journal of Politics* 50:864–95.
Corn, M. Lynne. 1986. "A Guide to Trust Funds, Special Accounts, and Foundations in the Fish and Wildlife Service Budget." Congressional Research Service. 30 May.
Corporation for Public Broadcasting. 1987. *Annual Report.* Washington, D.C.
Cothran, Dan A. 1986. "Some Sources of 'Budgetary Uncontrollability': The Interaction of Automatic Funding and Program Flexibility." *Public Budgeting and Finance* 6 (Summer): 45–62.
Crecine, John P., and Philip Bromiley. 1980. "Budget Development in OMB: Aggregate Influences of the Problem and Information Environment." *Journal of Politics* 42:1031–64.
Cuny, Thomas J. 1991. "Federal Credit Reform." *Public Budgeting and Finance* 11 (Summer): 19–32.
Davis, Joseph A. 1985. "Congress Tries for Compromise on Disputed Grazing Fee Issue." *Congressional Quarterly Weekly Report,* 24 August, 1676–78.
Davis, Otto A., M. A. H. Dempster, and Aaron Wildavsky. 1966. "A Theory of the Budgetary Process." *American Political Science Review* 60:529–47.
Davis, Phillip A. 1991. "East Meets West in Latest Fight over Grazing Fee Increase." *Congressional Quarterly Weekly Report,* 22 June, 1656–58.
———. 1992. "Drift New Ban, User Fee Repeal Sent to the White House." *Congressional Quarterly Weekly Report,* 10 October, 3153.
deLeon, Peter. 1987. "The Influence of Analysis on U.S. Defense Policy." *Policy Sciences* 20:105–28.
DeMaree, Allan T. 1982. "Infrastructure Chic: How to Judge the Jobs Bills," *Fortune,* 13 December, 122–24, 128.
DeMilner, Lawrence E. 1981. "Indexing with the Consumer Price Index: Problems and Alternatives." Congressional Budget Office, June 1981.
Demkovich, Linda E. 1981. "It's a Whole New Budget Ball Game, but Lobbyists Are Playing by Old Rules." *National Journal,* 10 October, 1806–9.
———. 1983. "Who Says Congress Can't Move Fast? Just Ask Hospitals about Medicare." *National Journal,* 2 April, 704–7.
———. 1984. "How to Run a Federal Energy Program without Spending Any Federal Money." *National Journal,* 18 February, 320–22.
———. 1985. "Administration Taking Aim at Subsidies for Hospitals' Medical Evaluation Costs." *National Journal,* 9 February, 309–11.
DeMott, Benjamin. 1990. *The Imperial Middle: Why Americans Can't Think Straight about Class.* New York: Morrow.

Dempster, M. A. H., and Aaron Wildavsky. 1979. "On Change: Or, There Is No Magic Size for an Increment." *Political Studies* 27 (September): 371–89.

DeMuth, Christopher C. 1980. "The Regulatory Budget." *Regulation* 4 (April): 29–46.

De Neufville, Judith I., and Stephen E. Barton. 1987. "Myths and the Definition of Policy Problems: An Exploration of Home Ownership and Public-Private Partnerships." *Policy Sciences* 20:181–206.

Derthick, Martha. 1975. *Uncontrollable Spending for Social Services Grants.* Washington, D.C.: Brookings.

———. 1979. *Policy Making for Social Security.* Washington, D.C.: Brookings.

Derthick, Martha, and Paul J. Quirk. 1985. *The Politics of Deregulation.* Washington, D.C.: Brookings.

Dexter, Lewis Anthony. 1970. *Elite and Specialized Interviewing.* Evanston, Ill.: Northwestern University Press.

Dion, Philip. 1983. "Rescuing Shaky REA May Be Harder Than Influential Rural Co-ops Say." *National Journal,* 5 May, 2310–13.

Doherty, Carroll J. 1990. "Who Will Dole Out Gulf Donations." *Congressional Quarterly Weekly Report,* 22 September, 3030.

Domke, William K. 1984. "Waste, Weapons, and Resolve: Defense Posture and Politics in the Defense Budget." *Policy Sciences* 16:371–90.

Donnelly, Harrison. 1982. "Creating Jobs: It's Not as Easy as It Seems." *Congressional Quarterly Weekly Report,* 20 November, 2871–78.

Downs, Anthony. 1972. "Up and Down with Ecology—The 'Issue-Attention Cycle.'" *Public Interest* 28 (Summer): 38–50.

Doyle, Jack. 1979. *Lines across the Land.* Washington, D.C.: Environmental Policy Institute.

Doyle, Richard, and Jerry McCaffery. 1991. "The Budget Enforcement Act of 1990: The Path to No Fault Budgeting." *Public Budgeting and Finance* 11 (Spring): 25–40.

Drews, Roberta. 1982. *Long-Term Costs and Their Treatment in the Federal Budget.* Congressional Budget Office. June.

Durant, Robert F. 1992. *The Administrative Presidency Revisited.* Albany: State University of New York Press.

Easton, David. 1951. *The Political System.* N.Y.: Alfred A. Knopf.

Eisinger, Peter. 1988. *The Rise of the Entrepreneurial State.* Madison: University of Wisconsin Press.

Eismeier, Theodore H. 1982. "The Power Not to Tax: A Search for Effective Controls." *Journal of Policy Analysis and Management* 1 (Spring): 333–45.

Eisner, Robert. 1986. *How Real Is the Federal Deficit?* New York: Free Press.

Ellwood, John W. 1985a. "Frequently Made Errors in Budgetary Research: A Critique and a Suggested Time-Series to Bring About More Accurate Models of Budget Behavior at the National Level." Prepared for delivery at the annual meeting of the Association for Public Policy Analysis and Management, Washington, D.C., 25 October.

———. 1985b. "The Great Exception: The Congressional Budget Process in an Age of Decentralization." In *Congress Reconsidered,* ed. Lawrence C. Dodd and Bruce I. Oppenheimer. 3d ed. Washington, D.C.: Congressional Quarterly Press.

Ellwood, John W., ed. 1982. *Reductions in U.S. Domestic Spending.* New Brunswick, N.J.: Transaction.

Elving, Ronald D. 1987. "Committee 'Finds' Funds for HUD, NASA, NSF." *Congressional Quarterly Weekly Report,* 3 October, 2407–8.

Eule, Julian N. 1987. "Temporal Limits on the Legislative Mandate: Entrenchment and Retroactivity." *American Bar Foundation Research Journal* 2 (Spring-Summer): 381–459.

Farmers Home Administration. 1980. "Agricultural, Rural Development, and the Farmers Home Administration." Mimeo.

Fenno, Richard F., Jr. 1966. *The Power of the Purse.* Boston: Little, Brown.

———. 1978. "Notes on Method: Participant Observation." In *Home Style: House Members in Their Districts.* Boston: Little, Brown.

———. 1986. "Observation, Context, and Sequence in the Study of Politics." *American Political Science Review* 80:3–15.

Ferejohn, John A. 1974. *Pork Barrel Politics.* Stanford: Stanford University Press.

Ferejohn, John A., and Keith Krehbiel. 1987. "The Budget Process and the Size of the Budget." *American Journal of Political Science* 31:296–320.

Fessler, Pamela. 1991. "Desert Storm Benefits Package Headed for Funding Battle." *Congressional Quarterly Weekly Report,* 9 March, 619–20.

Fischer, Gregory W., and Mark S. Kamlet. 1984. "Explaining Presidential Priorities: The Competing Aspiration Levels Model of Macrobudgetary Decision Making." *American Political Science Review* 78:356–71.

Fisher, Louis. 1975. *Presidential Spending Power.* Princeton: Princeton University Press.

———. 1980. "Techniques for Bypassing the Annual Appropriations Process." Congressional Research Service. 16 May.

Fitzgerald, A. Ernest. 1989. *The Pentagonists.* New York: Houghton, Mifflin.

General Accounting Office (GAO). 1978a. *Budget Authority for Foreign Military Sales Is Substantially Understated.* 27 July.

———. 1978b. *Consistent and Uniform Treatment of Inflation Needed in Program Cost Estimates Provided to the Congress.* 20 March.

———. 1978c. *Further Implementation of Full Funding in the Federal Government.* 7 August.

———. 1981. *Pitfalls in Interior's New Accelerated Offshore Leasing Program Require Attention.* 18 December.

———. 1983a. *Criteria for Recording Obligations for Defense Stock Fund Purchases Should Be Changed.* 19 August.

———. 1983b. *Improved Analysis Needed to Evaluate DOD's Proposed Long-Term Leases of Capital Equipment.* 28 June.

———. 1984a. *Improper Use of Industrial Funds by Defense Extended the Life of Appropriations Which Otherwise Would Have Expired.* 5 June.

———. 1984b. "Information on Repayment of the Government's Uranium Enrichment Program Costs and Audits of That Program's Financial Statements." Letter to Congressman John Dingell. 10 August.

———. 1985a. *Early Assessment of Interior's Area-Wide Program for Leasing Offshore Lands.* 15 July.

———. 1985b. *Managing the Cost of Government.* February.

———. 1985c. *Potential for Excess Funds in DOD.* 3 August.

———. 1986. *Loan Asset Sales: OMB Policies Will Result in Program Objectives Not Being Fully Achieved.* September.

———. 1987. *Federal Evaluation: Fewer Units, Reduced Resources, Different Studies from 1980.* January.

———. 1988. *Deficit Reductions for Fiscal Year 1989.* November.

———. 1989a. *Federal Financing Bank: The Government Incurred a Cost of $2 Billion on Loan Prepayments.* August.

———. 1989b. *Federal Office Space: Increased Ownership Would Result in Significant Savings.* December.

———. 1989c. *The National WIC Evaluation: Reporting and Follow-Up Issues.* December.

———. 1989d. *Operating Cash Requirement for Air Force Stock Fund Can Be Reduced.* April.

———. 1989e. *Strategic Petroleum Reserves: Analysis of Alternative Financing Methods.* March.

———. 1990. *Budget Issues: Capping of Outlays Is Ineffective for Controlling Expenditures.* September.

———. 1992a. *Program Performance Measures: Federal Agency Collection and Use of Performance Data.* May.

———. 1992b. *Foreign Assistance: Cost Reductions Possible from Improved Cash Transfer Management.* November.

———. 1993. *School Construction: Sallie Mae Financing Activities.* April.

Gilbert, George N., and Nancy L. Smith. 1976. "The Farmers Home Administration: Its Operation and Programs." Congressional Research Service. 24 March.

Gist, John R. 1975. *Mandatory Expenditures and the Defense Sector: Theory of Budgetary Incrementalism.* Beverly Hills, Calif.: Sage.

———. 1977. "'Increment' and 'Base' in the Congressional Appropriations Process." *American Journal of Political Science* 21:341–52.

———. 1982. "'Stability' and 'Competition' in Budgetary Theory." *American Political Science Review* 76:859–72.

Glaser, Barney G., and Anselm L. Strauss. 1967. *The Discovery of Grounded Theory.* New York: Aldine.

Gleeson, Michael E. 1980. "Budgeting for Federal Housing Programs: A Problem and What to Do About It." *Public Administration Review* 40:321–27.

Glicksman, Robert L., and George Cameron Coggins. 1984. "Federal Recreational Land Policy: The Rise and Decline of the Land and Water Conservation Fund." *Columbia Journal of Environmental Law* 9:125–236.

Gold, Steven. 1986. "State Income Tax Checkoff Programs: 1986 Update." *Fiscal Letter,* National Conference of State Legislatures, September, 8, 11.

Goodisman, Leonard. 1983. "Budgeting and Field Discretion in Disaster Relief." *Public Budgeting and Finance* 3 (Spring): 89–102.

Gordon, Michael R. 1983. "Stockman's Magic Touch." *National Journal,* 30 July, 1601.

Gould, George. 1986. Letter to Rudolph G. Penner, Director, Congressional Budget Office.

———. 1988. Letter to Senator Dale Bumpers.

Graham, George G. 1991. "WIC: A Food Program That Fails." *Public Interest* 103 (Spring): 66–75.

Gramlich, Edward M. 1990. *Benefit-Cost Analysis of Government Programs.* Englewood Cliffs, N.J.: Prentice-Hall.

Gurwitt, Rob. 1989. "States Try Ways to Stretch Money for Clean Water." *Governing,* February, 60–61.

Haas, Lawrence J. 1987. "When a Cut Is Not All That Unkind." *National Journal,* 24 October, 2681–82.

———. 1988a. "Bullish on Assets." *National Journal,* 30 April, 1122–26.

———. 1988b. "Dodging the Budget Bullet." *National Journal,* 1 October, 2465–69.

———. 1990. "Lost in Space." *National Journal,* 28 April, 1028–30.

———. 1991a. "Dan Rostenkowski's Secret Weapon." *National Journal,* 25 May, 1248.

———. 1991b. "Stalled Rescues." *National Journal,* 19 January, 162–64.

Hager, George. 1992. "Democrats Falter in Drive to Claim Peace Dividend." *Congressional Quarterly Weekly Report,* 28 March, 789–91.

Hale, George E., and Scott R. Douglass. 1977. "The Politics of Budget Execution: Financial Manipulation in State and Local Government." *Administration and Society* (November): 367–78.

Hartman, Robert W. 1983. *Pay and Pensions for Federal Workers.* Washington, D.C.: Brookings.

———. 1984. "Issues in Budgetary Accounting." In *Federal Budget Policy in the 1980s,* ed. Gregory B. Mills and John L. Palmer, 423–47. Washington, D.C.: Urban Institute.

Healey, Jon. 1993. "Panel Shifts Course on Nuclear Fund." *Congressional Quarterly Weekly Report,* 12 June, 1564.

Heclo, Hugh. 1984. "Executive Budget Making." In *Federal Budget Policy in the 1980s,* ed. Gregory B. Mills and John L. Palmer, 255–91. Washington, D.C.: Urban Institute.

Hedlund, Ronald D. 1984. "Organizational Attributes of Legislatures: Structure, Rules, Norms, Resources." *Legislative Studies Quarterly* 9 (February): 51–121.

Hirschman, Albert O. 1991. *The Rhetoric of Reaction.* Cambridge: Harvard University Press.

Hook, Janet. 1990. "Californians Feel a Backlash against Congressional Clout." *Congressional Quarterly Weekly Report,* 1 September, 2762–63.

House. *See* U.S. Congress. House.

Howard, Christopher. 1992. *The Hidden Welfare State: Tax Expenditures and Social Policy.* Ph.D. diss., Massachusetts Institute of Technology.

Huitt, Ralph K. 1963. "Congressional Organization and Operations in the Field of Money and Credit." In Commission on Money and Credit, *Fiscal and Debt Management Policies.* Englewood Cliffs, N.J.: Prentice-Hall.

Ippolito, Dennis S. 1984. *Hidden Spending: The Politics of Federal Credit Programs.* Chapel Hill: University of North Carolina Press.

Jefferson, Thomas. 1904–5. *The Works of Thomas Jefferson.* 12 vols. New York: G. P. Putnam.

Jones, L. R. 1991. "Policy Development, Planning, and Resource Allocation in the Department of Defense." *Public Budgeting and Finance* 11 (Fall): 15–27.

Jones, L. R., and K. J. Euske. 1991. "Strategic Misrepresentation in Budgeting," *Journal of Public Administration Research and Theory* 1 (October): 437–60.

Kamlet, Mark S., and David C. Mowery. 1980. "The Budgetary Base in Federal Resource Allocation." *American Journal of Political Science* 24:804–21.

———. 1985. "The First Decade of the Congressional Budget Act: Legislative Imitation and Adaptation in Budgeting." *Policy Sciences* 18 (December): 313–34.

Kane, Edward J. 1989. *The S and L Insurance Mess: How Did It Happen?* Washington, D.C.: Urban Institute.

Kanter, Arnold. 1972. "Congress and the Defense Budget: 1960–1970." *American Political Science Review* 66:129–43.

Kaplan, R. S., and R. Roll. 1972. "Investor Evaluation of Accounting Information: Some Empirical Evidence." *Journal of Business* 45 (April): 225–57.

Kaufman, Herbert. 1976. *Are Government Organizations Immortal?* Washington, D.C.: Brookings.

———. 1985. *Time, Chance, and Organizations.* Chatham, N.J.: Chatham House.

Keith, Robert, and Edward Davis. 1993. *The Senate's "Byrd Rule" against Extraneous Matter in Reconciliation Measures.* Congressional Research Service. 9 July.

Kellam, Susan. 1992. "Praise Is High, Funds Are Low for Welfare That Works." *Congressional Quarterly Weekly Report,* 27 June, 1876–81.

Kettl, Donald F. 1989. "Expansion and Protection in the Budgetary Process." *Public Administration Review* 49 (May/June): 231–39.

Kiel, L. Douglas, and Euel Elliott. 1992. "Budgets as Dynamic Systems: Change, Variation, Time, and Budgetary Heuristics." *Journal of Public Administration Research and Theory* 2 (April): 139–56.

Kiewiet, D. Roderick, and Mathew D. McCubbins. 1985a. "Appropriations Decisions as a Bilateral Bargaining Game between President and Congress." *Legislative Quarterly* 10 (May): 181–201.

———. 1985b. "Congressional Appropriations and the Electoral Connection." *Journal of Politics* 47:59–82.

———. 1985c. "Presidential Influence upon Congressional Appropriations Decisions." Prepared for delivery at the annual meeting of the American Political Science Association, New Orleans, 29–31 August.

———. 1991. *The Logic of Delegation.* Chicago: University of Chicago Press.

Kingdon, John W. 1966. "A House Appropriations Subcommittee: Influences on Budgetary Decisions." *Southwestern Social Science Quarterly* 47 (June): 68–78.

———. 1973. *Congressmen's Voting Decisions.* New York: Harper and Row.

———. 1984. *Agendas, Alternatives, and Public Policies.* Boston: Little, Brown.

Kirkland, Kenneth J. 1983. "'Creative Accounting' and Short-Term Debt: State Responses to the Deficit Threat." *National Tax Journal* 36 (September): 395–99.

Kirschten, Dick. 1989. "Robbing Peter." *National Journal,* 1 April, 827.

Kleit, Andrew N., and Richard L. Stroup. 1987. "Blackout at Bonneville Power." *Regulation* 11 (March–April): 30–36.

Koitz, David. 1985. "Social Security, Medicare, and the Unified Budget." Congressional Research Service. Printed by the Senate Budget Committee. September.

Kosterlitz, Julie. 1986. "A Tale of Survival." *National Journal,* 19 April, 934–37.

———. 1988a. "Graying Armies." *National Journal,* 12 March, 664–68.

———. 1988b. "Not Just Kid Stuff." *National Journal,* 19 November, 2934–39.

———. 1989. "Watch Out for Waxman." *National Journal,* 11 March, 577–81.

Kotlikoff, Laurence J. 1992. *Generational Accounting.* New York: Free Press.

Kotz, Nick. 1969. *Let Them Eat Promises.* Englewood Cliffs, N.J.: Prentice-Hall.

Kuntz, Phil. 1989a. "Expiring Federal Subsidies Raise a Policy Dilemma." *Congressional Quarterly Weekly Report,* 6 May, 1041–45.

———. 1989b. "VA-HUD Rider Would Increase FHA Mortgage-Loan Limit." *Congressional Quarterly Weekly Report,* 16 September, 2391–93.

———. 1990a. "Kentucky's Ford Leads Brigade of Members Pushing 'Extras.'" *Congressional Quarterly Weekly Report,* 20 October, 3485.

———. 1990b. "Pie in the Sky: Big Science Is Ready for Blastoff." *Congressional Quarterly Weekly Report,* 28 April, 1254–60.

———. 1991a. "Internal Affairs." *Where the Money Goes: A Guide to Congress' Spending Choices in the 1992 Appropriations Bills. Congressional Quarterly Weekly Report,* supplement to no. 49, 7 December, 111–18.

———. 1991b. "Senators Nick Funds for GAO, Assist Staff and Byrd." *Congressional Quarterly Weekly Report,* 15 June, 1559.

Lakoff, George, and Mark Johnson. 1980. *Metaphors We Live By.* Chicago: University of Chicago Press.

Lane, Ruth. 1990. "Concrete Theory: An Emerging Political Method." *American Political Science Review* 84:927–40.

Lau, Richard R., Richard A. Smith, and Susan T. Fiske. 1991. "Political Beliefs, Policy Interpretations, and Political Persuasion." *Journal of Politics* 53:644–75.

"Lawmakers Blast NASA Budget." 1989. *Congressional Quarterly Weekly Report,* 4 March, 444–45.

Leazes, Francis J. 1987. *Accountability and the Business State.* New York: Praeger.

Leigland, James. 1988. "Controls over Special Purpose Governments at State and Local Levels." Paper delivered at the annual research conference of the Association for Public Policy Analysis and Management, Seattle, 27–29 October.

LeLoup, Lance T. 1975. "Agency Policy Actions: Determinants of Nonincremental Change." In *Policy-Making in the Federal Executive Branch,* ed. Randall B. Ripley and Grace A. Franklin, 65–90. New York: Free Press.

———. 1978a. "Discretion in National Budgeting: Controlling the Controllables." *Policy Analysis* 4 (Fall): 455–75.

———. 1978b. "The Myth of Incrementalism: Analytical Choices in Budgetary Theory." *Polity* 10 (Summer): 488–509.

LeLoup, Lance T., and William B. Moreland. 1978. "Agency Strategies and Executive Review: The Hidden Politics of Budgeting." *Public Administration Review* 38:232–39.

Leonard, Herman B. 1986. *Checks Unbalanced: The Quiet Side of Public Spending.* New York: Basic Books.

Levi, Margaret. 1988. *Of Rule and Revenue.* Berkeley and Los Angeles: University of California Press.

Levine, Charles H., Irene S. Rubin, and George G. Wolohojian. 1981. *The Politics of Retrenchment: How Local Governments Manage Fiscal Stress.* Beverly Hills, Calif.: Sage.

Levine, Martin P. 1979. *The Long-Term Costs of Lower-Income Housing Assistance Programs.* Congressional Budget Office. March.

Litan, Robert E., and William Nordhaus. 1983. *Reforming Federal Regulation.* New Haven: Yale University Press.

Lowi, Theodore J. 1969. *The End of Liberalism.* New York: Norton.

McCall, George J., and J. C. Simmons. 1969. *Issues in Participant Observation.* New York: Random House.

McCubbins, Mathew D. 1991. "Party Politics, Divided Government, and Budget Deficits." In *Parallel Politics: Economic Policymaking in the United States and Japan,* ed. Samuel Kernell. Washington, D.C.: Brookings.

McDougall, Walter A. 1985. . . . *The Heavens and the Earth.* New York: Basic Books.

McNaught, William, and Jonathan Ratner. 1987. "Budgeting for Inflation in the Department of Defense." *Public Budgeting and Finance* 7 (Winter): 24–35.

Madison, James, Alexander Hamilton, and John Jay. 1961. *The Federalist Papers.* New York: New American Library.

Majone, Giandomenico. 1989. *Evidence, Argument, and Persuasion in the Policy Process.* New Haven: Yale University Press.

Malachowski, James, Samuel Bookheimer, and David Lowery. 1987. "The Theory of the Budgetary Process in an Era of Changing Budgetary Roles, FY48–FY84." *American Politics Quarterly* 15:325–54.

Mansbridge, Jane J., ed. 1990. *Beyond Self-Interest.* Chicago: University of Chicago Press.

March, James G., and Johan P. Olsen. 1989. *Rediscovering Institutions: The Organizational Basis of Politics.* New York: Free Press.

Maroni, Alice C. 1987. "Special Access Programs in the Defense Budget: Understanding the 'Black Budget.'" Congressional Research Service. 6 October.

Maroni, Alice C., and Raymond D. White. 1986. "Working Capital Funds in the Department of Defense: A Primer." Congressional Research Service.

Matlack, Carol. 1988. "A Harder Sell for Home-State Colleges." *National Journal,* 5 November, 2804.

———. 1990a. "Getting Their Way." *National Journal,* 27 October, 2584–88.

———. 1990b. "Zap! You're Taxed." *National Journal,* 3 February, 267–69.

———. 1991. "Barely Afloat." *National Journal,* 27 April, 988–92.

Matlack, Carol, and Scott Marshutz. 1987. "They Fly, We Cry." *National Journal,* 11 April, 879.

Matthews, Donald R. 1960. *U.S. Senators and Their World.* New York: Vintage.

Mautz, R. K. 1991. "Generally Accepted Accounting Principles and Federal Government Financial Reporting." *Public Budgeting and Finance* 11 (Winter): 3–10.

Mayhew, David R. 1991. *Divided We Govern.* New Haven: Yale University Press.

Meltsner, Arnold J. 1976. *Policy Analysts in the Bureaucracy.* Berkeley and Los Angeles: University of California Press.

———. 1987. *Policy Analysts in the Bureaucracy.* 2d ed. Berkeley and Los Angeles: University of California Press.

Meyers, Roy T. 1985. *The Budgetary Status of the Federal Reserve System.* Congressional Budget Office. February.

———. 1988. "Biennial Budgeting." In Senate Governmental Affairs Committee, *Proposed Budget Reforms: A Critical Analysis,* 71–118. April.

———. 1991. "The President's Fiscal Year 1992 Budget: Almost Quiet on the Budgetary Front." *Public Budgeting and Finance* 11 (Summer): 5–18.

———. 1992. "Federal Budgeting and Finance in 1991: The Future Is Now." *Public Budgeting and Finance* 12 (Summer): 3–15.

Michaelis, Laura. 1993. "Extension of Farm Programs through '95 Angers Critics," *Congressional Quarterly Weekly Report,* 29 May, 1361.

Milgram, Grace. 1979. "The Rationale for Assisted Housing." Congressional Research Service. 15 August.

Mills, C. Wright. 1959. *The Sociological Imagination.* London: Oxford University Press.

Mills, Mike. 1991. "Seeking a Safety Net for Highways." *Congressional Quarterly Weekly Report,* 20 July, 1974.

———. 1993. "In the End, Space Stations' Jobs May Be Its Strongest Card." *Congressional Quarterly Weekly Report,* 6 March, 507–8.

Modlin, Carey P. 1986. Memorandum to congressional spending committees. 6 March.

Moe, Ronald C., and Thomas H. Stanton. 1989. "Government-Sponsored Enterprises as Federal Instrumentalities: Reconciling Private Management with Public Accountability." *Public Administration Review* 49:321–29.

Moore, John. 1985. "Federal Hydropower: Repaying the Debt." Congressional Research Service. 3 May.

Morgan, Iwan. 1990. *Eisenhower versus "The Spenders".* New York: St. Martin's.

Morrison, David C. 1986a. "Managing the Warheads." *National Journal,* 6 December, 2935–39.

———. 1986b. "Pentagon's Top Secret 'Black Budget' Has Skyrocketed during Reagan Years." *National Journal,* 1 March, 492–98.

———. 1987a. "Dancing in the Dark." *National Journal,* 11 April, 867–73.

———. 1987b. "Fiddip-Faddle." *National Journal,* 10 October, 2576.

———. 1987c. "Overstocked." *National Journal,* 7 November, 2827.

———. 1989. "It Costs WHAT?!" *National Journal,* 5 August, 2012.

———. 1990a. "The Living Dead." *National Journal,* 6 December, 2846–50.

———. 1990b. "Threat Meltdown." *National Journal,* 17 March, 694.

———. 1991a. "Lost in Space." *National Journal,* 6 July, 1670–74.
———. 1991b. "Operation Feel Good." *National Journal,* 26 October, 2593–97.
———. 1991c. "Phony War Scenario Stirs India." *National Journal,* 6 April, 804–6.
———. 1992a. "Police Action." *National Journal,* 1 February, 267–70.
———. 1992b. "Smooth Operators." *National Journal,* 8 August, 1822–26.

Morrison, Sylvia. 1983. "Solvency of the Rural Electric Revolving Fund: An Economic Analysis of S. 1300 and H.R. 3050, 98th Congress." Congressional Research Service. 29 December.

———. 1988. "Rural Elective Cooperative Defaults: Origins, Current Status, and Legislative Implications." Congressional Research Service. October.

Morse, Ellsworth H., Jr. 1971. "Report of the President's Commission on Budget Concepts in Retrospect." *Public Administration Review* 31 (July–August): 443–50.

Mosher, Frederick C. 1984. *A Tale of Two Agencies: A Comparative Analysis of the General Accounting Office and the Office of Management and Budget.* Baton Rouge: Louisiana State University Press.

Mowery, David C., and Mark S. Kamlet. 1984. "Games Presidents Do and Do Not Play: Presidential Circumvention of the Executive Branch Budget Process." *Policy Sciences* 16 (March): 303–27.

Mudge, Richard R. 1982. *Major Financial Changes in the Highway Trust Fund since 1956.* Congressional Budget Office. November.

Muris, Timothy J. 1989. "The Uses and Abuses of Budget Baselines." Working Paper in Political Science, Hoover Institution. January.

Natchez, Peter B., and Irvin C. Bupp. 1973. "Policy and Priority in the Budgetary Process." *American Political Science Review.* 67:951–63.

National Aeronautics and Space Administration. 1985. *Spinoff 1985.*

National League of Cities. 1986. "The Case for General Revenue Sharing." Mimeo.

Nelson, Richard R., and Sidney G. Winter. 1982. *An Evolutionary Theory of Economic Change.* Cambridge: Harvard University Press.

Neustadt, Richard E. 1960. *Presidential Power.* New York: John Wiley.

Newlin, Eliza. 1991. "Objections to Boat Fee Swamp Congress." *National Journal,* 29 June, 1634–35.

North, Douglass C. 1990. *Institutions, Institutional Change, and Economic Performance.* New York: Cambridge University Press.

Novak, Viveca. 1992. "Window Dressing." *National Journal,* 11 November, 2610–12.

"Numbers in Reagan's Defense 'Cut' Proposal May Not Add Up." 1984. *National Journal,* 24 March, 551–52.

Office of Management and Budget. 1981. "Report on Strengthening Federal Credit Management." January.

———. 1989. *Budget of the U.S. Government, FY 1990, Historical Tables.*

Office of Technology Assessment. 1986a. *Research Funding as an Investment: Can We Measure the Returns?* April.

———. 1986b. *Technology, Public Policy, and the Changing Structure of American Agriculture.* March.

Oppenheim, John Edward. 1983. "Federal Response to Natural Disasters." Ph.D. diss., University of Michigan.

Orren, Karen, and Skowronek, Stephen. 1991. "Beyond the Iconography of Order: Notes for a 'New' Institutionalism," Paper presented to the annual meeting of the American Political Science Association, Washington, D.C., 30 August.

Ostrom, Elinor. 1986. "An Agenda for the Study of Institutions." *Public Choice* 48:3–25.

Paarlberg, Don. 1987. *Increasing Understanding of Public Problems and Policies.* Oak Brook, Ill.: Farm Foundation.

Padgett, John F. 1980. "Bounded Rationality in Budgetary Research." *American Political Science Review* 74:354–72.

Parker, Edwin B. 1981. "Economic and Social Benefits of the REA Telephone Loan Program." 24 March. Mimeo.

Patton, James M. 1985. "The Governmental Financial Reporting Entity: Review and Analysis." In *Research in Governmental and Non-Profit Accounting,* ed. James L. Chan, 1:85–116. Greenwich, Conn.: JAI Press.

Payne, James L. 1990. "The Congressional Brainwashing Machine." *Public Interest* 100 (Summer): 3–14.

———. 1991. *The Culture of Spending.* San Francisco: Institute for Contemporary Studies.

Phaup, Marvin. 1984. *New Approaches to the Budgetary Treatment of Federal Credit Assistance.* Congressional Budget Office, March.

———. 1985. *Government-Sponsored Enterprises and Their Implicit Federal Subsidy: The Case of Sallie Mae.* Congressional Budget Office. December.

Pitsvada, Bernard T. 1983. "Flexibility in Budget Execution." *Public Budgeting and Finance* 3 (Summer): 83–101.

Pitsvada, Bernard T., and Frank D. Draper. 1984. "Making Sense of the Federal Budget the Old-Fashioned Way—Incrementally." *Public Administration Review* 44: 401–7).

President's Commission on Budget Concepts. 1967. *Report of the President's Commission on Budget Concepts.* October.

President's Commission on the American Outdoors. 1986. *Report of the President's Commission on the American Outdoors.* December.

Rapp, David. 1986. "PIK Certificates Prove Popular with Farmers and Lawmakers." *Congressional Quarterly Weekly Report,* 13 September, 2139–42.

———. 1987a. "The CCC Plows a Furrow for Other Spending." *Congressional Quarterly Weekly Report,* 23 May, 1052–57.

———. 1987b. "Farmer and Uncle Sam: An Old, Odd Couple." *Congressional Quarterly Weekly Report,* 4 April, 598–603.

———. 1987c. "Senate Agriculture Resorts to 'Paper' Savings." *Congressional Quarterly Weekly Report,* 24 October, 2619.

———. 1987d. "Using Some Fancy Footwork, Farm Committees Find Funds." *Congressional Quarterly Weekly Report,* 17 October, 2532.

———. 1987e. "Whitten Seldom Wastes an Opportunity . . . Especially When It Comes to Agriculture." *Congressional Quarterly Weekly Report,* 23 May, 1054–55.

———. 1992. "The Medicaid Shell Game: Too Good to Last." *Governing,* January, 62.

Rauch, Jonathan. 1984. "Women and Children's Food Program Is 'Off Limits' to Reagan Budget Cutbacks." *National Journal,* 17 November, 2197–99.

———. 1985a. "Aspin's Persistence and Budget 'Magic' Pay Off in Cuts in Military Pensions." *National Journal,* 12 October, 2305–10.

———. 1985b. "Congress, Worried about Huge Budget Deficits, Eyes an UNCOLA Strategy." *National Journal,* 19 January, 152–55.

———. 1985c. "Like Magic." *National Journal,* 21 September, 2168.

———. 1986a. "The Appropriator." *National Journal,* 12 July, 1708–12.

———. 1986b. "Pawnshop Budgeting." *National Journal,* 9 August, 1944–47.

———. 1986c. "Promises, Promises." *National Journal,* 20 September, 2289.

———. 1989. "Counterrevolution." *National Journal,* 2 August, 2142–45.

———. 1991. "The Golden Fleece." *National Journal,* 18 May, 1168–71.

Reischauer, Robert D. 1982. "The Federal Budget: Subsidies for the Rich." In *The Federal Budget: Economics and Politics,* ed. Michael J. Boskin and Aaron Wildavsky, 235–62. San Francisco: Institute for Contemporary Studies.

Rhyne, Elizabeth. 1980. "The Congressional Budget Office and Food Stamps Reform." Kennedy School of Government case program.

Richardson, Joe. 1981. "Food Stamps: Funding Crises and Appropriations Ceilings." Congressional Research Service. 17 December.

Rickards, Robert C. 1984. "How the Spending Patterns of Cities Change: Budgetary Incrementalism Reexamined." *Journal of Policy Analysis and Management* 4 (Fall): 56–74.

Riker, William H. 1980. "Implications from the Disequilibrium of Majority Rule for the Study of Institutions." *American Political Science Review* 74:432–46.

———. 1986. *The Art of Political Manipulation.* New Haven: Yale University Press.

Rivlin, Alice. 1992. *Reviving the American Dream.* Washington, D.C.: Brookings.

Rossiter, Clinton. 1956. *The American Presidency.* New York: New American Library.

Rotherham, James A. 1985. "The Railroad Retirement Program: A Case Study in the Deficit Dilemma." *Public Budgeting and Finance* 5 (Autumn): 40–57.

Rothman, Robert. 1985. "House OKs Three Memorials to 'Forgotten' War Veterans." *Congressional Quarterly Weekly Report,* 9 November, 2312.

Rovner, Julie. 1988. "Certain Low-Income Programs Are Winners in Budget Process." *Congressional Quarterly Weekly Report,* 9 April, 952.

———. 1991. "Both Chambers Join the Battle over Medicaid Financing." *Congressional Quarterly Weekly Report,* 23 November, 3459.

———. 1992. "Drugmakers Back User Fee Bill to Speed FDA Drug Approval." *Congressional Quarterly Weekly Report,* 19 September, 2825.

Rubin, Alissa J. 1991. "$40 Billion 'Mission to Earth': Big Money, Little Scrutiny." *Congressional Quarterly Weekly Report,* 11 May, 1185–91.

Rubin, Alissa J., and Jill Zuckman. 1991. "House Revives Space Station with Cuts to Housing." *Congressional Quarterly Weekly Report,* 8 June, 1492–94.

Rubin, Irene. 1993. *The Politics of Public Budgeting.* Chatham, N.J.: Chatham House.

Ruggles, Patricia. 1990. *Drawing the Line.* Washington, D.C.: Urban Institute.

Rundquist, Barry S., ed. 1980. *Political Benefits: Empirical Studies of American Public Programs.* Lexington, Mass.: D. C. Heath.

Safire, William. 1978. *Safire's Political Dictionary.* New York: Ballantine.

Sample, V. Alaric. 1992. "Resource Planning and Budgeting for National Forest Management." *Public Administration Review* 52:339–46.

Samuelson, Robert J. 1981. "Administration Slips and Stumbles in Efforts to Cut Off-Budget Spending." *National Journal,* 12 June, 1067–71.

Savage, James D. 1988. *Balanced Budgets and American Politics.* Ithaca, N.Y.: Cornell University Press.

———. 1991. "Saints and Cardinals in Appropriations Committees and the Fight against Distributive Politics." *Legislative Studies Quarterly* 16 (August): 329–47.

Schattschneider, E. E. 1960. *The Semisovereign People.* New York: Holt, Rinehart, and Winston.

Schick, Allen. 1966. "The Road to PPB: Stages of Budget Reform." *Public Administration Review* 26:243–58.

———. 1973. "A Death in the Bureaucracy: The Demise of the PPB." *Public Administration Review* 33:146–56.

———. 1975. "The Appropriations Committees versus Congress." Congressional Research Service. August.

———. 1978. "Contemporary Problems in Financial Control." *Public Administration Review* 38:513–19.

———. 1980. *Congress and Money.* Washington, D.C.: Urban Institute.

———. 1983. "Incremental Budgeting in a Decremental Age." *Policy Sciences* 16:1–25.

———, ed. 1984. *Making Economic Policy in Congress.* Washington, D.C.: American Enterprise Institute.

———. 1990. *The Capacity to Budget.* Washington, D.C.: Urban Institute.

Schneider, Anne, and Helen Ingram. 1993. "Social Construction of Target Populations. Implications for Politics and Policy." *American Political Science Review* 87:334–47.

———. 1990. "Behavioral Assumptions of Policy Tools." *Journal of Politics* 52:510–29.

Schulman, Paul R. 1975. "Nonincremental Policy Making: Notes toward an Alternative Paradigm." *American Political Science Review* 69:1354–70.

———. 1988. "The Politics of 'Ideational Policy.'" *Journal of Politics* 38:263–91.

Schussheim, Morton H. 1974. "Rural Housing Programs—A Progress Report." Congressional Research Service. 23 April.

Searing, Donald D. 1991. "Roles, Rules, and Rationality in the New Institutionalism." *American Political Science Review* 85:1239–60.

Seidman, Harold. 1988. "The Quasi World of the Federal Government." *Brookings Review* 6 (Summer): 23–27.

Senate. *See* U.S. Congress. Senate.
Sharkansky, Ira. 1965. "Four Agencies and an Appropriations Subcommittee: A Comparative Study of Budget Strategies." *Midwest Journal of Political Science* 9 (August): 254–81.
Shepsle, Kenneth A., and Barry R. Weingast. 1981. "Political Preferences for the Pork Barrel: A Generalization." *American Journal of Political Science* 25:96–111.
Shillingsburg, John D. 1979. *Loan Guarantees: Current Concerns and Alternatives for Control.* Congressional Budget Office. January.
———. 1982. *The Federal Financing Bank and the Budgetary Treatment of Federal Credit Activities.* Congressional Budget Office. January.
Singer, Neil M. 1984. *Modifying Military Retirement: Alternative Approaches.* Congressional Budget Office. April.
Smigel, Erwin O. 1969. "Sample, Method, and Techniques." In *The Wall Street Lawyer.* Bloomington: Indiana University Press.
Smith, Marvin M. 1983. *Accrual Accounting for Military Retirement: Alternative Approaches.* Congressional Budget Office.
Smith, Richard A. 1984. "Advocacy, Interpretation, and Influence in the U.S. Congress." *American Political Science Review* 78:44–63.
Smith, Robert W. 1989. *The Space Telescope.* New York: Cambridge University Press.
Smith, Steven S. 1989. *Call to Order.* Washington, D.C.: Brookings.
Smithies, Arthur. 1955. *The Budgetary Process in the United States.* New York: McGraw Hill.
Solomon, Burt. 1987. "Our Facts, Their Facts." *National Journal,* 6 June, 1457–61.
Staats, Elmer B. 1967. "Coverage of the Budget—Government-Sponsored Enterprises." *Staff Papers and Other Materials Reviewed by the President's Commission.* October.
Stanfield, Rochelle L. 1978. "The Battle of the Bulge in HUD's 1979 Budget. *National Journal,* 7 January, 18.
———. 1981a. "For the States, It's Time to Put Up or Shut Up on Federal Block Grants." *National Journal,* 10 October, 1800–1805.
———. 1981b. "Numbers Crunch—Data Funds Cut Just When More Statistics Are Needed." *National Journal,* 28 November, 2119–21.
———. 1983. "Public Facilities Needs Not Enormous." *National Journal,* 23 April, 860.
Stanton, Thomas H. 1990. "Increasing the Accountability of Government-Sponsored Enterprises." *Public Administration Review* 50:590–93.
———. 1991. *A State of Risk.* New York: Harper Business.
Starobin, Paul. 1987a. "House Panel OKs $58 Billion for Housing, NASA, Veterans." *Congressional Quarterly Weekly Report,* 27 June, 1379.
———. 1987b. "Panel Would Charge 'User Fee' for Gulf Escort." *Congressional Quarterly Weekly Report,* 17 October, 2507.
———. 1987c. "Pork: A Time-Honored Tradition Lives On." *Congressional Quarterly Weekly Report,* 24 October, 2581–91.
———. 1989a. "Committee Balks at 'Reforms' Pegged to Off-Budget Deal." *Congressional Quarterly Weekly Report,* 1 July, 1620–21.

———. 1989b. "Obscure Trigger-Tax Provision Imperils Aviation Budget." *Congressional Quarterly Weekly Report,* 8 April, 745–46.

———. 1993a. "Bringing It Home." *National Journal,* 27 March, 742–45.

———. 1993b. "Connie's Prizefight." *National Journal,* 26 June, 1642–45.

Steiner, Gilbert Y. 1976. *The Children's Cause.* Washington, D.C.: Brookings.

Steuerle, C. Eugene. 1992. *The Tax Decade.* Washington, D.C.: Urban Institute.

Stewart, Charles III. 1988. "Budget Reform as Strategic Legislative Action: An Exploration." *Journal of Politics* 50:292–321.

———. 1989. *Budget Reform Politics: The Design of the Appropriations Process in the House of Representatives 1865–1921.* New York: Cambridge University Press.

Stockman, David A. 1986. *The Triumph of Politics.* New York: Harper and Row.

Stone, Deborah A. 1988. *Policy Paradox and Political Reason.* Glenview, Ill.: Scott, Foresman.

———. 1989. "Causal Stories and the Formation of Policy Agendas." *Political Science Quarterly* 104 (Summer): 281–300.

Stone, Peter H. 1993. "Called to Account." *National Journal,* 17 July, 1810–13.

Straussman, Jeffrey D. 1988. "Rights-Based Budgeting." In *New Directions in Budget Theory,* ed. Irene S. Rubin, 100–123. Albany: State University of New York Press.

Stubbing, Richard A., with Richard A. Mendel. 1986. *The Defense Game.* New York: Harper and Row.

Surrey, Stanley S., and Paul R. McDaniel. 1980. "The Tax Expenditure Concept and the Legislative Process." In *The Economics of Taxation,* ed. Henry J. Aaron and Michael J. Boskin. Washington, D.C.: Brookings.

———. 1985. *Tax Expenditures.* Cambridge: Harvard University Press.

Sweeney, Naomi. 1967. "Major Recent Criticisms of the Federal Budget." In President's Commission on Budget Concepts, *Staff Papers and Other Materials Reviewed by the President's Commission,* 17–47.

Szanton, Peter L. 1985. "OMB's Defense Cop-Out." *Foreign Policy* 58:99–114.

Tarpgaard, Peter T. 1982. *Building a Six Hundred-Ship Navy: Costs, Timing, and Alternative Approaches.* Congressional Budget Office. March.

Taylor, Andrew. 1992. "Bill Establishing New Overseer for Fannie, Freddie Clears." *Congressional Quarterly Weekly Report,* 10 October, 3138.

Taylor, Stephen J., and Robert Bogdan. 1984. *Introduction to Qualitative Research Methods: The Search for Meanings.* 2d ed. New York: Wiley.

Thomas, William. 1986. *Budgeting for Defense Inflation.* Congressional Budget Office. January.

Towell, Pat. 1986. "House Votes Bill to Trim Military Retirement." *Congressional Quarterly Weekly Report,* 26 April, 923–26.

———. 1990. "Recruiting Defense Dollars for Environmental Duty." *Congressional Quarterly Weekly Report,* 7 July, 2133–35.

———. 1992. "Bush Signs Defense Measure with SDI Cut, Cancer Funds." *Congressional Quarterly Weekly Report,* 10 October, 3190.

Tucker, Harvey J. 1982. "Incremental Budgeting: Myth or Model?" *Western Political Quarterly* 35:327–38.

Tufte, Edward R. 1977. "Political Statistics for the United States: Observations on Some Major Data Sources." *American Political Science Review* 71:305–14.

Twight, Charlotte. 1989. "The Political Economy of the National Defense Stockpile." *Policy Studies Review* 8 (Summer): 774–99.

U.S. Congress. House. Committee on Post Office and Civil Service. Various dates. "Current Salary Schedules of Federal Officers and Employees together with a History of Salary and Retirement Annuity Adjustments." Published annually.

U.S. Congress. House. Committee on the Interior. 1983. "Bureau of Indian Affairs Budget Request for FY84." 24 February.

U.S. Congress. Senate. Committee on Agriculture, Nutrition, and Forestry. Subcommittee on Agricultural Credit and Rural Electrification. 1981. *Proposed Changes in the REA Program.* 14 May.

U.S. Congress. Senate. Committee on Veterans Affairs. 1981. "Cost-Savings Legislation." 6 May.

U.S. Department of Agriculture. 1984. *A Brief History of the Rural Electric and Telephone Programs.* December.

———. 1985. *A Brief History of the Farmers Home Administration.* February.

U.S. Department of Housing and Urban Development. Office of Policy Development and Research. 1986. *1986 Report to the Congress on the Federal National Mortgage Association.*

U.S. Department of Treasury. 1990. *Report of the Secretary of the Treasury on Government Sponsored Enterprises.* May.

Walker, Jack L., Jr. 1977. "Setting the Agenda in the United States Senate." *British Journal of Political Science* 7 (October): 423–45.

Wanat, John. 1974. "Bases of Budgetary Incrementalism." *American Political Science Review* 68:421–28.

Wander, W. Thomas. 1982. "Patterns of Change in the Congressional Budget Process, 1865–1974." *Congress and the Presidency* 9 (Autumn): 23–49.

Weaver, R. Kent. 1986. "The Politics of Blame Avoidance." *Journal of Public Policy* 6 (October-December): 371–98.

———. 1988. *Automatic Government: The Politics of Indexation.* Washington, D.C.: Brookings.

Webber, Carolyn, and Aaron Wildavsky. 1986. *A History of Taxation and Expenditure in the Western World.* New York: Simon and Schuster.

Wehr, Elizabeth. 1984a. "Rural Co-ops Bill Threatened with Stiff Senate Opposition." *Congressional Quarterly Weekly Report,* 26 May 1281–82.

———. 1984b. "Rural Utility Co-ops Fighting to Save Federal Loan Program." *Congressional Quarterly Weekly Report,* 14 January 53–58.

Weimer, David L. 1992. "Political Science, Practitioner Skill, and Public Management." *Public Administration Review* 52:240–45.

Weimer, David L., and Aidan R. Vining. 1992. *Policy Analysis: Concepts and Practice.* 2d ed. Englewood Cliffs, N.J.: Prentice-Hall.

Wheeler, Porter K. 1978. *Highway Assistance Programs.* Congressional Budget Office. February.

White, Joseph, and Aaron Wildavsky. 1989. *The Deficit and the Public Interest.* Berkeley and Los Angeles: University of California Press.

Whiteman, David. 1985. "The Fate of Policy Analysis in Congressional Decision Making: Three Types of Use in Committees." *Western Political Quarterly* 38:294–311.

Wildavsky, Aaron. 1964. *The Politics of the Budgetary Process.* Boston: Little, Brown.

———. 1975. *Budgeting: A Comparative Theory of Budgetary Processes.* Boston: Little, Brown.

———. 1984. *The Politics of the Budgetary Process.* 4th ed. Boston: Little, Brown.

———. 1992. *The New Politics of the Budgetary Process.* 2d ed. Glenview, Ill.: Scott, Foresman.

Wildavsky, Aaron, and Bill Cavala. 1970. "The Political Feasibility of Income by Right." *Public Policy* 18 (Spring): 321–54.

Wilson, James Q. 1973. *Political Organizations.* New York: Basic Books.

Witte, John F. 1985. *The Politics and Development of the Federal Income Tax.* Madison: University of Wisconsin Press.

Wood, Lance D., Elliott P. Laws, and Barry Breen. 1981. "Restraining the Regulators: Legal Perspectives on a Regulatory Budget for Federal Agencies." *Harvard Journal on Legislation* 18 (Winter): 1–33.

Wright, Joseph R. 1986. "Loan Asset Sale Guidelines and Credit Reform." Office of Management and Budget memorandum for cabinet officers and agency heads. 8 July.

Zuckman, Jill. 1991a. "Earth vs. Space." *Where the Money Goes: A Guide to Congress' Spending Choices in the 1992 Appropriations Bills. Congressional Quarterly Weekly Report,* supplement to no. 49, 7 December, 145–55.

———. 1991b. "Mikulski Trims Carefully to Pay Cost of *Freedom.*" *Congressional Quarterly Weekly Report,* 13 July, 1890–91.

———. 1992. "Jobless Benefits Reform Bill Draws Add-ons, GOP Fire." *Congressional Quarterly Weekly Report,* 9 May, 1256–57.

Zuckman, Jill, and Alissa Rubin. 1991. "Social Program Lobbyists Dig In As NASA Looks to Senate." *Congressional Quarterly Weekly Report,* 15 June, 1578–79.

Index